COMPUTER-AIDED DATA ANALYSIS

COMPUTER-AIDED DATA ANALYSIS

A PRACTICAL GUIDE

WILLIAM R. GREEN

Placer Development Limited
Vancouver, British Columbia

A Wiley-Interscience Publication

JOHN WILEY & SONS

New York • Chichester • Brisbane • Toronto • Singapore

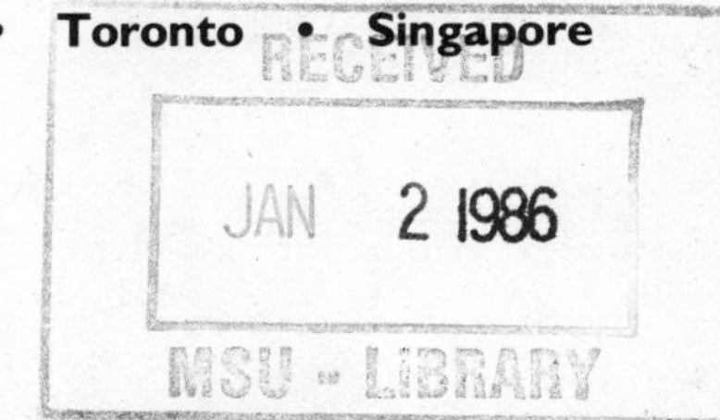

Library of Congress Cataloging in Publication Data:

Green, William R.
Computer-aided data analysis.

"A Wiley-Interscience publication."
Bibliography: p.
Includes index.
1. Multivariate analysis—Data processing. I. Title.

QA278.G75 1985 519.5'35 84-21931
ISBN 0-471-80928-4

Printed in the United States of America

10 9 8 7 6 5 4 3 2 1

PREFACE

This book was written to provide an introduction to the data analysis techniques in common use in the applied sciences. The algorithms can be easily implemented on a computer, and most people who have access to a computer may find that many programs are already available to perform these tasks. The emphasis here will be on the effective use of computer methods—merely having a set of working programs does not guarantee that the nonspecialist computer user will find efficient procedures for analyzing a particular set of data. There are a great many books in print giving the mathematical operations—and programming techniques for implementing them—but very little has been published to help people learn how to use such methods effectively.

For the past 10 years, I have been involved in attempts to train geologists, engineers, market analysts, and others in computer methods. While these people may be very familiar with statistical concepts, and be used to working with computer output, they often have not been directly involved in running computer programs. The general experience is that everyone has to learn the "tricks of the trade" the hard way, by trial and error. If they are lucky, experienced users in the same organization may be able to help speed up this process. The purpose of this book is to make such experience more widely available.

The advent of "personal" computers and other inexpensive hardware means that many more people are now running their own computer studies, while in the past they would have relied on expert staff in a computer department to do this work. Professionals in geology, forestry, agriculture, commodities and stock trading, and many other fields are becoming computer users. They cannot of course devote full time to learning computer methods, as their primary functions remain in other areas.

There are two main groups who may find this book useful. The first consists of those who wish to use a computer to aid in data analysis, but who are not themselves computer experts (students and people in professional occupations, for example). For these people, my intention is to show the capabilities they should look for in the programs available to them, and to provide practical suggestions on how to use standard programs. The second group consists of analysts and programmers who develop data analysis systems. I hope they will gain insight into how their programs might be applied, to aid in future enhancements.

After the introduction in Chapter 1, the book is divided into three main sections. The first deals with the basics of analyzing data on a computer. Chapter 2 discusses the preparatory stages, which include developing an understanding of the computer system and how to use it. In addition, the data must be put into a computer-compatible form, which is frequently taken for granted, although of fundamental importance in obtaining useable results. In Chapter 3, frequency distributions are introduced, with simple data displays such as histograms providing the key. Chapter 4 moves on to the problem of investigating data with more than one variable. Here, correlation matrices and two-variable scatter plots are of great value. Chapter 5 contains suggestions for designing programs to allow these basic tools to be used effectively. In addition to flexible analysis software, a good set of utility routines (for data sorting, selection, listing, etc.) is essential.

Many problems in analysis involve data which have a spatial component, that is, which can be located on a map. Generally this involves plotting data on a two-dimensional coordinate system, which is the general topic of Part II. Chapter 6 outlines the principles of computer graphics. In Chapter 7, the requirements for effective application of graphics to data analysis are studied. Chapter 8 deals with specific techniques for combining the basic statistical methods with plotting to determine spatial structure and locate anomalous data. In Chapter 9 this is extended by considering additional methods for enhancing the visual impact of computer plots.

Part III is a brief review of more advanced analysis techniques. Chapter 10 covers advanced statistical methods. These include geostatistics, which allows rigourous statistical procedures to be applied in spatial data analysis. In addition, Chapter 10 contains an overview of powerful multivariate methods like factor analysis, and considers the application of computer graphics to aid in interpreting the results. Chapter 11 considers special analysis methods designed for array-oriented data, including time-series analysis and image analysis for remote sensing. Finally, in Chapter 12 the subject turns to interpretation of the data, which frequently involves an excercise in model-building.

Throughout the book are example applications of these methods, drawn largely from the earth sciences, but also including other types of data. The nature of the data in the examples is secondary to the techniques, which are quite general. A review of principles for effective use of computer methods is given in appendix A, along with an outline of a working data analysis system, given in Appendix B. Finally, there is a list of references and sources of more detailed information on many of the specialized topics introduced here, and a glossary of basic terms used in data processing and computer graphics.

It is a great help to any computer user to be able to draw on the experience of others. I have been fortunate in this regard, since I have received a great deal of useful advice from associates at Chevron and Placer. As this book stems from my work at these companies, I am indebted to all who have helped me. While they are too numerous to list here, I would like to extend my thanks to each one.

A few people deserve special thanks. Bart Cramer (of Chevron in Houston) showed me many useful techniques for plotting data, taught me the great power of simple tools such as histograms and scatter plots, and demonstrated the advantage of a flexible approach. Bill Robertson (of Chevron in Calgary) was also a valuable source of practical ideas. At Placer, Peter Kowalczyk, Jerry Thornton, and Bruno Barde provided a thorough test of many of the basic concepts in this book, and helped in developing an easy-to-use set of programs. Peter Bradshaw instigated the general concept of providing an interactive analysis system for occasional computer users at Placer.

The encouragement I received from my superiors for learning and developing new ideas was also a valuable asset. At Chevron, Paul Skakun, Dave Peacock, Al Singleton, and Garth Greenwood, among others stand out in this regard. At Placer, Ed Rychkun and John Brunette have given me the freedom to develop new ideas. If there are any names I have omitted, I will apologize in advance.

In preparing the manuscript, the Univac 1100 was indispensable, and Al Kemp helped me to prepare some of the figures: their assistance is greatly appreciated. The plotting program CPS1 (from Radian Corporation, of Austin, Texas) has been invaluable to Placer as a company, and to me in preparing the computer graphics displays in this book.

Finally I must thank my family (Nunzia, Cristina, and Daniel) for their support.

WILLIAM R. GREEN

British Columbia, Canada
January 1985

CONTENTS

COMPUTER-AIDED DATA ANALYSIS

CHAPTER 1

APPLICATIONS OF DATA ANALYSIS

Throughout history, man has sought to increase his knowledge and understanding of his surroundings. Such efforts usually begin with observations of some natural event, followed by attempts to define the underlying causes of that event. A natural extension of these acts is an attempt to predict when (or where) particular events will occur. Although pure curiosity is a strong incentive, more practical motives are often involved as well. For example, early astronomical studies produced economic benefits by predicting the seasons, but must also have infused feelings of intellectual achievement in primitive astronomers.

In the broadest sense, data analysis can be considered to include all such studies. The observations we wish to study constitute the "data" (following the Latin, an individual observation is a "datum"). The normal definition of "analysis" is the separation of a whole into parts. In this context there may be many aspects to analysis, including identification of recurring patterns, definition of previously unknown features, and determination of the causes of the phenomenon under investigation.

The ultimate goal is a complete understanding of an event and all of its physical processes. Since the universe may be considered infinitely variable, if viewed on a sufficiently fine scale, it is necessary to define these processes in terms of simplified physical models. The final result of data analysis, then, may be a set of parameters that is consistent with the data.

SCIENTIFIC DATA ANALYSIS

The scientific approach to data analysis is largely a matter of defining rules to make the processes of acquiring and studying data repeatable. This implies that anyone trained in a particular field should be able to obtain the same data by following the same observational procedures, and should get the same results from the same set of data. Many branches of mathematics were developed to formalize analysis, and indeed we might consider mathematics itself to be an embodiment of the rules necessary for studying data. The other sciences can be viewed as the principles needed to model phenomena.

Organized scientific studies have been going on for centuries, and much of our present knowledge of the universe has been derived from the great volumes of data collected in the past. Many current projects aim to refine the historical work by increasing the accuracy of the observations and improving the analysis techniques. As a result, many sciences are very dependent on sophisticated electronic devices to acquire data, and powerful computers to analyze the data and reduce them to an understandable form. Often the methods of analysis are not in themselves new, although the volumes of data treated are orders of magnitude greater than would have been considered manageable even fifteen years ago.

Modern capabilities for collecting enormous volumes of data have resulted in a great reliance on statistical analysis methods. The statistical behavior of a set of data (e.g., the range and distribution of values) is first determined, while particular data values are studied only in relationship to this "average." In some fields, there are so many data that individual values may never be looked at on their own. In seismic exploration, the raw data are the amplitudes of seismic waves taken at short increments of time, and at many locations on the ground. A typical survey might have several hundred "records," each containing 200,000 or more "samples."

Progressive improvement in data acquisition and analysis eventually results in a need to revise the physical explanation of the phenomenon. This often results from observation of previously undetected subtle behavior not accounted for in current theory. There are many examples of this effect in scientific history. The Ptolemaic model of planetary motions proved adequate for centuries, but was replaced by Kepler's model of elliptical orbits which provided a better explanation for deviations from circular motion. Newton's laws of motion were a marvel when first developed, but had to be extended by Einstein to include the relativistic effects first observed in the late 19th Century.

AIMS OF DATA ANALYSIS

Once a scientific problem has been defined, the first step is to record observations of the events involved. After a number of data have been collected (perhaps over a period of time or at different locations), it may be possible to determine if there are recognizable patterns. If so, data can be extrapolated to predict future events, or to infer useful properties related to the observations. There were a number of notable successes quite early in man's history, including the prediction of the motions of the sun and moon, the discovery of areas suitable for agriculture, and the location of mineral resources.

The first aim of analysis, then, could be described as finding whether a set of data is in any sense predictable. This can be defined as determining the "structure" of the data. There may be many components to the structure; the key problem is to find those that are most significant. The characteristics of a set of data that has a structural component might include a tendency to take on preferred values, a similarity to adjacent values (in time or space), and a dependence on the value of other variables observed at the same location.

Finding a structural component in a set of data often implies that the data values are functionally related to another variable which defines position. This might be time (day to day variations in temperature or stock prices, for example), linear position (air pollution measurements along a highway), spatial position (population per unit area throughout a country), or indeed any coordinate system that is relevant to the problem. The structure is that part of the measured value which can be predicted knowing the coordinates of the observation in the chosen coordinate system.

If a structure can be identified, it can be removed from the data to produce a "residual" field. In many cases, the first level of attack on the residuals is to search for unusual values (those much higher or lower than the average, for example). These abnormal events are called "anomalies." The next step is to determine if the anomalies themselves contain a structural component that might be used to refine the physical model.

Strong structural features in the data may obscure the presence of secondary effects which are equally interesting. A classic example can be drawn from astronomy. A planetary orbit is dominated by the gravitational attraction of the sun, although small perturbations due to other bodies in the Solar System can also be detected. A path that takes account only of the sun must be worked out before these variations can be studied as a separate occurrence. In fact, this type of analysis led to the discovery of the outer planets, by indicating the approximate part of the sky in which to look. It is widely believed that there are still other planets to be discovered beyond Pluto, since our current knowledge of the orbits of the outer planets cannot be totally explained in terms of the identified bodies.

In some cases, identification of anomalies is an important step in itself, since they can point to areas of intrinsic interest. In exploring for minerals, geochemical measurements of trace element concentrations in rock or soil samples are frequently used in the first stages. After accounting for regional trends, the geologist might locate all of the high values for one element on a map to delineate areas for more detailed study. There are many possible variations, of course, such as examining ratios, or requiring that several elements have coincident anomalous readings. The key principle is that recognition of the unusual situation can be an incentive for further investigation.

Another type of structure may be present if the data can be grouped into distinct classes based on the data values. In this case, it may not be possible to predict values without first accounting for the characteristics of the groups. In the geochemical example, the "background" levels used to search for anomalies may be very different when samples from different types of rock are considered. When this is the case, the groups may be determined by independent observation, as when a geologist notes the predominant type of rock. Failing this, grouping may be attempted by investigating the statistical behavior of data. This approach is the aim of multivariate statistical methods such as factor analysis. These techniques are widely applied in analysis of the spectral data recorded by the LANDSAT satellites. Data clustering and pattern recognition can often be used to indicate areas suitable for agriculture or mineral development, by comparing poorly explored territory to locations whose potential is known.

Another problem in isolating the significant features of the data is the presence of observation errors. While these may be systematic functions of the data collecting procedure, more often they can be considered to be random "noise" added to a real "signal." The first objective of analysis is to remove the noise so that later studies can assume the data to be error-free. A major goal of any data collection procedure is to reduce the magnitude of the errors as much as possible. In general, however, one cannot expect to record noise-free data (due to the physical limitations of the instruments and the presence of natural background "noise" levels).

In any study, there is always the possibility that an unknown phenomenon will be present. In prehistoric times, the causes of everyday events were unknown, so the first steps in studying the universe naturally dealt with events such as weather, seasons, and the motions of celestial bodies. In modern science, new phenomena may not be apparent until considerable effort has been expended in analysis. In some fields, a major aim of analysis is in fact to detect previously unknown events (for example the ongoing search for new particles in high-energy physics). In other cases, discoveries have been made accidentally during the investigation of totally different problems. The first pulsar was detected in 1967 during a radio-telescope search for new quasars, which are an entirely different type of body.

MODELING AND DATA INTERPRETATION

We are as interested in "why" things happen as "how," so explanations of the causes of observed events are a major goal of any analysis. The process of finding a physical explanation for observed data is often called "interpretation."

Even if a true understanding of the physical process has not been reached, a great deal can often be achieved by studying the available data. The development of astronomical knowledge provides an illustration. It is now well known that early societies (for example the Mayans and the builders of Stonehenge) had detailed records of planetary motions and could predict eclipses by extrapolating from observed patterns. The true nature of the dynamics of the Solar System was not made clear until much later, when Kepler developed his laws of motion in the 17th Century.

If analysis can successfully isolate different components in data, and if the sources of the phenomenon are at least partly understood, it may be possible to interpret data in terms of a model of the phenomenon. Before any data can be effectively interpreted, a relationship between the observations and their sources must be defined. This will not be exactly known, and in fact may be completely wrong, if the prevailing theory later proves to be invalid. It is the task of the interpreter to see if the data fit the theory, and, if not, to seek ways to extend or modify the model to compensate for discrepancies.

As an application of data interpretation, consider seismological studies of the earth's structure. The pertinent data are sets of earthquake records from seismographic stations, showing a number of seismic waves arriving at different times. The amount of time it takes for a given wave to travel from the earthquake source to the station is strongly related to the depths of the structural boundaries (which reflect or bend seismic waves). The data are also influenced by other factors, which must be included as parameters of the physical model. A typical model defines the earth as concentric layers (i.e., inner and outer core, mantle, and crust), for which density, temperature, and seismic velocity are known functions of depth. One objective of the interpretation is to define the depths of the boundaries between the layers.

An alternate problem might be to assume current estimates for the boundary positions to be correct, and to seek to improve the model values for seismic velocity or density.

The problem of interpretation is then to relate the effects of variations in the model (i.e., the sources) to variations in the data. One approach is to calculate the expected observations consistent with the data, given a known functional relationship. This is called the "direct" problem in modeling physical phenomena. An alternate method is to solve the related "inverse" problem: to define the nature of the sources (i.e., the parameters of the model) from the observations. The inverse solution is usually considerably more difficult, as it requires a more detailed knowledge of the physical processes, and more elaborate measures to guard against the influence of spurious components in the data.

As an example, consider a geophysicist who wishes to relate a set of surface gravity measurements to buried ore bodies. After first isolating a local anomaly by removing an estimated regional component, a first model might attribute the entire anomaly to a single large body. One approach to interpretation would then be to calculate the gravity response of such a body, given some assumptions about its size, depth, and density (i.e., to solve the "forward" problem for gravity). If significant differences between the real data and the theoretical response of the model remain, additional sources (perhaps smaller and shallower) might be added to the model. The gravity effect of the model is then recomputed, with a new comparison to the data. This process could be repeated a number of times, until an acceptable "fit" of the model to the data is achieved.

Using the same example, an alternate approach would be a solution of the "inverse" problem for the given gravity anomaly. In this case, the relationship of observed gravity to a source body is applied in the opposite direction. The calculations start with the gravity data, and the results are the parameters of a variable number of sources (size, density, depth) of some assumed shape. It is important to note here that a physical model is built into the inverse calculation, which means the results can only be valid within all of the assumptions of that model. As before, if the results are not reasonable, a revised model may be required. This decision is frequently dependent on the judgement of the interpreter, and cannot be considered absolute.

An inherent limitation in many interpretation problems is that a number of different models may fit the data equally well. This lack of "uniqueness" can be treated in two ways. First, the number of parameters in the model may be reduced, in effect producing a class of models of which only one provides a "best" fit to the data. A more rigorous approach is to calculate the range of model parameters which define the set of all acceptable models.

In either event, the result may be that the data will provide little useful information on their own, if the range turns out to be large. This is equivalent to saying that a unique solution will be found only for a very restricted type of model. For example, in a gravity exploration survey, there are an infinite number of models which fit the data. The only common parameter that can be uniquely determined from the local gravity anomaly is the total mass of the source bodies. The solution to this dilemma lies in considering other available information at the same time. In our example, geologic constraints must be applied to the model to obtain a useful interpretation of the gravity data.

Interpretation of data in terms of a physical model might be viewed as the final stage of analysis, or as a separate operation which relies on data analysis to extract the components of the data which are pertinent to the model. In either case, it demands accurate application of both the mathematical techniques used to prepare the data for interpretation and of the physical principles associated with the phenomenon. Both operations can be very complex, and it is rare to find scientists who are expert in both areas. As a result, it is common to have different people involved in the two operations. It is essential, however, that a data analyst have at least a background knowledge of the physical problem, and that the interpreter understand the basic mathematical procedures. If this is not the case, it is very possible (indeed probable) that the analyst will provide inappropriate (although accurate) data to the interpreter, who will accept them on faith.

Although interpretation is based on physical principles, in many cases it cannot be as rigidly defined as the mathematical procedures of statistical analysis. A scientist's intuition and practical experience often must be applied to reduce a complex set of data to understandable form. The goal of exact repeatability cannot be attained in such cases. Although this is unfortunate, it is an inevitable result of the fact that we are always dealing with a simplified picture, not the complete reality.

THE ROLE OF THE COMPUTER

Many of the steps taken in analyzing a set of data require mathematical operations. Although these can be done manually (if the volume of data is not too great), the use of a computer is essential to achieve effective results. As more routine and repetitive tasks are delegated to the computer, the analyst will have more time to pursue alternate methods, investigate anomalies, and develop a complete understanding of the data. This often means that a more detailed study can be done in the time available to complete the analysis, and that more confidence can be placed in the results.

The primary advantage of using a computer in data analysis is this reduction of the time spent on repetitive mathematical calculations. In fields where great volumes of data must be studied, the use of a computer is mandatory, since manual calculations would take years (if not lifetimes).

Another major contribution from the computer is its ability to store large amounts and different types of data. Interdisciplinary studies which simultaneously examine data from a variety of sources are becoming more common. With current "database" techniques for cross-referencing and selecting subsets of data, a computer can provide almost unlimited combinations of data to be tested. This allows the analyst a free rein in asking "what if" questions about the interrelationships of the data.

Following the problem of large sets of data a little further, the computer provides a number of convenient methods for converting data into manageable forms for the analyst and interpreter. Statistical summaries are often very useful, but the real power comes when computer "graphics" displays are produced. Adapting the old adage that a picture is worth a thousand words, we might say that a computer generated plot can replace a million numbers. As we shall see later, compression and summarization of data is an invaluable tool in all phases of data processing, from initial verification and error checking to final evaluation of interpreted results.

Despite its enormous "number-crunching" power, a computer is not a complete analysis system in itself. The experience and judgement of the human analyst cannot be totally replaced. The real world is so complex that it will never be possible to completely define all possible variations to a given problem within the confines of a computer program. The ability to look beyond the limitations of a current model and redefine the parameters of a problem is essential in many cases. Anyone using a computer must always bear in mind that its results are only valid within the assumptions incorporated in the current model.

These fundamental limitations of computers have often discouraged nonspecialists from using them. A feeling may arise that restrictions in some areas necessarily make the whole procedure suspect. As a result, jobs for which the computer is ideally suited continue to be handled manually.

Another problem can arise from the opposite viewpoint: that the computer's answers can always be taken as complete and perfectly accurate. One can easily reach its conclusion when presented with computer printouts filled with detailed statistics and other calculations given to seven or eight significant figures. The process by which the machine reduces several hundred pages of numbers to a detailed contour map may seem so magical that no thought is given to the possibility the map is not completely correct (or for that matter what "correct" means in this context).

The best situation of course is to have both the computer and the human user make a full contribution. This means that the computer can take over the jobs of data handling, calculation, and display, while the analyst concentrates on evaluating the results. It is pointless to expect the computer to provide final answers, and senseless to waste the time of highly trained people on routine jobs. The interplay of man and machine is a fundamental aspect of this process, which must be considered by both the developers and users of computer systems. To properly define the transition points where human intervention is needed, there must be a full understanding of the restrictions of computer programs, and a thorough knowledge of the particular problem under investigation.

Having completed an overview of the aims of data analysis, the remainder of this book will deal with methods for using a computer to make these tasks easier. My aim is to illustrate the functions of an effective computerized analysis system. In designing such a system, the key principle is that computer programs should be set up to encourage use of the machine, without demanding total dependence on built-in assumptions. Scientific reasoning requires a flexible approach: using a computer should increase the ability to test different theories, not restrict choices to predetermined paths.

PART I

BASIC DATA ANALYSIS USING A COMPUTER

This section covers the basic procedures for analyzing data with a computer. To do this requires a knowledge of both statistics and fundamental principles of computer systems.

CHAPTER 2. INITIAL STEPS IN COMPUTER DATA ANALYSIS

To understand how a computer may be used, it is important to have some understanding of how it works. The first part of this chapter outlines basic principles of data processing. Before data analysis begins, it is necessary to have the required data accessible to the computer programs. The results of any analysis are worthless if erroneous data have been used in the study.

Entering and validating data in a computer file may often be taken for granted, although these tasks are perhaps the single most important steps in analysis.

CHAPTER 3.
BASIC STATISTICAL ANALYSIS

One of the fundamental steps in understanding a set of data is determining the distribution of values. This is usually achieved by calculating basic measures such as mean and standard deviation, and by producing a graphical display in the form of a histogram. Producing histograms with different parameters is an effective way of studying both the overall features, and of isolating extreme values. If the data approximate a normal distribution, a number of higher level statistical measurers can be applied.

CHAPTER 4.
MULTIVARIATE DATA ANALYSIS

The methods presented in Chapter 3 are extended to consider those situations where more than one variable is involved. The primary problem is then determining if the variables are functionally related to each other. For numeric data, a correlation matrix provides a quick measure of interdependence. Many problems can be reduced to two variables, allowing the use of scatter plots and simple curve fitting to estimate the relationship of the variables.

CHAPTER 5.
EFFECTIVE USE OF COMPUTERIZED ANALYSIS SYSTEMS

To gain the full benefit from a computer's power, the user needs to develop procedures for using a variety of different programs. In addition to basic tools such as histograms and scatter-plots, programs for sorting data, selecting specific fields, and listing subsets of data are often required. This chapter discusses ways of improving analysis software to make these tasks easier, and suggests methods for taking advantage of utility functions to supplement the basic results.

CHAPTER 2

INITIAL STEPS IN COMPUTER DATA ANALYSIS

Before data can be analyzed on a computer, two preliminary steps are required. First, the analyst must acquire a basic knowledge of how to use the available computer systems. This step is of course necessary only for the first use of a particular system, although a reasonable level of experience may be necessary for efficiency. Second, is it necessary to have the data in a form which the computer understands. This must be done for every project. In this chapter, the basic principles of computer systems are reviewed, and the methods and problems associated with preparing data for computer analysis are discussed. In later chapters, we will assume an understanding of these initial topics.

PRINCIPLES OF COMPUTER DATA PROCESSING

Computers are now so widespread that the majority of people working in commercial or scientific fields have had at least some exposure to them. It is important that a user understand how a computer works in addition to what it can do if he or she is to use it effectively. In this section, basic concepts and terms used in data processing are defined for readers not familiar with computers. This will necessarily be a sketchy account: anyone wishing more details should consult one of the many books on principles of computers (some examples are listed in the References). While it is desirable to describe these ideas in nontechnical language, in any discussion of this type it is virtually impossible to completely avoid the use of jargon. The basic terminology will be used in later chapters, since in many cases it provides a convenient shorthand, which should streamline the discussion.

To begin, we must note that a "computer" is really a "system," composed of a number of separate parts. These are normally grouped into two main types: hardware (the electronic and mechanical equipment), and software (the coded instructions which control the functions of the hardware).

1. Hardware

The electronic devices which store data and do calculations are collectively knows as *hardware*. There are three major functions that the hardware must perform, each involving special types of equipment: computation, input/output, and data storage. The separate components can be combined in a single unit, but these functions can still be considered independent when visualizing the operation of the system.

a. The Central Processing Unit (CPU)

The ability to do calculations is the essence of a computer. This function requires a number of hardware components, usually considered as a single entity called the Central Processing Unit (or CPU). The CPU is responsible for all of the operations performed by the system, including loading programs and data into memory, doing calculations, and transferring "output" to the appropriate places. Other pieces of hardware attached to the CPU are called peripherals.

Unlike the arithmetic we are used to, a computer does its work in terms of "binary" numbers. This means that everything is reduced to a 0 or 1 representation, a pattern which is emulated electronically by high or low voltages, or by opposite states of magnetic polarity. All data stored in the system and used by the CPU for calculations are in this "bit" form. A bit is a binary digit, which can have a value of either 1 or 0. A group of bits treated as single entity is called a "byte." A byte is generally the number of bits needed to represent a single character (very often 8 bits make up 1 byte, although other values are possible). A "word" is a group of bits needed to store a single number, typically 32 or 36 on large computers. Storage and retrieval of data is usually done on a word basis (i.e., whole words are transferred as a unit).

This internal configuration is seldom apparent to anyone using the computer, since it always translates strings of 0's and 1's to conventional letters or numbers before the "user" sees them. When the data are in a character format (such as a computer file containing the text of this book), an arbitrary coding scheme is used to translate each byte into a character. Numeric data can be stored more efficiently by expanding the string of bits as a series of powers of 2:

$$1110101 = 1(1)+0(2)+1(4)+0(8)+1(16)+1(32)+1(64) = 117$$

A computer's internal handling of numbers can take two forms. A numeric value may be considered as an integer, in which case the entire string of bits in a word will be converted using the power of two expansion. Alternately, it may be treated as a "floating point" number (a decimal number between 0 and 1 multiplied by some power of 10) by breaking the word into two integers. Typically, seven or eight bits are used for the exponent, and the rest for the mantissa. In any numeric expansion, one bit is interpreted as a sign, to allow for negative values.

There is a subtle problem associated with this scheme for coding numbers in that the "precision" of the stored values is limited. Treating a 36-bit word as a floating point number means that only about seven significant digits can be carried. Even worse, this value is effectively reduced when a series of numeric operations are performed, as "round-off" errors tend to accumulate. In some applications, the effect of this problem is reduced by using "double-precision" for numeric data (i.e., two words are considered as a single number).

b. Input/Output Devices

In order to do any useful calculations, a computer must be able to transfer data in and out of the system. This capability is provided by Input/Output (or I/O for short) devices, such as display terminals, tape and disk readers ("drives"), lineprinters, and plotters. Many of these can alternately be used for input and output. Terminals (also called CRT for cathode ray tube, or VDT for video display terminal) are a good example: they can be used for most data entry jobs, and for receiving printed or graphical results of computations. Some devices, however, are designed only for very specific jobs, and belong to only one half of the I/O function. An example is a plotter, which is used to display the graphical output from various programs, but generally has no input capability.

I/O devices tend to break down more often than other components, since they have more mechanical functions than most strictly electronic equipment. For example, many printers use moving chains which strike the paper, and are thus are much more prone to wear and tear than a memory chip which is subject only to electrical activity. This is becoming more of a concern to nonspecialists. The use of "personal" computer systems results in moving hardware (and associated maintenance problems) from large computer centers into individual offices. The responsibility for keeping the systems operational usually moves at the same time. This includes routine tasks such as loading paper and connecting printers, as well as making repairs (or contacting a repairperson).

c. Data Storage

Given the ability to transfer data from place to place, the system must also be able to store data. The hardware devices for data storage can be grouped into two types. Computer "memory" is reserved for very fast data retrieval of instructions and data used during the operation ("execution") of programs. Because of the demand for ultra-high speed, memory capacity in any computer must be limited, so facilities are also needed to store data and programs which are not currently active. A major function of some I/O devices is to transfer data between memory and these secondary devices.

Secondary storage is usually handled by a combination of magnetic tapes and magnetic "disks." The computer "reads" existing data from a storage device into memory, and "writes" new data from memory to storage. Tapes can store enormous amounts of data, but are relatively slow to read, since they must be processed sequentially from beginning to end. In addition, manual intervention of a computer operator is needed to load a tape onto a tape drive, so that data can be read into the system. Disks provide an intermediate stage between memory and tapes. Data access is quite fast, although not fast enough to keep up with the CPU (hence the need to transfer data to memory). Capacity is much greater than memory, although not comparable to tapes. Disks are something like a continuously spinning phonograph record, with a number of sensors which allow data to be read from different areas without a sequential search from the start. In effect, a single disk "pack" is subdivided into many "sectors" ("tracks," "segments," and other terms are also common). This means that data from a particular part of a disk can be located directly, with a great savings in the time needed to transfer a given amount of data.

A set of data which is to be considered as a separate entity is usually called a "file." Many files can be stored on a single tape or disk. On tape, they will be arranged sequentially so that they can be located by searching from the beginning. On disk, the location of a given file usually bears no relationship to the physical partitioning of the disk (often a single file will actually be stored in many small segments on a disk). As we shall see in the next section, this does not pose a problem to anyone using the computer, since the ability to locate a given disk file is provided by software. Another function of the software is to allow individual "records" to be extracted from the file (a "record" here means the set of data associated with a single event or location).

2. Software

The apparent intelligence of the computer merely reflects the abilities of the people who write its programs. Their instructions control the functions performed by the hardware, and are collectively described by the complementary term *software*. We often speak also of *programs,* which are collections of instructions (sometimes termed pieces of software) designed to perform a specific task. The total set of software, then, consists of a number of different programs.

A basic requirement of software is that it allow instructions to be written in a form other than the series of bits that the hardware understands. The coding of binary instructions for the hardware is called "machine language," while the software is written using any of a number of "programming languages." The ability to translate from a programming language into machine language is therefore an essential function of the software available on any computer. Translation programs are generally called "compilers." Frequently used languages include FORTRAN (for Formula Translator; a language widely used in scientific applications), COBOL (oriented towards business reports and accounting), and Basic (often used as the operating language for small computers). Pascal (also common in microcomputers), and APL (noted for its compact mathematical syntax), are becoming increasingly popular.

Although many different programming languages are in use, it is common for a software "system" to be written in a single language. That is, a large set of programs used in conjunction with one another are usually written in the same language. This avoids problems in translating between languages, and generally allows a programmer to be more efficient, as common algorithms can easily be shared by several programs. In many cases this also gives a strong incentive to continue development of programs in a particular language. If a switch is made, the capability of using existing routines may be lost, offsetting the potential advantages of any new language. There may also be a large volume of software available (from commercial sources or technical publications) in one particular language, and not in others. In scientific data analysis, for example, a vast number of FORTRAN programs are readily available, so this language remains the most heavily used, despite the attractive features offered by some of its competitors.

Software is frequently distinguished into two types: "system" and "applications" software. System software is generally supplied by the computer manufacturer to provide the fundamental instructions for operating the computer system. The "operating system" is another term used to denote the collection of programs which control the functions of the hardware. Applications software is the set of programs that perform the tasks required by the users of the computer system. Programs in this group are generally developed by the users themselves, or acquired from organizations which specialize in software development.

The operating system of any modern computer is just as important as the hardware for providing the ability to do calculations. The operating system controls all the activities of the hardware, and is the indispensable link between the applications programs and the CPU. Among other things, the system software must locate particular programs and data on disk files, load them into memory, and send output to the desired devices. Most computers larger than a desk-top personal computer have the capability of performing several tasks at the same time. This is another function performed by the system software, demanding a continual monitoring of all concurrent "jobs." System "resources" such as memory and access to the CPU are continually redistributed among the active jobs to maximize the total amount of work being completed.

A number of utility functions are also usually included in the system software. Among these are routines to monitor disk space allocated to each user, record the usage of particular programs or devices, copy files from disk to tape, and so on. In general, users need not worry about the details of such programs, since they are tightly integrated into the system. The main concern should be that the capabilities are known, and relatively easy to use, so that the full power of the system can be tapped.

Local applications programs can also take advantage of much of the system software. First of all, the system software provides the necessary compilers to translate "source code" from the language used in programming into machine instructions. There is usually an intermediate step, where the local program is "linked" to the "library" of system software. This allows many standard functions to be simply called from existing software, without requiring each program to provide the complete instructions. One example is the use of mathematical functions such as square roots and exponentials, which can usually be performed by a one-line instruction which gets the function from the system library.

In addition to libraries of system software, most computer installations have applications libraries. These are used in exactly the same way, but contain frequently used functions designed for the particular types of jobs that run on that machine. A common example is a library of plotting subroutines, which allow many standard types of computer graphics output to be created by simple calls.

3. Firmware

A third term has come into vogue in recent years: *firmware* denotes programs that are permanently encoded in storage devices; they are in effect a hybrid of hardware and software. The usual role of firmware components is to provide particular hardware devices with extended capabilities for common operations. The effect is that some functions normally provided by conventional software are "built-in" to the equipment for immediate recall by function keys or other external prompts.

One example is the use of microprocessors as "intelligence" for computer terminals. Firmware components provide such functions as storing extra command lines and displaying the position of the "cursor." Another command use of firmware is in computer graphics devices. For effective computer plotting, it is convenient to place some intelligence in the output devices. When a graphics terminal or plotter can decipher symbol codes, scale the plot, and isolate sections of the plot, it is often possible to greatly reduce the amount of data that must be transferred from the computer. This is especially important in cases where the plotting device is at a remote location and the plotted data must be transmitted over long-distance communications lines.

Firmware is also largely responsible for the impressive capabilities now available in small personal computers. In many cases, a simple operating system and language compiler are incorporated, to be immediately available as soon as the machine is turned on. Specialized programs can also be installed via firmware, allowing the manufacturer to provide the capabilities of a large program without having to deliver the source code for the program to each buyer.

4. Interfaces

The links between different components in a computer system are called interfaces. An interface can be hardware, such as the I/O "channels" used for data transfers; or software, such as the operating system, which can be viewed as the interface between the applications programs and the rest of the system.

The primary hardware interface between the computer user and the machine is a computer terminal. The user sends information to the computer by typing on a keyboard, and receives messages from the system on a video screen. A typical terminal displays 24 lines of 80 characters each, or about half a page of text at a time, including both the typed entries from the keyboard, and the output from the computer. The effectiveness of the user's interaction with the system is a function of the physical characteristics of the terminal (e.g., the amount of glare on the screen, and the "feel" of the keyboard), and the system software which controls I/O at the terminal. The amount of the screen that can be used for input, the ease of correcting typing errors, and the speed of output to the terminal are among the factors which contribute to the user's degree of satisfaction with the entire system. These factors are also influenced by other components of the system besides the terminal itself.

A "control" language provides the essential interface between the user and the system software. Each operating system has its own command language, with specific rules of syntax that must be learned by the user. Most of a novice's training goes into learning these rules, which include specific commands to run a program, create a data file, and so on. Conventions for allowed file names must also be committed to memory. The commands for heavily used system programs (listing a file, summarizing the contents of a collection of files, etc.) must also be learned.

Access to files (for simple examination, addition or correction of data, etc.) is usually supplied by a system "text editor." This is a program that displays portions of a file on a terminal screen, and allows revisions to be made. Changes are often simply a matter of retyping the desired parts of the display (by moving the cursor to the appropriate places), and signalling the completion of corrections with a special key. In addition to (or instead of) such a "full-screen" operation, revisions can be done as a search for specific strings of characters (e.g., "change all occurrences of 1000 to 2000"). Editing programs also allow insertion or deletion of blocks of text, and generally provide extensive "back-up" facilities to recover data in the event of inadvertent deletions.

The interface between the user and the applications programs is also important. This is the portion of each program which gets information from the user. There can be a great range here, from programs which ask detailed questions before reading parameters, to those which assume that a complex set of instructions will be entered without any help. If programs are easy to use, and allow fast input of important parameters, productivity is increased, since more jobs can be prepared by the user in a fixed period of time.

5. Machine "Intelligence"

A point which cannot be emphasized too much is that a computer does not "think," and never makes independent decisions. The machine is in effect no more than a calculator, albeit an enormously fast and powerful one. Even in dealing with special systems for "artificial intelligence," it is the software and not the hardware that provides the apparent reasoning ability of the machine. When limitations, awkward procedures, and related problems are encountered, restrictions written into the programs are usually responsible. Although such restrictions may be needed to allow for physical limitations in the hardware, there are ways of implementing them that ensure minimal external effect. If a user encounters difficulties, the solution is to consult the program developer about improving the software, rather than to consider the problem an unavoidable part of using the computer. Admittedly there are cases where the restrictions are in the system software, which the computer manufacturer may be reluctant to modify.

This is more than just an abstract comment: even experienced computer users often continue to use unnecessarily complicated procedures because of a feeling that "the computer has to have it this way." There may well be better methods already in existence (although poorly documented), or available through minor changes. A small investment of time in searching for simpler methods may eventually pay large dividends.

6. Data Flow Through a Computer System

All operations that use a computer can be visualized in three basic steps: input, processing, and output. "Input" implies that a set of data is available to the computer system, and thus involves entering data into computer files. "Processing" designates the operation of programs which use the input as raw material and perform various calculations. "Output" is the result of processing, and can be new data files, printed messages, graphical data, or a combination of these.

In order to analyze data on a computer, it is first necessary to determine if the facilities are available to perform these three steps. If the data are not already in a computer file, they must be entered into the computer system. Programs that can do the desired processing must be located (or developed), and user must learn how to operate them. Finally, the output requirements need to be defined, taking into consideration the limitations of the particular computer system. There is no point in undertaking an extensive computer mapping project, for instance, if the available equipment cannot produce the number of maps required in a reasonable amount of time.

7. Distributed Processing

Due to the ever decreasing cost of computer hardware, many organizations have a variety of machines deployed for data processing. As we might logically expect, each device tends to be used for tasks for which it is best suited. The end result is that the data processing tasks are shared among a variety of devices, instead of being concentrated in one central system. This is called "distributed processing."

Distributed processing often involves a "network" of computers in different locations, especially in large organizations with a number of offices. Using high-speed communications services, it is possible to use a computer thousands of miles away as though it were in the same building. Smaller machines at each local site can be used for such tasks as entering data, creating printer listings, and controlling special devices (such as a plotter or digitizer), while a more powerful system at a central office provides the capability for managing large data files, and extensive "number-crunching."

"Distributed processing" originally meant having various satellite devices linked to a large computer. All operations were controlled by the central machine; that is, data would be passed to a particular device automatically when the appropriate operation was requested. The proliferation of cheap microcomputers has changed this basic form, however. Since a microcomputer can work on its own, or be used as a terminal for a larger machine, the choice of where to do many tasks is now up to the user. There is a considerable danger of making the wrong choice, and losing some of the efficiencies afforded by using the computer in the first place.

PREPARING DATA FOR COMPUTER ANALYSIS

Before we begin analyzing data, they must be in a form suitable to the chosen procedure. To begin with, some type of permanent record is essential, to allow the observations of different people (or different instruments) to be combined. These records must also be in a logically defined form, to enable an analyst who was not involved in collecting the data to extract the desired information without ambiguity. To ensure the goal of repeatability, unexplained items must be avoided.

These basic rules are especially important when a computer is used to study data. Although the analyst may be able to understand incomplete data by considering the context, we cannot expect the machine to apply the same level of judgment. The primary rule in preparing data for a computer is to ensure that the information is complete and unambiguous, since the computer cannot "read between the lines."

The starting point of any project, then, is the recording of data. When analysis with a computer is involved, the next requirement is to convert the data from its original form into the strings of bits that the computer can read. This is termed "data entry," and is mandatory regardless of whether the data consist of readings from an electronic device or subjective impressions noted during an experiment. The procedure normally is in two stages:

encoding the data in binary form, and "loading" the data into a storage device. Accurate data entry may often be taken for granted, but is of fundamental importance. No matter how sophisticated the analysis methods, the results are only as good as the input data. This principle is often succinctly stated as "garbage in, garbage out," a phrase which should remain in all computer users' minds.

1. Strategies for Preparing Computer Data Files

Before setting up a computer file, some thought must be given to the data that will be placed in it. As a general rule, any information related to the problem at hand should be included in the file. If some data are judged unimportant and so excluded, the ability to try new approaches in analysis may be lost. If the early stages of analysis suggest a need to use additional data, much time can be lost waiting for a second phase of data entry. This can often take much longer than one might expect, since new and old data will need to be merged. In addition, the setup time for data entry is also repeated, and this may well be the largest factor in completing the job.

In cases where data are recorded automatically, there might be less freedom to define how much information to include in the stored data. Once again, though, the primary rule is not to prejudge the results by deciding that only certain items are significant ahead of time. This decision is after all one of the basic aims of analysis.

Obviously it is not always possible to collect all pertinent data at the same time, or to record everything that might be of interest later. The physical limitations of the recording process have to be considered, along with the time constraints that are often externally imposed on the study. In such cases, the basic rule must be modified to account for these other factors.

2. Procedures for Loading Data into Computer Files

The traditional method of encoding data for computer use was "key-punching" alphanumeric characters on paper cards, which would then be read into the computer system by a "card-reader." Nowadays, punch machines have been largely replaced by "data-entry" terminals, which are used in the same fashion, but store data directly on magnetic discs. This allows easy recall for correction, and much faster data transfer to the main computer.

This procedure provides a very flexible method of data translation, since any combination of letters and numbers is allowed. The operation of "keying" data consists in essence of typing the information as a duplicate from a paper original. To guard against typing errors, the usual practice is to "verify" the data. To do this, the operator keys from the original a second time, while a program in the data entry device compares each character to that received the first time. This method of duplicate entry results in coded data that has very few errors when compared to the original. Of course, it cannot detect errors in the original form, which may be quite prevalent if manual methods are involved.

In many scientific studies which use monitoring instruments to take "observations," it is now common for the instrument to directly record the data on magnetic tape or disks. In these cases, errors due to manual transcription are eliminated, although there is still the possiblity of encountering "bad" tapes or disks which cannot be read later. There is also the chance of instrument malfunction or external "noise" introducing errors in the data.

Often the data to be studied are largely computer generated, and cannot be compared to any original for error checking. Lengthy calculations are often needed as a preliminary stage, so that the input to a particular program may bear little resemblance to the original "observed" value. For example, raw gravity meter readings must be corrected for instrument drift, the effects of latitude, elevation, and topography before any analysis can begin.

3. Merging Different Sets of Data

One problem which can arise in any study is that other data not recorded concurrently may also be needed in the analytical study. Such data must be entered into the computer independently, and merged with the associated data. During this operation, it is very easy to introduce errors if the merging program cannot unambiguously determine which data are meant to be associated with each other.

The need to merge data can arise in many ways. The original data may be in different reports, which must be keyed separately. When automatic recording devices are used, access to other data might not be posssible at the time of recording. For example, in recording spatial data, the sample values must also have location information for analysis. Accurate coordinates of the sample points may not be known until surveying is completed at a later date.

The key to successful merging is to have unique identifiers on each record in each file. The procedure is then to sort the files according to the value of the identifier, so that a merging program can use the identifier to determine when records match. This approach is necessary to account for the possibility that the separate files have different numbers of records. In the example presented earlier, consider the case where many more locations were surveyed than had gravity readings taken. The program which combines the data will sequentially read through both sets of data, comparing the identifier fields to decide when records are to be merged as a single record in the output file. In such cases, it may be necessary to have options to include only complete records in the output, or to write out all input data, leaving blank spaces as required.

4. Error Checking

Regardless of how the data were obtained and entered into a computer file, it is essential that a thorough error-checking procedure be completed before true analysis begins. This might involve manual comparison of computer listings to original forms, calculation of summary statistics, and computer plotting. As we shall see, these are in fact many of the basic tools for analysis, and can be applied in detecting errors as well as in finding structure or real anomalies.

If a certain type of data is used repeatedly, it may be possible to write a program to check for specific errors. This requires that certain constraints on the data items be checkable, for example that values correspond to entries in a table, or lie within stated numeric bounds. This also requires that the format of the records be fixed (or allowed to vary only in a controlled fashion). For example, a geologist might note descriptive parameters of rock samples collected in mineral exploration. Tables of codes can be defined for recording the type of rock, along with its color, crystal structure, texture, and other pertinent information. After entering the data into the computer, an error-checking program can compare all entries to the allowable values for each parameter. From the printed messages of violations produced by the program, corrections can be made to the file (and error-checking repeated as necessary). Any type of data with a restricted number of allowable entries can be checked in this fashion (vegetation types in environmental monitoring, religion, political affiliation in a census, and so on).

Another type of error check can be made if the data are known to be smoothly varying (i.e., if discontinuities in recorded values are not expected). In this case, all values can be compared to adjacent locations, and thresholds of acceptable differences tested. These methods may be totally automatic, or may require inspection of various computer-generated displays which show adjacent data in proper orientation. As before, any data which do not appear to "fit" the expected pattern must be checked before proceeding to the full analytical study.

Whenever an automatic error-checking method is applied, it is essential that an analyst look at the results. It is possible to program the computer to reject such data, but this is a very dangerous practice. The possibility that a computer-detected "error" is really valid data pointing to a significant anomaly cannot be discounted. The judgment of the analyst must be retained in the process of correcting the data. If not, the ability to use past experience in making decisions on the validity of the data is lost. When the volume of data is large, it may not be possible to check each value, and an automatic procedure will be mandatory. This usually means that averages will be used instead of individual readings, so this is not a severe limitation. The large number of data also means the statistical estimates will be more reliable, and the significance of an individual point reduced.

Once all required data have been entered into computer files and a thorough search for errors completed, the true analysis process can begin. Throughout the study, it is very important to bear in mind that errors may still be present in the data. It is virtually impossible to guarantee that all errors have been located ahead of time. While searching for the causes of anomalous data, error sources must always be considered. It should never be assumed that data are 100 percent correct, and the process of testing for errors should never be taken for granted.

5. Databases

To analyze data quickly and efficiently, the methods for locating particular data files should be as simple and reliable as possible. As we noted earlier, a computer's operating system provides the means for creating data files, writing data into files, and reading data when requested. Each system has its own naming conventions and methods for listing the names of files currently available.

Sets of data in a computer are called "databases." This term usually implies that there are some common aspects to the entries. The prices of all stocks on the New York Stock Exchange might reside in one database, while information on unemployment, GNP growth, and other economic indicators would be in another. The information in a database is accessed with a software package known as a "database system" or "database management system" (DBMS). Such programs have the ability to select specific categories of data, particular records, etc. In Chapter 5, we will see the importance of such techniques in studying the interrelationships among different variables.

Complete database systems also contain methods for indexing data. This can be a great help in identifying the contents of computer files, especially if the standard naming conventions do not allow lengthy or multilevel entries for a complete description. We will return to this topic in Chapter 5, as well. The database system will also provide the capability to make corrections, merge new fields or records, combine data from different files, and so on. These utility functions are very useful in the initial preparation of a database, and are often required during analysis as well, to add the results of analysis to the original data.

CHAPTER 3

BASIC STATISTICAL ANALYSIS

Most analytical studies involve data with more than one variable. Although the objective of the study may be to find a functional relationship between variables, each must be examined independently prior to this stage of analysis. Without an understanding of the separate variables, proper evaluation of the interrelationships between them is impossible. In this chapter, we look at the basic statistical tools used to study the behavior of a single variable.

Recall that a primary objective of analysis is to find predictable components in the data. If the observed values are completely random, there is no hope of successful prediction (and little value in performing the analysis). Fortunately, virtually all physical phenomenon that can be expressed by a numeric measure have a tendency to take on preferred values. Many natural constraints are involved in limiting the possible values. For example, temperatures cannot fall below absolute zero, and concentrations of elements in any material must be in the range of 0 to 100 percent. Besides such natural extremes, it is common to see a grouping of values around some central value. For any location, the daily temperature will vary around the average taken over a year, with at least some degree of predictability according to the season.

A vast array of mathematical tools, considered as the distinct subfield of "statistics," can be applied to define these preferential tendencies. This book is not intended as a text in statistics, so mathematical details are generally omitted from the following discussion. Any introductory book on statistics can provide more detailed information.

BASIC STATISTICAL MEASURES

The determination of the statistical behavior of any variable starts with a calculation of the average value of all the measurements. Next, and equally important, is a measure of the tendency for individual "samples" to deviate from the average. An average value, and average deviation, can be calculated in several ways, using different mathematical formulae. The most commonly used measures are the arithmetic "mean" and "standard deviation." The arithmetic mean is a simply the sum of all values, divided by the number of samples, or

$$X = \frac{\text{sum}(x)}{\text{N}} \qquad 3.1$$

where x denotes an individual sample value and N is the total number of samples. The standard deviation is defined as

$$S = SQRT \frac{\text{sum}((x\text{-}X)**2)}{(N\text{-}1)} \qquad 3.2$$

Note that S is calculated from the square of the differences of individual values from the mean (instead of the actual differences) to prevent positive and negative displacements from cancelling each other. Note that the standard deviation is always taken as the positive square root of the "variance" (i.e., the variance is obtained from Eq. 3.2 by omitting the square root). To allow comparisons of relative variability between different variables, a "coefficient of variation" may be calculated, by taking the ratio of the standard deviation to the mean.

Equation 3.2 can also be written as

$$S = SQRT \frac{(\text{sum}(x**2) - (\text{sum}(x))**2 / N)}{(\text{N-1})} \qquad 3.3$$

which is a more convenient form for use on a computer since it does not require a prior calculation of the mean. As a result, all necessary quantities for computing the mean and standard deviation can be accumulated with one "loop" through the available data. In a computer program, a "loop" means a repeated operation which is performed sequentially on all members of an "array" of data.

The extreme minimum and maximum values are often useful in basic analysis as well. They are easily found by testing each value against the current extremes in the same loop used to set the mean. The four basic quantities determined by this first pass through the data can be used throughout the analysis process. Setting parameters for effective display, and testing data to be used in more complex calculations, are common applications.

FREQUENCY DISTRIBUTIONS

Although the mean and standard deviation give an immediate summary of variations in data, they cannot provide details of variations among samples. This requires the calculation of a "frequency distribution," which shows the number of samples which have each particular data value. If a continuous range of values is possible, all values in a specified range are considered the same. For example, in examining temperature charts, measurements might be rounded off to the nearest two degrees in counting frequencies, even if originally recorded to 0.1 degree of accuracy.

The use of frequency distributions is fundamentally related to the concepts of probability. The distribution shows the percentage of total "samples" that fall within a given range of numeric values. If the group of samples being analyzed is representative of the complete "population," this may be taken as a measure of the probability that any given sample will belong to a particular class. A "probability density function" is a mathematical equation that allows the distribution to be calculated; that is, to compute the percentage of values expected within any given range. These theoretical models define the complete range of values in terms of a few basic parameters like the mean and standard deviation.

If a set of data has a known distribution, a great deal of useful information can be easily derived. A frequent problem in data analysis is then to test whether a distribution is of a particular type. Rigorous statistical tests have been developed for many types of distributions by means of probability theory. Alternately, a visual judgement may be made by overplotting the theoretical curve on the observed data. Some applications will be discussed later.

GRAPHICAL DISPLAYS

1. The Histogram

Frequency distributions are best presented graphically. A very common form is the frequency histogram, as shown in Figure 3.1. This is a two-dimensional

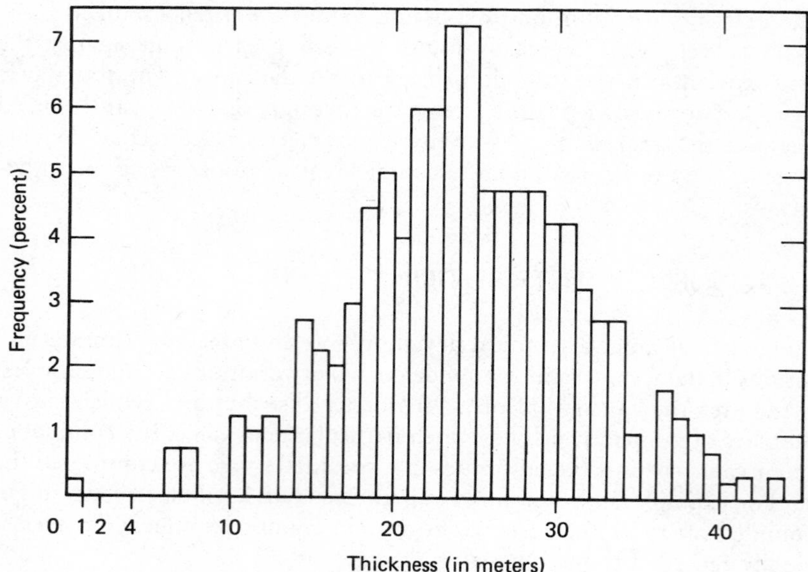

FIGURE 3.1. A histogram display. This example shows the distribution of vein thickness in a mineral deposit. (Reproduced from *Mining Geostatistics* by A. G. Journel and C. Huijbregts, by permission of Academic Press (London), copyright 1978, Academic Press (London) Ltd.)

graph, where one axis represents the data value and the other is the number of samples which have that value. The Y axis of the plot is frequently expressed in terms of the percentage of total samples, rather than as an absolute count.

Creating a histogram is largely a simple counting process. A number of "classes" are defined in terms of subranges of the numeric value. These may be set to cover the complete range of the data, or perhaps a restricted range derived from the mean and standard deviation, or from inspection of a previously drawn histogram. The numeric limits of each class are then computed by subdividing the complete range into a predetermined number of subintervals. Alternately, the numeric range of each class may be preset, in which case the number of classes is computed from the minimum and maximum values.

Once the classes have been defined, each data value is examined in turn, and tested against the class boundaries to find the class to which it belongs. The "count" value for that class is then increased by one. The final step is to display the results, which might be a simple tabulation of the counts for each class, a bar-scale-type of diagram, or perhaps a plotted line. The bar-scale format in Figure 3.2 is commonly used for computer output, as it can be generated with simple printed characters and displayed on a terminal screen or printer. Histograms which use plotted lines can also be computer generated, but require graphic output devices for the display, and thus are not as widely used. The cost of computer graphics is rapidly decreasing, however, and even microcomputers can now produce true "computer graphics." As a result, printer-type displays will eventually be supplanted.

2. Effective Use of Histograms

Although a histogram can be created completely automatically, it is often necessary to change some of the basic parameters to arrive at the most useful display. Since data can have a wide variety of possible distributions, a histogram program must have considerable flexibility to accommodate these differences.

The parameters that influence the appearance of a histogram are:

1. The "range," that is, the minimum and maximum numeric values to be included
2. The number of classes used for counting values
3. The "size" of a class (i.e., the range of numeric values to be treated as a unit in counting values)
4. Transformations of numeric values (scaling, taking logarithms or exponentials, etc.)

For a given range, class size and the number of classes are dependent on each other, so only one of these parameters can be predefined.

It is often useful to produce a number of histograms of a given variable by varying these basic parameters. A histogram covering the complete range of data values is always needed to identify samples outside the main distribution. All extreme values should be investigated as possible errors or true anomalies. When the range is broad, the histogram will have poor resolution, or may be excessively long if the class size, rather than the number of classes, was fixed. To supplement the basic histogram, the range may be restricted to allow portions of the distribution to be examined in more detail. The subrange might be determined from the basic statistics (e.g., $X - 3*S$ to $X + 3*S$), or simply supplied to the program as parameters entered by the user. Figure 3.2 demonstrates the process using data obtained from a geologic survey (geochemical analyses of stream sediment samples). The nature of the example is not significant to the process, as the histogram form can be used for any type of data.

Two types of common problems are evident in these examples. First there

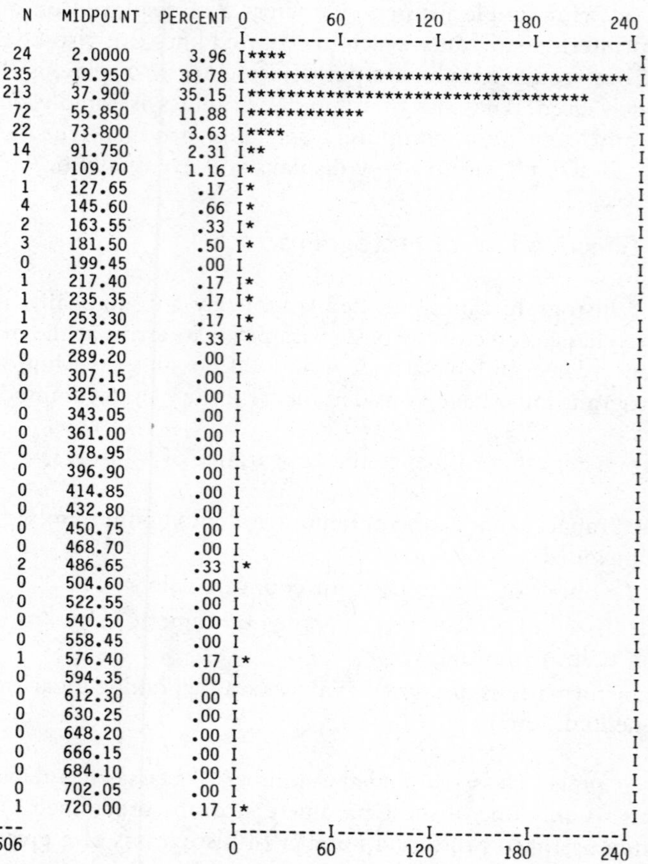

N MIDPOINT PERCENT 0 60 120 180 240
24 2.0000 3.96
235 19.950 38.78
213 37.900 35.15
72 55.850 11.88
22 73.800 3.63
14 91.750 2.31
7 109.70 1.16
1 127.65 .17
4 145.60 .66
2 163.55 .33
3 181.50 .50
0 199.45 .00
1 217.40 .17
1 235.35 .17
1 253.30 .17
2 271.25 .33
0 289.20 .00
0 307.15 .00
0 325.10 .00
0 343.05 .00
0 361.00 .00
0 378.95 .00
0 396.90 .00
0 414.85 .00
0 432.80 .00
0 450.75 .00
0 468.70 .00
2 486.65 .33
0 504.60 .00
0 522.55 .00
0 540.50 .00
0 558.45 .00
1 576.40 .17
0 594.35 .00
0 612.30 .00
0 630.25 .00
0 648.20 .00
0 666.15 .00
0 684.10 .00
0 702.05 .00
1 720.00 .17
606
0 60 120 180 240

FIGURE 3.2*a*. Histogram showing extreme data values (outliers) of concentration of copper in stream sediment samples.

is the case where occasional values are extremely large compared to the mean (Fig. 3.2*a*). The usual result is that the great majority of samples are combined into one or two classes, obscuring the details of the distribution. By excluding such "outliers," much better resolution of the main part of the graph is obtained. The other difficult situation occurs when the majority of samples have the same value, and thus unavoidably end up in the same class (Fig. 3.2*b*). The vertical scale used to plot all other classes is then greatly suppressed. In this case, the preferred value may be excluded, or the vertical scale adjusted to "clip" the single high value, and preserve detail throughout the plot. If the clipping option is used, it is important to identify

```
  N    MIDPOINT  PERCENT 0         190       380       570       760
                         I---------I---------I---------I---------I
749     1.0000     82.04 I*************************************** I
 70     2.0000      7.67 I****                                    I
 33     3.0000      3.61 I**                                      I
 20     4.0000      2.19 I*                                       I
 14     5.0000      1.53 I*                                       I
  4     6.0000       .44 I*                                       I
  1     7.0000       .11 I*                                       I
  0     8.0000       .00 I                                        I
  8     9.0000       .88 I*                                       I
  1     10.000       .11 I*                                       I
  1     11.000       .11 I*                                       I
  1     12.000       .11 I*                                       I
  1     13.000       .11 I*                                       I
  2     14.000       .22 I*                                       I
  0     15.000       .00 I                                        I
  0     16.000       .00 I                                        I
  1     17.000       .11 I*                                       I
  0     18.000       .00 I                                        I
  0     19.000       .00 I                                        I
  1     20.000       .11 I*                                       I
  1     21.000       .11 I*                                       I
---                      I---------I---------I---------I---------I
908                      0         190       380       570       760
```

FIGURE 3.2*b*. Histogram with the majority of samples in one class.

values which exceed the maximum plotted value to ensure that these extremes are still considered in interpreting the plot.

Figures 3.2*c* and *d* show the histograms obtained after taking these corrective steps. Much more detail is evident in both cases.

The problem of a majority of samples in one class often arises when the procedure for measuring the numeric value in question has a lower "detection" limit. This means that all values below some threshold cannot be distinguished, and are reported as a constant value. In trace element analyses of geologic or environmental samples, this is a common occurrence because of the physical limitations of the laboratory procedures. Considering that concentrations of a few parts per million (or even parts per billion) may be significant, research efforts toward reducing the detection limits are well justified. There is of course no guarantee that the problem will ever be completely solved.

The example above of a data distribution with occasional very large values, compared to a dominantly low population, is quite common in nature. Such distributions are called "skewed" to indicate the lack of symmetry expected in many of the theoretical models. Examples include concentrations of trace elements in the earth's crust, magnitudes of earthquakes, peak runoff heights of rivers, and many others. As we noted earlier, one method for studying the distribution of such data is to produce a number of histograms allowing different parts of the range to be displayed with different resolution. An alternate, and often simpler, approach is to apply a transformation which

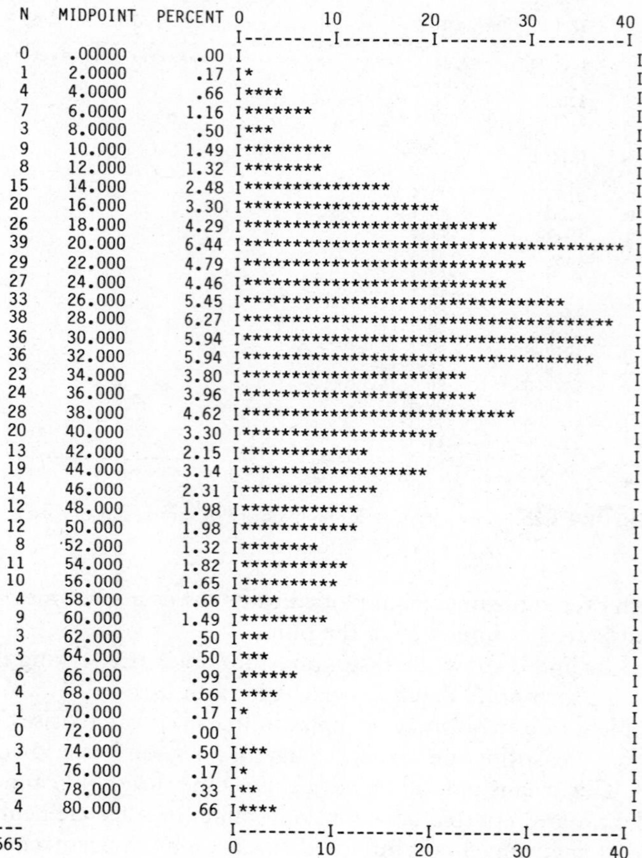

N	MIDPOINT	PERCENT
0	.00000	.00
1	2.0000	.17
4	4.0000	.66
7	6.0000	1.16
3	8.0000	.50
9	10.000	1.49
8	12.000	1.32
15	14.000	2.48
20	16.000	3.30
26	18.000	4.29
39	20.000	6.44
29	22.000	4.79
27	24.000	4.46
33	26.000	5.45
38	28.000	6.27
36	30.000	5.94
36	32.000	5.94
23	34.000	3.80
24	36.000	3.96
28	38.000	4.62
20	40.000	3.30
13	42.000	2.15
19	44.000	3.14
14	46.000	2.31
12	48.000	1.98
12	50.000	1.98
8	52.000	1.32
11	54.000	1.82
10	56.000	1.65
4	58.000	.66
9	60.000	1.49
3	62.000	.50
3	64.000	.50
6	66.000	.99
4	68.000	.66
1	70.000	.17
0	72.000	.00
3	74.000	.50
1	76.000	.17
2	78.000	.33
4	80.000	.66
565		

FIGURE 3.2c. Data for Fig. 3.2*a* with extreme values removed.

reduces the range. A simple and effective procedure is to take logarithms of the values and set the range and class boundaries in terms of the transformed values. Figure 3.3 shows the effect. Note that the midpoint values for each class may still be shown in original units to allow easy comparison to other data.

Many natural phenomenon appear to follow a "lognormal" pattern, which means that the distribution of log-transformed values has a "normal" distribution curve. When dealing with lognormal data, the basic statistical measures should be supplemented by their logarithmic counterparts. A mean and standard deviation can be computed from the log values, of course, but it is preferable to express these measures in the original units. Transforming

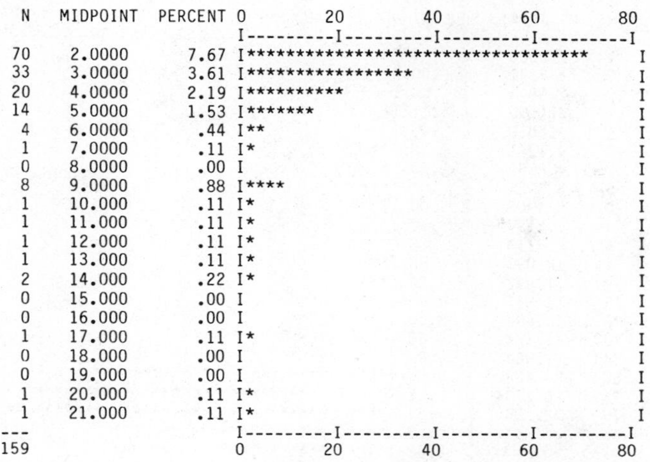
```
 N   MIDPOINT  PERCENT 0         20        40        60        80
                       I---------I---------I---------I---------I
 70   2.0000     7.67  I***********************************    I
 33   3.0000     3.61  I******************                     I
 20   4.0000     2.19  I***********                            I
 14   5.0000     1.53  I********                               I
  4   6.0000      .44  I**                                     I
  1   7.0000      .11  I*                                      I
  0   8.0000      .00  I                                       I
  8   9.0000      .88  I****                                   I
  1   10.000      .11  I*                                      I
  1   11.000      .11  I*                                      I
  1   12.000      .11  I*                                      I
  1   13.000      .11  I*                                      I
  2   14.000      .22  I*                                      I
  0   15.000      .00  I                                       I
  0   16.000      .00  I                                       I
  1   17.000      .11  I*                                      I
  0   18.000      .00  I                                       I
  0   19.000      .00  I                                       I
  1   20.000      .11  I*                                      I
  1   21.000      .11  I*                                      I
---                    I---------I---------I---------I---------I
159                    0         20        40        60        80
```

FIGURE 3.2*d*. Data for Fig. 3.2*b* with the largest class removed.

the log "mean" back to an arithmetic value gives the "geometric mean," which is often defined as

$$X_G = N\text{th root}(x_1 * x_2 * x_3 * \cdots * x_N) \qquad 3.4$$

where x_1, x_2, . . ., are the individual sample values.

It is very much easier to compute the geometric mean by applying Eq. 3.1 on the log values, and transforming the result, than to ue Eq. 3.4 directly. One cannot simply convert the log standard deviation, however, since a logarithm is a nonlinear transformation (i.e., the logarithm of a sum is not equal to the sum of individual logarithms). In arithmetic terms, the value at one log standard deviation above the geometric mean will have a greater offset than the value at one log standard deviation below. To express the variance properly, two arithmetic values are needed. One method is to compute the arithmetic equivalents to the points one log standard deviation above and below the log mean. This pair of values (sometimes called the dispersion) is written with the mean as $X_G(N_1,N_2)$ (e.g., 520(750,360)).

3. The Cumulative Frequency Plot

An alternative presentation which contains the same information as a histogram is the cumulative frequency diagram. The construction of a cumulative frequency diagram begins with the same counting procedure used for

```
  N   MIDPOINT  PERCENT 0         20        40        60        80
                        I---------I---------I---------I---------I
  1    2.0000      .17 I*                                        I
  0    2.3171      .00 I                                         I
  0    2.6844      .00 I                                         I
  1    3.1099      .17 I*                                        I
  0    3.6030      .00 I                                         I
  3    4.1741      .50 I**                                       I
  2    4.8359      .33 I*                                        I
  5    5.6025      .83 I***                                      I
  0    6.4907      .00 I                                         I
  3    7.5197      .50 I**                                       I
  5    8.7118      .83 I***                                      I
  4    10.093      .66 I**                                       I
  8    11.693     1.32 I****                                     I
 15    13.547     2.48 I********                                 I
 20    15.694     3.30 I**********                               I
 40    18.182     6.60 I********************                     I
 54    21.064     8.91 I***************************              I
 60    24.404     9.90 I******************************           I
 74    28.273    12.21 I*************************************    I
 76    32.755    12.54 I**************************************   I
 55    37.947     9.08 I****************************             I
 51    43.963     8.42 I**************************               I
 38    50.933     6.27 I*******************                      I
 27    59.007     4.46 I**************                           I
 14    68.361     2.31 I*******                                  I
 12    79.199     1.98 I******                                   I
 10    91.754     1.65 I*****                                    I
  7    106.30     1.16 I****                                     I
  3    123.15      .50 I**                                       I
  4    142.68      .66 I**                                       I
  3    165.29      .50 I**                                       I
  2    191.50      .33 I*                                        I
  1    221.86      .17 I*                                        I
  4    257.03      .66 I**                                       I
  0    297.77      .00 I                                         I
  0    344.98      .00 I                                         I
  0    399.67      .00 I                                         I
  2    463.03      .33 I*                                        I
  1    536.43      .17 I*                                        I
  0    621.48      .00 I                                         I
  1    720.00      .17 I*                                        I
---                    I---------I---------I---------I---------I
606                    0         20        40        60        80
```

FIGURE 3.3. Data for Fig. 3.2*a* with log transform applied.

the histogram. Next we must convert the counts to frequencies (simply divide by the total number of samples) and add the individual frequencies in sequence to produce an accumulating value (which starts at 0 and ends at 1.00). Once again, the results are plotted as an X-Y graph, with one axis ranging from 0 to 100 percent, and the other representing the data values within the chosen range. The data value represents the maximum in the class, since the cumulative frequency is a measure of all data contained in the class. For a histogram, it is more common to plot the data value representing the midpoint of the class, thus considering it as an "average" value.

Although no new information is incorporated, this format is sometimes easier to interpret. In cases where a given percentage of the highest values is to be selected, the appropriate "cutoff" value may be read directly from

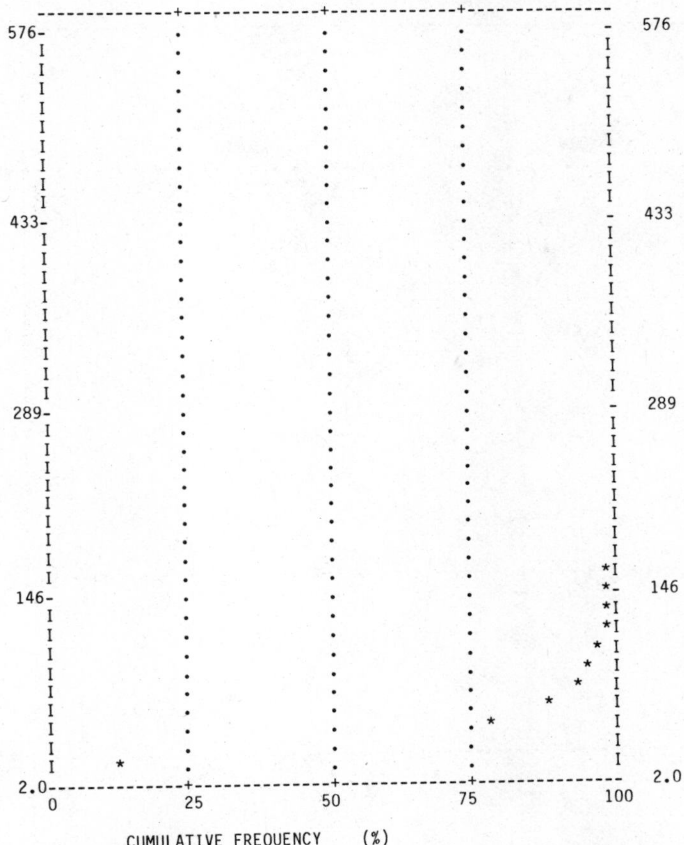

FIGURE 3.4a. Cumulative frequency plot corresponding to Fig. 3.2.

the graph. The cumulative curve may mask small clusters of high values, however, so in general it is advantageous to produce both types of displays.

The parameters that control the appearance of the cumulative frequency plot are the same for the histogram, since we are merely displaying the same data in a slightly different form. The same types of problems are also evident when difficult sets of data are encountered. As we might expect, the same types of solutions prove to be effective. Some examples are shown in Fig. 3.4, drawn from the same data as the histograms in Fig. 3.2 and 3.3.

For both types of display, the aim in adjusting the parameters of the graph is to fully utilize the available range. In effect, the resolution of the graph is reduced if the great majority of the data are contained in a few

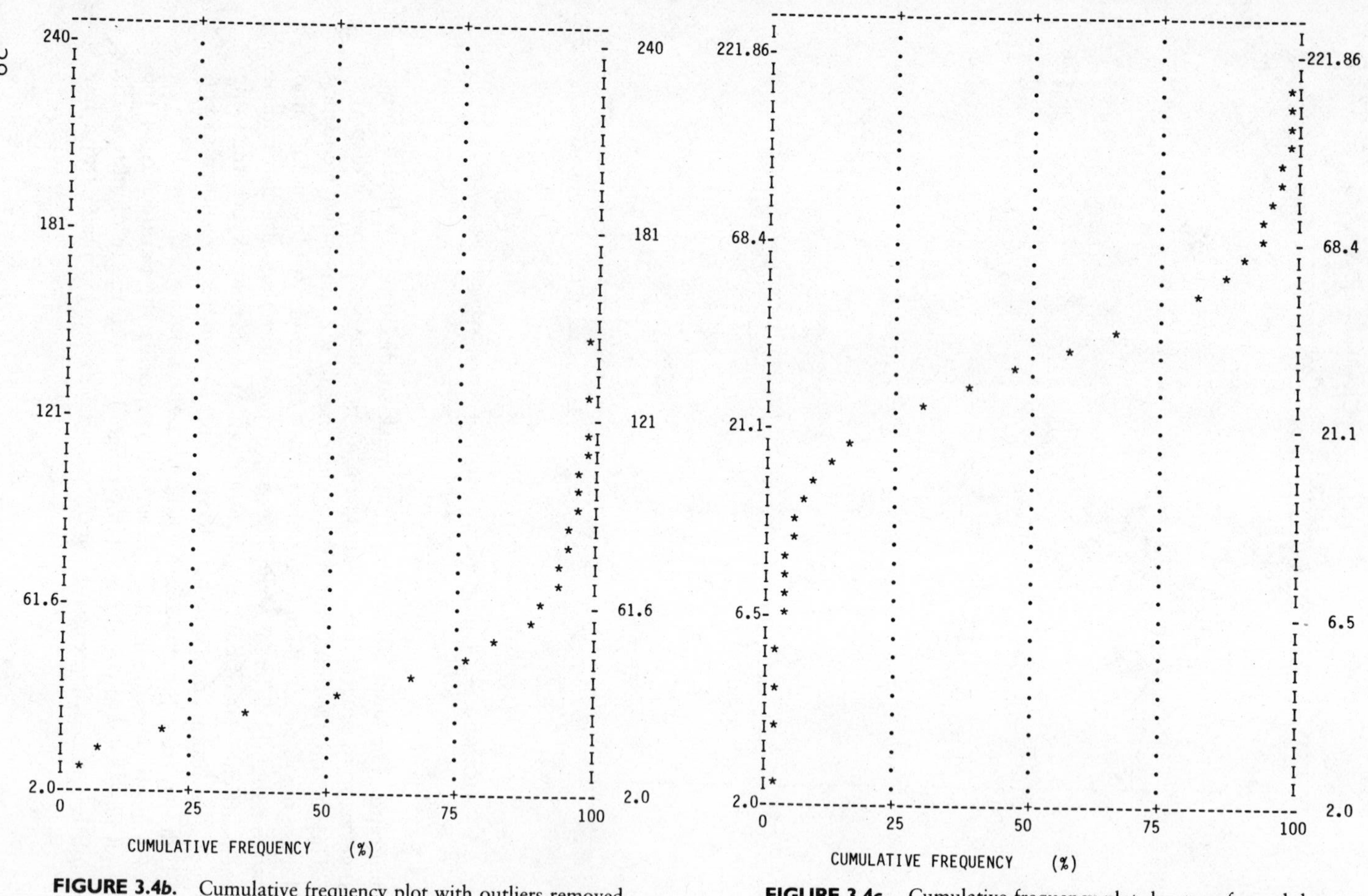

FIGURE 3.4*b*. Cumulative frequency plot with outliers removed.

FIGURE 3.4*c*. Cumulative frequency plot: log-transformed data.

classes, with a consequent reduction of the value of the graph in isolating interesting features of the distribution.

THE NORMAL DISTRIBUTION

A number of different theoretical distributions have been developed. Perhaps the most common is the "normal" (or Gaussian, after Karl Gauss) distribution, which has the probability density function

$$f(x) = \exp\left(\frac{-(x\text{-}X)**2/(2S**2))}{S * (SQRT\ (\ 2\text{pi})}\right) \qquad 3.5$$

where X, S, and x are defined as above (mean, standard deviation, and sample value). The normal distribution is the mathematical description of the classic "bell" curve used in a wide variety of statistical processes to describe data which tend to group about a fixed value (Fig. 3.5).

Many natural phenomena have distributions that are at least approximately normal, and a great deal of mathematical research has gone into investigating the properties of this distribution. As a result, many sophisticated statistical tests can be applied to data that are "normal," allowing an analyst to quickly derive a detailed understanding of the data. The following discussion outlines the basics of statistical decision making, but is by no means a complete representation of the full range of applications.

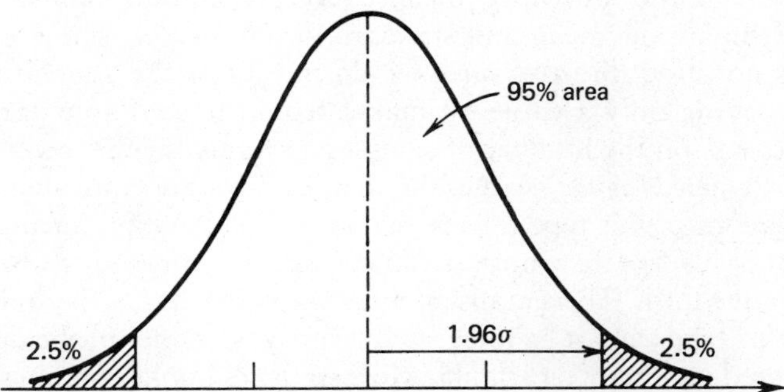

FIGURE 3.5. The normal distribution. Ninety-five percent of all values lie within 1.96 standard deviations of the mean value. (Reproduced from *Time Series and Systems Analysis with Applications* by S. M. Pandit and S. M. Wu, copyright 1983 John Wiley & Sons, by permission of the publisher.)

I. Statistical Decisions

The mean and standard deviation, which are the basic parameters of a normal distribution, are never exactly known, since they are derived from a finite subset of a potentially infinite number of data. In dealing with these estimated values, a primary question is to define the "error" in the estimates. Another way of looking at this problem is to define the possible range of values that the true mean (of the complete population) can have, given the value derived from the available samples. This may be a vital factor in situations where economic decisions must be based on the data. For example, in developing a producing mine from a body of mineral ore, the average "grade" of the ore largely determines the potential profit to be made. The possible range that the true average may have must also be considered in determining the risk in proceeding with development (if there is a 30 percent probability that the true grade is below the value needed to break even, there is an equivalent chance that the mine developer will not recover his investment).

By exploiting the properties of the normal distribution, the errors in the basic statistical values can be quantified. One simple approach is to compute the "confidence" limits for the mean at some specified level of accuracy. For example, the 95 percent confidence limits on a mean value are a pair of entries which define the a range of values which have a 95 percent probability of containing the true mean. The formula for computing the limits is

$$XL = X \pm [T(N\text{-}1,P/2)] * S/SQRT(N) \qquad 3.6$$

where $T(N\text{-}1, P/2)$ is the Student's T distribution. The parameters of the T distribution are the desired significance level (P), and the number of samples used to estimate the mean and standard deviation (N). The normal distribution is not used directly, since we do not know the standard deviation exactly, having only a value estimated from the available data. The dependence of T on the number of samples accounts for the uncertainty in S. Note that when N is very large, the distributions are equivalent.

Calculations of this type require the normal distribution (or the equivalent T distribution for data whose variance is only estimated) to be expressed in cumulative form. This entails an integration of Eq. 3.5 Exponential functions of this type cannot be integrated directly, so tables of the distributions must be used instead of a formula. Most statistics books contain such tables, calculated for a range of values of P and N.

Another common practice is to calculate the probability that the true mean is above (or below) a given value. In the ore grade example, an obvious choice would be the "cutoff" grade which determines whether the ore can be recovered profitably. This procedure is often termed "hypothesis" testing, since the basic question can be posed as a true or false situation. For example, we might define the hypothesis as "The average grade is greater than 1.5 percent." The problem is then to decide if this statement is true or false. This is in effect the same problem as finding confidence limits, with the distinction that we may be interested in only one side of the confidence region. A two-sided test is used when we require the mean to be within a given range of some fixed value. For example, the acceptable weight of a container might be defined as any value within two percent of the stated amount.

The decision to accept or reject the hypothesis is based on the probability that the estimaed value is inside the "region" defined by the cutoff values. The usual practice is to fix the "significance level" of the test (at say 95 percent), which allows use of the tabled T distribution in a manner similar to the confidence limit calculation. Since the decision is dependent on the available data, there is always the possibility that the statistical analysis will indicate the wrong choice. There are two types of errors that can arise:

Type I: Reject the basic hypothesis when it is in fact true.

Type II: Accept the basic hypothesis when it is false.

In decision making, these types of errors may have considerably different impacts. In the mining exploration problem, a Type I error would arise if the estimated grade is significantly lower than the true value. In deciding not to proceed with development, the "loss" to the company is the exploration expense and the lost opportunity. If development proceeds, while the ore grade is in fact below the cutoff (a Type II error), the loss could be very much larger (since mine development might easily be more expensive than exploration by a factor of 10 to 100).

This situation of having a limited number of samples to represent a large population is very common, and so statistical decision making is an important tool in many fields. In addition to the geologic sampling case discussed earlier, we might consider the great variety of polls (e.g., voter preference, TV ratings) which estimate averages for an entire country from a few thousand people. In astronomy, only a very limited number of objects can be directly observed, even though cosmologists wish to understand the universe as a whole. The effectiveness of new medical procedures must be judged from a limited number of test cases, while their value depends on widespread application.

2. Probability Graphs

Considering the powerful statistical tools available through the normal distribution, a natural problem is to determine whether a given set of data are indeed normal. Although statistical procedures are available to make this

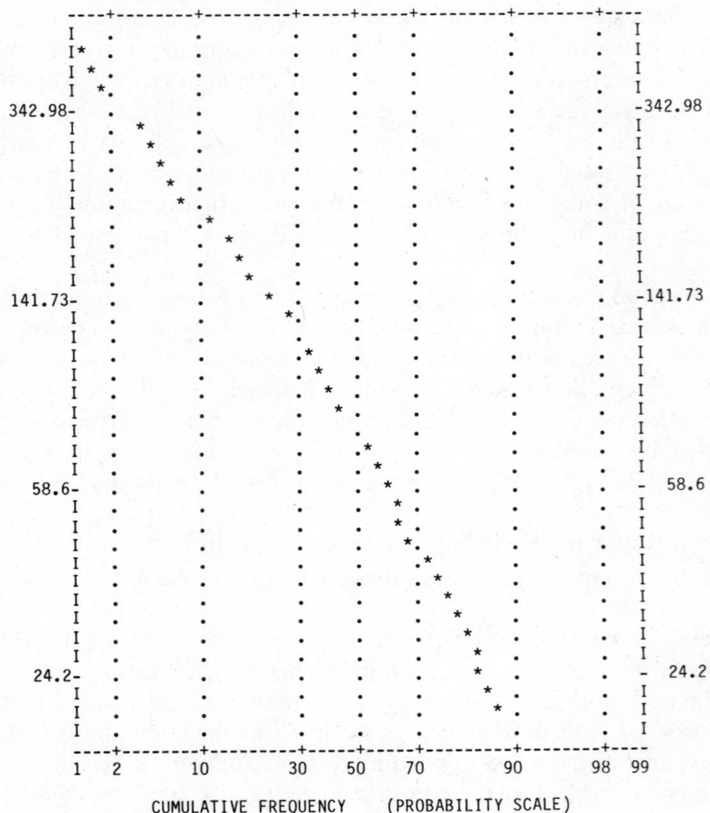

FIGURE 3.6. Probability plot.

determination, perhaps the simplest method is the graphical display shown in Fig. 3.6. This "probability plot" is simply a cumulative frequency curve, plotted on a axis scaled to represent the normal distribution. If the data are normal, the plot will be a straight line. In addition to demonstrating the nature of the distribution, the graph has a number of other useful properties, as we shall see later.

Probability graphs can be constructed manually, given a table of cumulative frequencies and preprinted paper. "Log" probability paper is also available to test the possibility of lognormal distributions. Note that the example displays the values "top-down," that is, the maximum value is plotted at the low end of the frequency scale. The summing of frequencies could equally well be applied in the other direction, of course—the choice is essentially a matter of custom in particular types of application.

These graphs can be easily constructed on a computer, as well. A simple addition can be made to any program which plots cumulative frequency diagrams, to automatically do the necessary scaling of the frequency axis. Since the exponential function involved in the normal distribution is not easily computed, a table of values is required. The values in the table are probabilities corresponding to fixed increments of the standardized variable Z (original values transformed so that mean equals zero and standard deviation equals one). The program must set the number of printing positions to use for the "probability" axis, and the range of values to be plotted. Note that 0 and 100 percent cannot be represented, since the curve extends to infinity in both directions. Once these values are fixed, each print position can be assigned a probability value. In plotting the graph, each cumulative frequency is tested against these values to decide where to plot the current value. A logarithmic display can also be easily produced by supplying an option for the program to transform all values prior to accumulating sums for the classes.

If a reasonable straight line can be fit to the data on the probability graph, the parameters of the distribution can be obtained by inspection. The mean value is the intercept of the fitted line with the 50 percent line. The standard deviation is found by picking the intercepts at 16 and 84 percent, since a basic property of the normal distribution is that 68 percent of the samples will lie within one standard deviation of the mean. Note that if log probability paper is used, this procedure will yield the geometric mean and dispersion.

3. Multiple Populations

A probability graph that is not a straight line does not necessarily indicate that the distribution is not normal. In many cases the data will contain samples from different sources, each with a normal distribution. If the parameters of the distributions are different, the graph will show curvature in the transitions between populations. Figure 3.7 is an example of this situation. Note that the corresponding histogram (Fig. 3.8) shows a departure from the "bell" shape as well, although in many cases the separation may be much more apparent on the probability plot. In addition, the parameters of the separate populations can be estimated by fairly simple graphical constructions (see the discussion in the book by A. J. Sinclair for applications).

Multiple populations are an unavoidable problem in many types of analysis. Surface geochemical measurements indicate the total concentrations of given elements, which might reflect several different geologic events. The individual sources will, in general, not make a uniform contribution to each sample. For instance, the majority of samples in a geochemical survey may have low concentrations of gold, representative of the dominant rocks in

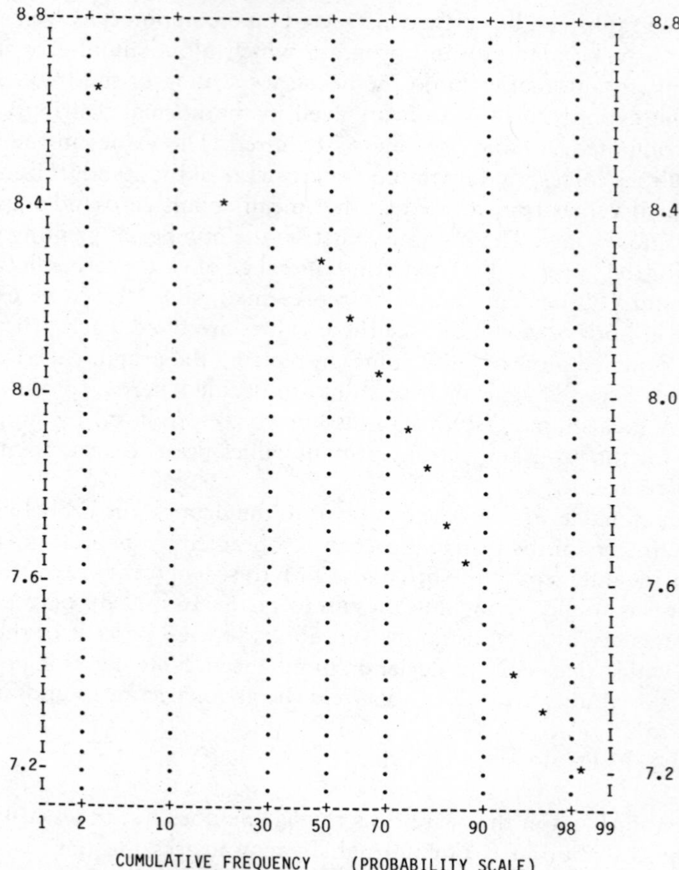

FIGURE 3.7. Probability plot showing possible multiple populations.

the region, while the remainder are influenced by local mineralized zones. In a study of environmental quality, there may be many different sources of pollution, each having distinct characteristics. In some cases the problem may be somewhat alleviated by the use of other data which might also be related to the discrete populations. For example, the occurrence of particular types of rocks may be another indication of mineralization, which could be used to supplement the geochemical analyses.

If more than one population is evident, one primary goal of the analysis can be achieved if the samples in each population can be identified. This may be simple, if the distributions are well separated to begin with, or very difficult, if there is a considerable overlap. If a separation is possible, the

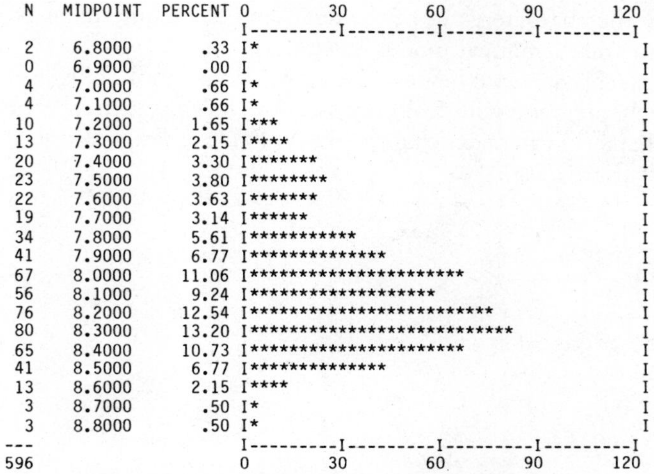

N MIDPOINT PERCENT 0 30 60 90 120
2 6.8000 .33 I*
0 6.9000 .00 I
4 7.0000 .66 I*
4 7.1000 .66 I*
10 7.2000 1.65 I***
13 7.3000 2.15 I****
20 7.4000 3.30 I*******
23 7.5000 3.80 I********
22 7.6000 3.63 I*******
19 7.7000 3.14 I******
34 7.8000 5.61 I***********
41 7.9000 6.77 I**************
67 8.0000 11.06 I**********************
56 8.1000 9.24 I******************
76 8.2000 12.54 I*************************
80 8.3000 13.20 I***************************
65 8.4000 10.73 I**********************
41 8.5000 6.77 I**************
13 8.6000 2.15 I****
3 8.7000 .50 I*
3 8.8000 .50 I*
---
596 0 30 60 90 120

FIGURE 3.8. Histogram corresponding to Fig. 3.7.

analysis proceeds to study the relationships of the different groups. Regardless of the method used to segregate groups of samples, it is important to determine whether the groups are significantly different from one another. A statistical judgement can be made by testing the hypothesis that the difference in the mean values for each group is zero.

In Chapter 5, procedures for selecting subsets of data and examining their spatial patterns are discussed. Applications of computer graphics to study spatial relationships between groups will be presented in Chapter 8.

4. Non-parametric Statistics

As we noted earlier, a normal distribution for any set of data must be defined in terms of the mean and standard deviation. All of the statistical decisions are then dependent on these parameters. If the distribution is not truly normal, or if the parameters can only be roughly estimated, these judgements may be considered suspect. Fortunately, a vast body of experience indicates that the normal distribution works in practice for many types of data.

There are still cases, however, where the assumption of normality is overly restrictive and potentially dangerous. A great deal of recent work in mathematics has been in the field of "non-parametric" (or "distribution-free") statistics, which attempts to overcome this problem. The major goal of these techniques is to provide the types of decision-making procedures available through classical statistics, without making any assumptions about the nature of the data distribution. In other words, statistical judgements are based solely on the characteristics of the data, and the requirement that the data "fit" some mathematical model is removed.

These techniques are beyond the scope of this book, however, so in succeeding chapters we will deal only with the basic statistical model covered in this chapter. In the next chapter, the methods are extended to the problem of multivariate data.

CHAPTER 4

MULTIVARIATE DATA ANALYSIS

Many scientific problems involve the simultaneous recording of a number of different measurements related to a particular event. In such situations, the basic procedures for statistical analysis of a single variable must be extended to study the interrelationships of multiple variables. In mathematics, this is usually termed "multivariate analysis." 'This chapter considers the basic procedures and how they can be effectively performed on a computer.

THE NATURE OF MULTIVARIATE DATA

Any situation where the value of more than one variable is recorded may be termed a multivariate problem. In one sense, all problems are of this type, since in addition to the recorded variables, additional information will always be collected to describe the location of the readings. Here location is taken in the broadest sense, to mean any designation of "place" that uniquely identifies different samples; for example the time of an event, or its position in space. The location (or coordinate) variables are usually considered as being independent of the observed phenomenon, so in common practice multivariate problems are those for which there is more than one dependent variable. Multivariate techniques may also be required to examine functional relationships between coordinates and a single measured variable.

The data associated with a given event may then be considered as one of two general types. The first category is the "coordinate" information, which specifies attributes of the location where (or when) the information was recorded. The second main category is the variables which are associated with the phenomenon. As noted above, these may be defined as the "dependent" variables. A major aim of analysis is to determine the nature of this dependence. These variables may be functionally related to each other, as well as to the location of the observations. The functional relationships are often used in attempts to define a common source, which might be the ultimate objective.

1. Numeric and Descriptive Data

In analyzing multivariate data, it is often necessary to make another type of division of the variables. "Numeric" fields can be used for the full range of statistical calculations outlined in the previous chapter. This category includes any variable which can be expressed as a number in a meaningful sequence of values. Often we must also deal with "descriptive" data, or variables which take on discrete values that cannot be translated into a conventional numeric series. A geologist collecting rock samples may note the type of rock, the dominant minerals contained in it, its color and texture, and a variety of other information that is usually recorded in the form of arbitrary codes. Sociological studies provide a number of other examples. Surveys of voting patterns, religious preferences, and similar items deal largely with data of this type, and as a result different statistical methods must be applied.

In a computer data file, descriptive fields are usually in "character" form, since they may contain letters and other non-numeric symbols. A discrete variable might be coded as a set of numbers, although it is still treated in terms of unique and independent values, rather than as part of a meaningful numeric sequence. True numeric data can be "integer" or "real." In most cases, "real" numbers are used for all types of statistical data, in order to allow a continuous range of values. Integer fields are often computed during analysis to store counts of samples and other information which have only whole number values.

2. Analysis of Descriptive Data

The standard statistical methods assume that the data have a continuous distribution of values, and thus can only be applied to numeric data. When faced with the problem of relating descriptive and numeric data, the standard approach is to subdivide data into groups based on the values of the descriptive fields. Statistical analysis of the associated numeric data is performed on each group. The resulting summary statistics for each group may then be compared, using statistical significance tests. To do this type of analysis efficiently, a good procedure for isolating the different groups is required. This involves a number of considerations of practical program design and data storage, which will be discussed in Chapter 5, where examples with descriptive data are included. In the remainder of this chapter, we consider the methods for studying the relationships of the numeric fields.

THE TWO-DIMENSIONAL CASE

The simplest multivariate problem of course is having two variables to study instead of one. This often involves one dependent variable and one coordinate; for example the price of gold recorded over a period of time. In many cases, we might wish to study two dependent variables that could also be related. For example, prices of gold and silver may be compared to see if they are related to each other, independent of their historical behavior.

Although we have used the term "dependent variable," this should not be taken to mean that such a value is completely controlled by the independent variables. There may be unknown factors not included in the available data. For example, metals prices are influenced by public confidence in the economy and numerous other unquantifiable factors, in addition to past history, values of associated commodities, etc. The general result is partial interdependence of different variables, which leaves us with the problem of interpreting the significance of the unexplained variations.

1. Curve Fitting and Correlation

The first step in testing for a functional relationship is usually to find the equation of a straight line which "fits" the two variables. If we call one variable x and the other y, we must determine the values of a and b in the equation

$$y_1 = a + bx \qquad 4.1$$

The criteria for defining a and b is that the error in the estimate (y_1) be minimized, when all values of y are considered. In practice, we minimize the sum of the squared quantity $(y-y_1)$, in order to avoid cancellation of positive and negative differences. Other criteria might also be used, for example taking the absolute value of $(y-y_1)$, but in general these do not lead to a simple mathematical formulation. This is a classic minimization problem, solved by taking partial derivatives with respect to a and b and setting the result to 0. The result is

$$b = \frac{\text{sum}(x*y) \ - \ (\text{sum}(x)*\text{sum}(y))/N]}{[\ \text{sum}(x**x) \ - \ (\text{sum}(x)**2/N} \qquad 4.2$$

$$a = Y - bX$$

where Y is the mean value of y, X is the mean value of x, and N is the number of samples.

Merely finding the equation of the line does not indicate how well it "fits" the data. A common statistical measure is the "correlation coefficient," which has a magnitude that varies between 0 (no relationship) and 1 (y_1 is an exact prediction of y). It is computed as

$$R = SQRT \frac{\text{sum}(y_1\text{-}Y)**2}{\text{sum}(y\text{-}Y)**2} \qquad 4.3$$

In this form, it represents the ratio of the "explained" variation to the total variation in y. An alternate form is

$$R = \frac{\text{Cov}(x,y)}{\text{S}(x) \ * \ \text{S}\ (y)} \qquad 4.4$$

where Cov(x,y) is the "Covariance" between x and y, and $S(x)$ represents the standard deviation of x. The covariance is calculated as

$$\text{Cov}(x,y) = \frac{\text{sum}(x-X) \ * \ \text{sum}(y \ - \ Y)}{N} \qquad 4.5$$

The correlation coefficient can also be expressed in terms of the slope of the "regression" line, as

$$R = b * \frac{S(x)}{S(y)} \qquad 4.6$$

This allows R to be computed without prior calculation of X and Y, so that all the quantities related to the relationship of x and y can be obtained with one loop through the data. Note also that R can take on negative values if y has an inverse relationship with x (i.e., y tends to decrease as x increases). In fact, R will have the same sign as b, since $S(x)$ and $S(y)$ are strictly positive quantities.

This formulation assumes that all "error" in the estimate of y is in y itself: that is, x is treated as the independent variable, and is considered to be perfectly accurate. When data errors may be present in both x and y, (or when they are mutually dependent on some other variable), the simple regression line is not the optimum function for testing the correlation between x and y. In this situation, alternate mathematical procedures can be used to distribute the error equally between the x and y variables. A straight-line fit is still produced, and a correlation can be obtained as before (as the ratio of explained variation to total variation).

Most observations are subject to some degree of error, of course, although the relative accuracy of each variable may be different. The simple regression model is then seldom completely valid, although very often it is more than adequate, considering the statistical nature of the data. Note also that the "error" in the least-squares procedure includes both the uncertainty of observations and true variations in the relationship of x and y. Choosing the proper procedure then requires estimates of the expected measurement errors, as well as some knowledge of the physical relationship of x and y. For more discussion of this topic, consult the references (for example, the book by Acton).

2. The Two-Dimensional Scatter Plot

In addition to calculating a correlation coefficient, it is very useful to graphically display the relationship of the two variables. A two-dimensional "scatter plot" is the usual form, as shown in Fig. 4.1. Here the axes of an X-Y graph represent the values of the two variables, and a set of discrete points are plotted using pairs of values from individual samples to determine position on the plot. The quality of the fitted line can also be visually judged by overplotting the calculated value y_1.

This type of analysis need not be restricted to linear functions. Least-squares theory can equally well be applied to fitting a higher order curve to the data. This approach is usually restricted to relatively low order polynomials (maximum degree four or perhaps five), since extreme fluctuations in the computed value (y_1) are likely to result from using higher powers of x in the calculation. In any event, the intent of fitting a function is to define a simple trend to explain the gross characteristics of the relationship, which should preclude the use of complex functions.

If a higher order curve has been used, it is still possible to define a correlation coefficient using Eq. 4.3. It is important to identify the function used to estimate y since the value of R will naturally be different for each choice. To distinguish the basic value derived from the straight line fit, it is often termed the "linear correlation coefficient." Note that the covariance

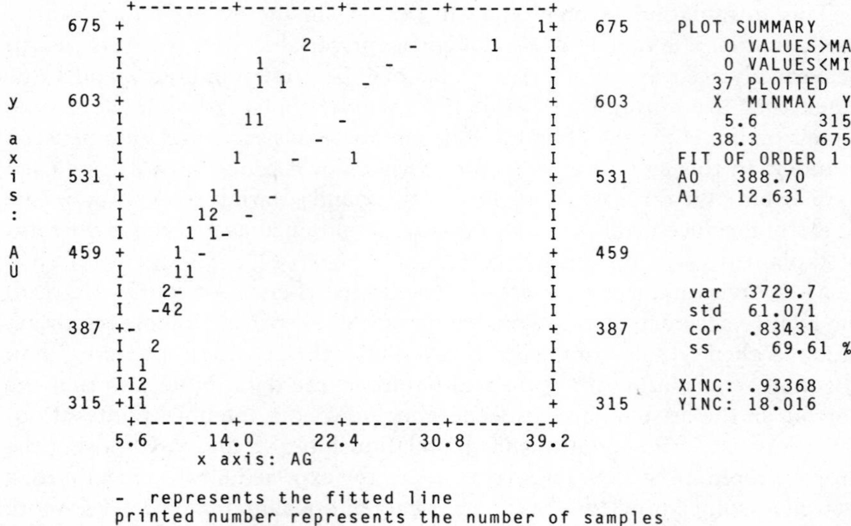

FIGURE 4.1. A two-dimensional scatter plot: prices of gold and silver 1980–1982.

formulation (Eq. 4.4) represents only the linear measure, as does the form in Eq. 4.6 which relates R to the slope of the fitted line.

A simple scatter plot can easily be created on a computer printer, although these graphs can also be plotted using computer graphics. This allows considerably more detail, and results in a more aesthetically pleasing result. Special devices are required, however, which means that not all computer users have access to this type of output. Examples of true computer graphics will be included in Part II, after the subject has been properly introduced in Chapter 6.

As we found earlier in considering histograms and frequency plots, the value of a graph is enhanced if the data effectively cover the plotted area. As in the one-dimensional case, this may not be true of first attempts that include the complete range of values. It is valuable to produce such plots to see if extreme values in each variable tend to correspond. To examine parts of the two-dimensional distribution in more detail, a scatter plot program requires options similar to those in a histogram routine: the ability to reset the ranges and to apply transformations to the data. In this case, of course, there are twice as many parameters since these options should operate independently on each variable.

A program to print scatter diagrams must be somewhat more complicated than a histogram printing routine since it has to consider the values of two

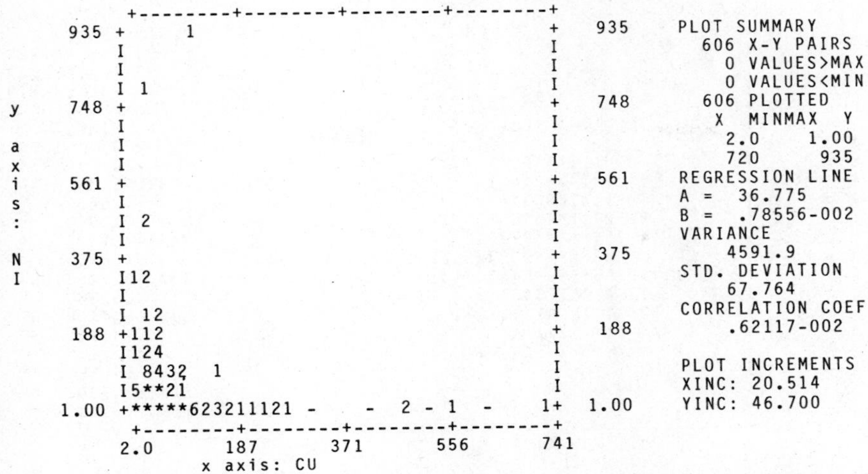

FIGURE 4.2a. Scatter plot showing effect of outliers: nickel vs. copper in stream sediments.

variables. In the single variable cases, data are organized into classes first. The printing segment simply proceeds sequentially through the list of counts for each class, printing the class value and count (or a scaled version of it) on successive lines. A scatter plot uses a two-dimensional array, each cell representing a range of values in both *x* and *y*. Each sample can be assigned to a cell by testing the *x*, *y* values against the cell boundaries. The array

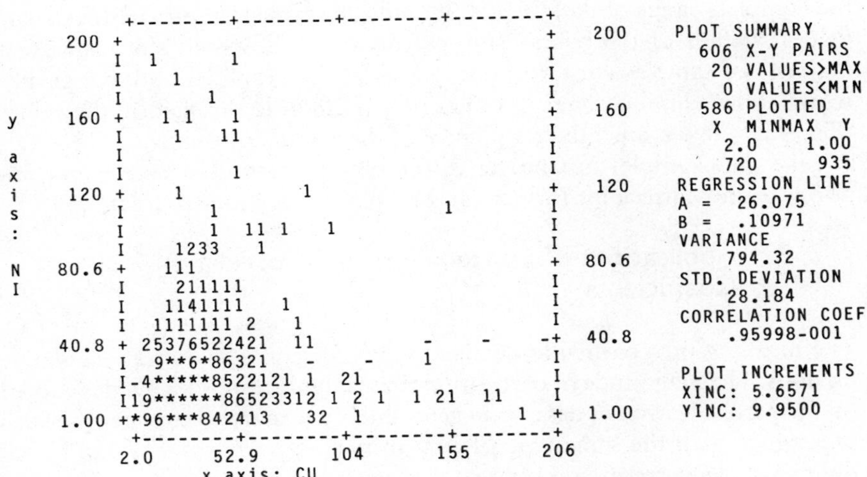

FIGURE 4.2b. Extreme values removed from data in Fig. 4.2*a*.

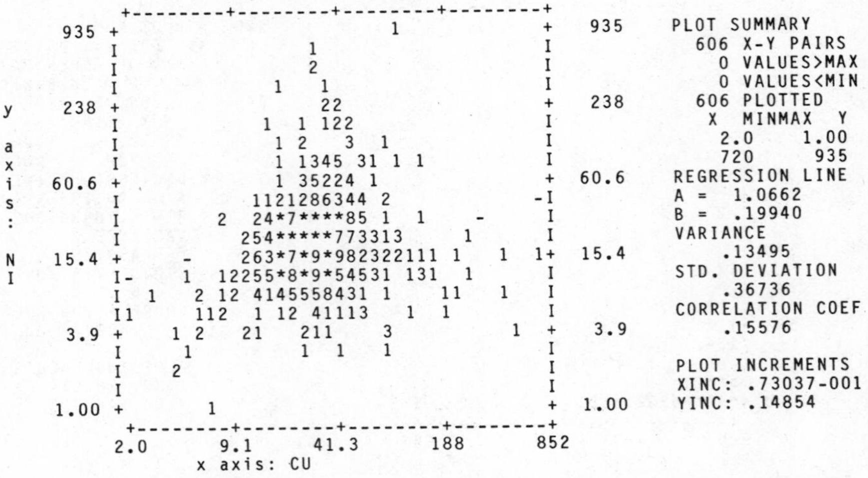

FIGURE 4.2c. Log-transformed version of Fig. 4.2*a*.

can be used to hold the number of samples, or simply a character to indicate whether or not any samples are located in it. In printing, a single character represents each cell, usually the number of samples, thus giving an indication of the density of data in different regions of the plot.

Figure 4.2 contains examples of different scatter plots drawn for the same set of data, in this case concentrations of copper and nickel in stream sediment samples from southwestern British Columbia. The plot which includes the complete range of data (Fig. 4.2*a*) indicates some samples with extreme values. Details of the relationship are obscured, however, since the great majority of samples cluster in one corner of the graph. Additional graphs which show a limited range of values (Fig. 4.2*b*) or log-transform the values (Fig. 4.2*c*) give a much better picture of the dominant trends.

Like the examples in Chapter 3, the type of data used here is not important: the scatter plot format can be used for any numeric data.

3. Applications of Scatter Plots and Correlation Coefficients

The meaning of a particular correlation coefficient is seldom immediately obvious. The magnitude of correlation that is significant is highly dependent on the particular type of data, so in general it is necessary to consider previous experience with the same type of data in making such judgements. In addition, while a correlation coefficient is a rigorously defined statistic, it cannot always be clearly interpreted without examining the scatter plot. If either

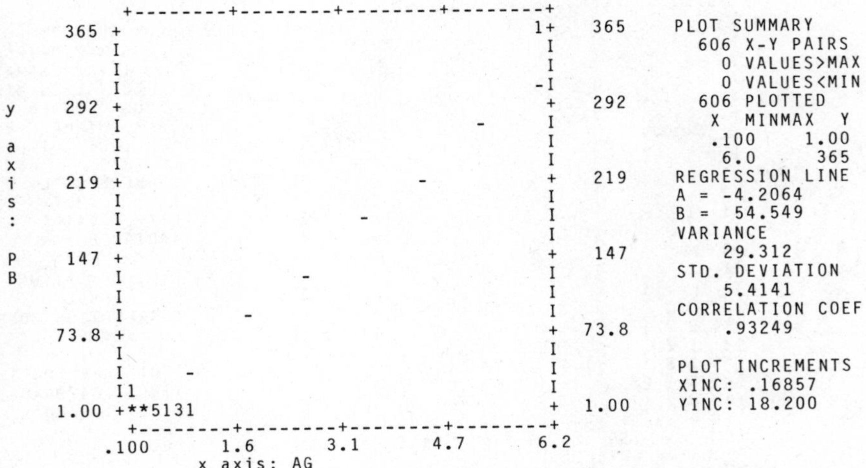

FIGURE 4.3*a*. Effect of outliers on the correlation coefficient in a full range of data: lead vs. silver in stream sediments.

(or both) of the variables have lognormal characteristics, the coefficient should be computed for both original and transformed data.

"Outliers" may also be a problem. Occasional samples that have extreme values for both variables may have a strong contribution to the coefficient. In such cases, it may indicate a strong relationship, which in fact disappears when the outliers are excluded from the calculation. This effect can be seen in the scatter plots shown in Fig. 4.3. In the plot of all data (Fig. 4.3*a*), a correlation coefficient over 0.9 is indicated. Excluding the single sample containing the maximum values for both variables reduces the value to below 0.3 (Fig. 4.3*b*). Note also that the log version is much less influenced by the single outlier (Fig. 4.3*c*).

One of the primary uses of scatter plots is to check for the existence of multiple populations among the available samples. If multiple peaks can be seen in the individual histograms, it is likely that the scatter plot will show discrete clusters as well. In addition, a scatter plot may show groupings not readily apparent in the separate analyses of the variables. The existence of multiple populations is likely to cause a low correlation coefficient, since a single line cannot adequately represent more than one trend. This is another case where the the computed correlation should be used with caution. This effect can be seen in Fig. 4.2, where a very low correlation coefficient is indicated, while the plot shows two definite trends in the data. We will return to the problem of subdividing the samples into the appropriate groups in the next chapter.

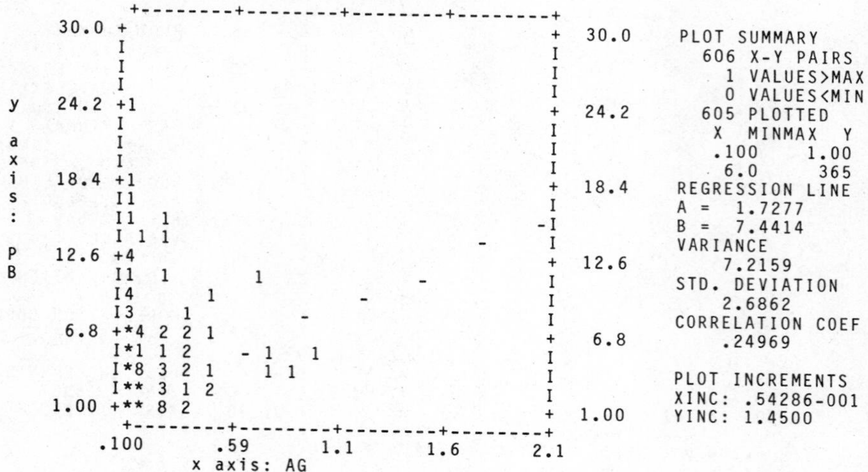

FIGURE 4.3*b*. Extreme values removed in calculating *R*.

Scatter plots are also frequently used to compare different measurements of the same variable. This may be necessary to calibrate a new instrument, for example, or to provide a test of accuracy by duplicate measurements, or to compare preliminary estimates to final results. To simplify the interpretation of the plot, the two axes should have the same scale and cover the same range of values. It is also useful to plot a 1:1 line (i.e., the line *Y*

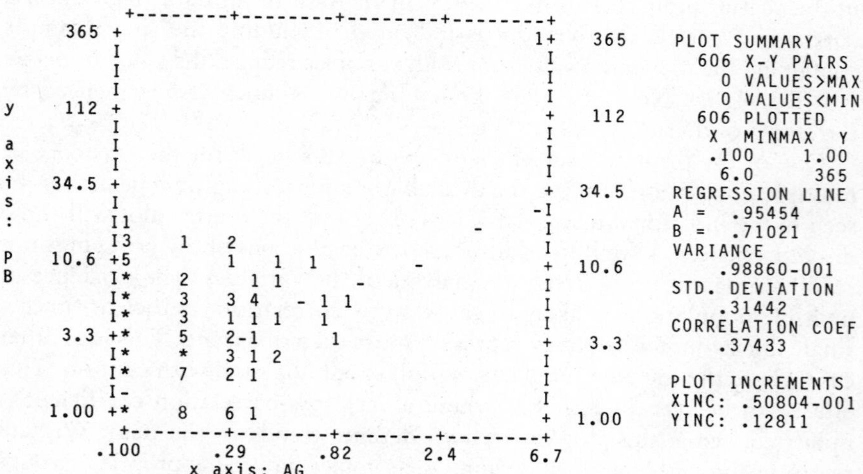

FIGURE 4.3c. Log transformed equivalent of Fig. 4.3*a*.

= X), since any significant departure of the regression line indicates a bias in one of the measurements. These options might all be set by a single program parameter if they are used extensively.

4. Singled-Valued Data

The usual applications of scatter plots involve multivalued data, that is, data for which many values of the dependent variable *(y)* may correspond to the same *x*. This is not a requirement, and the same procedures may also be used for single-valued data. Although the representation is the same, the graphs are often called "profile" plots, since the values can be connected sequentially in a line diagram. A computer program for scatter plots can be used for profiles, although a routine which assumes sequential single values may be computationally more efficient, since assigning data to cells is once again a one-dimensional problem.

Figure 4.4 shows an example of plotting single-valued data. In this case, the *x*-axis is time, and the *y*-axis is the price of gold taken at the end of each month. In working with such "time series," it is often desirable to predict future values by using cyclic functions. A great number of choices are possible, of course. Simple polynomials can provide recurring patterns. The example shows the modeling of the gold price by a polynomial of order four, which is able to follow many of the highs and lows in the data. It is more common to use sums of trigonometric functions (such as Fourier series), however, since the dependence on a fundamental "period" can be expressed

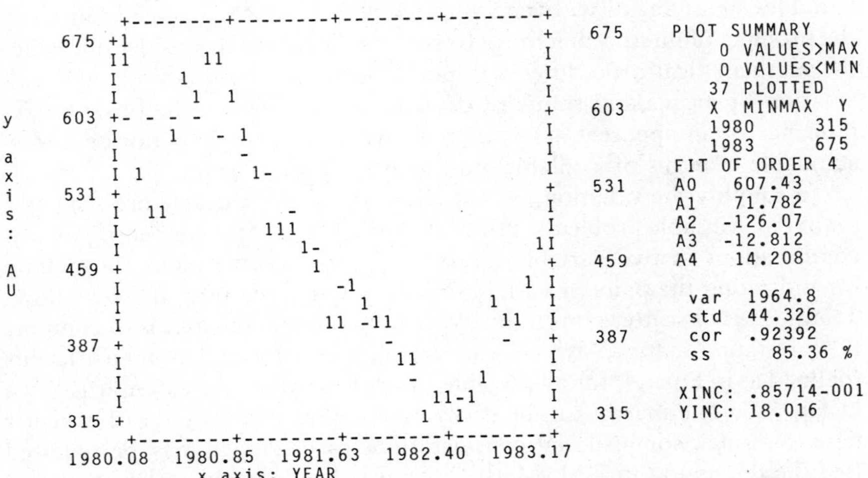

FIGURE 4.4. "Profile" plot for the price of gold from 1980 to 1982.

more easily. Time-series analysis is a complex field in itself, requiring a great variety of sophisticated mathematical algorithms and computational procedures. An outline is given in Chapter 11.

In many cases, a number of profile plots are to be compared, for example the prices of several stocks over the current year. Such multiple time series might also be displayed in the simplistic form shown here, but can be more easily interpreted when several curves can be displayed on the same graph. This requires true computer graphics, which will be introduced in Part II. More sophisticated examples of two-dimensional data display will therefore be delayed until then.

THE N-DIMENSIONAL CASE

It is often necessary to investigate the behavior of more than two variables, of course. A basic problem in multivariate studies is conceptual: it is often difficult to visualize even three-dimensional problems, let alone situations where many more variables are involved. Most of our experience involves working with two-dimensional graphs, such as the frequency plots and scatter diagrams we have previously considered. It is seldom practical to build three-dimensional models, so real objects are commonly represented by projection onto a flat surface. As soon as we have a variable measured at various points in space, we have in effect created a four-dimensional problem, and a simple display of the data distribution may prove very difficult, if not impossible.

There are a number of statistical methods designed to investigate many variables simultaneously. Even with such techniques for summarizing data, the problem of interpreting the perceived relationships is considerable, since the mathematical procedures are much more complex than a simple calculation of means and standard deviations. In addition, the physical significance of an apparent association of many variables may not be understandable in terms of available models of the phenomenon.

To simplify the situation, we can often study a N-variable problem as a set of two-variable problems. Where N is at all large, the number of possible combinations of two variables is unmanageable, so we require a method for indicating the pairs of variables that appear to be related. This allows a limited set of scatter plots to be created. A common practice is to compute a "correlation matrix," which is in essence a set of correlation coefficients (defined as in Eq. 4.4) for all possible pairs of variables. An example is given in Fig. 4.5. The matrix can be easily be computed for any set of numeric data, although some special considerations for accuracy may be required (see the discussion in P.M. Mather's book). As we noted earlier, the level of correlation deemed significant is data dependent, so we must rely on past

Correlation matrix for 606 records with 8 variables

	ZN	CU	PB	NI	CO	AG	MN	FE
ZN	1.000	.012	.472	.108	.272	.548	.108	.350
CU	.012	1.000	-.004	.006	.038	.049	.069	.151
PB	.472	-.004	1.000	-.016	.002	.932	.009	.036
NI	.108	.006	-.016	1.000	.773	-.015	-.025	.205
CO	.272	.038	.002	.773	1.000	-.009	.117	.594
AG	.548	.049	.932	-.015	-.009	1.000	.057	.068
MN	.108	.069	.009	-.025	.117	.057	1.000	.252
FE	.350	.151	.036	.205	.594	.068	.252	1.000

FIGURE 4.5. Example correlation matrix for multivariate data concentrations of trace elements in sediment samples.

experience to some extent. In dealing with new types of data, a first-level approach might be to select the five largest coefficients for more detailed analysis. This should only be a starting point, however, since we may find that the high coefficients are largely due to outlying values, as noted earlier. Recall also that a low correlation coefficient may result when the data contain multiple populations, which individually may have strong associations of the variables.

To go beyond the pairing approach of correlation matrices and scatter plots requires advanced statistics which consider the problem in the true multidimensional sense. The mathematical methods are considerably more complex, and will not be considered in detail here. Chapter 10 has a brief introduction to some of the more commonly used techniques. Some practical considerations for computer implementation will also be reviewed in Chapter 10.

In addition to these mathematical methods, multivariate analysis often relies on graphical displays. The simple two-dimensional scatter plot is a common example, although many other techniques have been developed for special types of data. Like multiple-time series, true computer graphics are required. Chapter 10 will also consider some graphical methods for multivariate analysis.

CHAPTER 5

EFFECTIVE USE OF COMPUTERIZED ANALYSIS SYSTEMS

As we have seen in previous chapters, data analysis with a computer may involve a number of different operations. A generalized procedure for analyzing any set of data is as follows:

1. Enter data into a computer file.
2. Summarize and list this file to check for errors.
3. Select subsets of data for analysis.
4. Perform statistical analysis.
5. Plot results of analysis.

The problems of data entry and verification were described in Chapter 2. It is worth reiterating that data errors cannot always be easily detected, and may still be encountered during the analysis phase. Statistical analysis may be as simple as computing means and standard deviations, or as complex as the multivariate techniques outlined in Chapter 10. In many cases, steps 3 and 4 are repeated in an iterative fashion, as initial statistical analyses may indicate the existence of multiple populations to be investigated independently. The value of plotting data will not be discussed until Part II, as it requires an understanding of computer graphics. Many of the general principles outlined here will also apply to procedures for computer plotting.

At all levels, the user must specify his requirements to the computer, and receive output information in a readily understandable form. Making these tasks easy is largely a function of software. An effective program often requires more lines of code for these operations than for performing its basic algorithms. Efficient use of a computer demands more than just installing individual programs, however, since many different procedures may be needed for a single study. As a result, analysis "systems" should be designed to allow simple transitions between component programs. In addition, the separate programs should have a consistent form of operation, to reduce the time required to learn how to use them. In this chapter, rules for developing such systems are developed. In addition to specific analysis programs, system utility programs can often be applied to great advantage. Sorting data, searching through files, and printing files are also important functions of a complete data analysis system. The ability to use existing software for these tasks can be a great aid in developing new applications.

PRINCIPLES FOR DESIGNING ANALYSIS PROGRAMS

1. Parameter Specification

Although there are many ways for a user to enter instructions, it is impossible to define a single method and set rigid rules for writing programs. The great diversity of computing environments and problems to be solved with a computer demands different strategies. A large organization with a powerful computer system and expert support staff is very likely to operate in a different fashion from a small company using a minicomputer. Computer programs designed for experts can assume a fair level of knowledge on the part of the user, and dispense with extensive prompts and explanatory messages. Such programs demand a high level of training and experience, however, and thus are not suited for occasional use by nonexperts. In designing any system, it is very important to first identify the intended users. If the programs are of the "expert" variety, novice users will likely have difficulty applying them. On the other hand, a great deal of effort can be wasted in developing a self-tutoring type of system, if the users do not need the extra instructions.

Figure 5.1 illustrates different methods for specifying parameters, as might be used to define the range of values to plot in a scatter diagram. The simplest form (in terms of programming effort), is shown in Fig. 5.1*a*, where a "fixed format" parameter entry is used, requiring each value to be entered on a predefined part of a line of text. A variation which allows rapid entry is to use a list of values separated by commas or blanks. In Fig. 5.1*b*, the values

```
(a) Fixed format parameter record

     >RUN SCPLOT
     >      0.0   100.0  10.0     50.0
      123456789 123456789   123456789     (column number)

      Variation:
     >RUN SCPLOT
     >0,100,10,40

(b) Named parameter list

     >RUN SCPLOT
     >XMIN=0,XMAX=100,YMIN=10,YMAX=40

(c) Interactive parameter solicitation

     >RUN SCPLOT
      Enter the minimum and maximum values for the
      X and Y axes of the plot, in that order
     >0,100,10,40

(d) Interactive parameter solicitation with defaults

     >RUN SCPLOT
      Parameters for the scatter plot are:
       XMIN = 0.0       minimum value for X axis
       XMAX = 120.0     maximum value for X axis
       YMIN = 0.0       minimum value for Y axis
       YMAX = 40.0      maximum value for Y axis
      To use the current values, enter a blank line
      To change any values, enter a list such as
        XMIN=0,YMIN=0        etc
     >XMAX=100,YMIN=10
```

FIGURE 5.1. Methods for supplying program parameters. Example: defining minimum-maximum values for axes of a scatter-plot. Other parameters, such as the data file name, are not shown. Lines preceded by a > are entered by the user. (*a*) Fixed format parameter record; (*b*) named parameter list; (*c*) interactive parameter solicitation; (*d*) interactive parameter solicitation with defaults.

are defined by a parameter list, which is more flexible since the parameters can be entered in any order. The use of descriptive names helps ensure that reasonable values will be given, since the association of numeric values with program variables is explicitly given. Another advantage of the named list is that it is easier to adapt existing parameter files, since the names can be used as keywords. These benefits more than offset the extra typing required to enter the parameter list. The user must still be aware of the definitions of the various parameters prior to running the program, however.

An interactive format is shown in Fig. 5.1*c*. This is designed to aid a novice user, since the program describes the information it needs before reading the values. In Fig. 5.1*d*, the program provides a higher level of help by first setting "default" values that the user can selectively replace. This "menu" form is the most convenient to use, but also requires the most programming time. It can also take longer to run, when the time for the interactive question and answer session is compared to a procedure of simply reading many parameters from one compact list.

Another basic decision is whether the programs are to run in a "batch" or "interactive" mode. Batch (or background) jobs are generally submitted to the computer to run as resources are available, while the user goes on to another task. "Interactive" (foreground) processing means that the user enters instructions at a terminal and the required calculations are performed immediately. The choice of mode depends on the power of the computer, the volume of data to be handled, and the complexity of the computations. In the batch mode, of course, explanatory messages in the program are of no help, since the user has already entered the parameters. Programs run in batch are then necessarily in the "expert" category.

In the early days of computers, all jobs were run in the batch style, with programs, parameters, and data all contained in a deck of punched cards submitted via a card reader. Today, files on disk have replaced the cards, and revisions are entered on a terminal. A simple system command (dependent on the particular computer) is used to start "execution" of the job. This mode requires that all data and parameters needed by the program be present, since the user loses contact with the job once it is submitted. In running batch jobs, it is therefore necessary to know how to define data files, how to set parameters, and other details of the program operations. This implies that the user must be experienced, or prepared to consult program documentation to learn how to set up a job.

With the great speed of modern computers, many jobs that were previously run in background mode can now be completed fast enough to be processed during a foreground "session." This does not mean that the program must be rewritten in a fully interactive mode. The batch form can be still be used, so long as all parameters are predefined. The procedure is for the user to set up a file containing the parameters, run the program, look at results, and revise the parameters if required. This situation can lead to some confusion as to the meaning of the word "interactive." We might define "interactive processing" as any procedures run at a terminal for immediate evaluation by the user. This does not necessarily mean that the programs are fully interactive, in the sense that the user is instructed by the program, and has the ability to specify parameters at key stages of the calculations.

2. Interactive Definition of Parameters

Interactive programs can eliminate much of the need for expert knowledge, since the program can "prompt" the user for information as required. Errors in parameters can also be trapped, and reentered as necessary, without the expense of a complete run that might contain worthless results, or the delay of waiting for a job that stopped early because of a simple error. In some situations, operations that might require several batch runs can be combined into one, since the user can look at intermediate results before setting parameters for the next stage. An interactive, self-instructing program is much more difficult to program than a batch-oriented program that does the same job, since all of the prompts, and many of the error checks, must be added to the batch version.

Until quite recently, the concept of analyzing large volumes of data interactively was for most people a remote dream because of the limitations of and workload on computers. With dramatic decreases in hardware costs, and impressive advances in capabilities (especially for minicomputers and microprocessors), it has become possible for most data processing jobs to be done interactively. The availability of effective software may still be a problem: limitations in the programs may dictate the range of applications to which the system can be successfully adapted. The cost of writing software may also impose serious constraints on developing improved programs.

It may seem desirable to have a data analysis program that could process all types of data without demanding a great level of expertise from the user. It is very unlikely that such a system will ever be developed, however, because of a very fundamental problem: the great variety of data types, and the widely different procedures required for data analysis, make it very difficult to develop truly general-purpose software. Having too wide a scope often causes the program to be loaded down with options extraneous to any individual problem.

A point which may easily be overlooked is that the total cost of developing a fully interactive system may never be paid back in increased efficiency. In many cases, a combined approach of interactive parameter submission with background execution can give nearly the same increase in productivity at a much lower cost (e.g., little additional software, and fewer specialized devices like graphics terminals). A simple hardware upgrade may have much more impact than installing a number of interactive programs. A careful evaluation of potential benefits is essential before commitment should be made to a major new system.

Keeping in mind the difficulties outlined above, specification or selection of an interactive software system should incorporate the following general principles:

1. User response should be menu oriented, allowing definition of several parameters with one transmission to the computer. This is especially important on multiuser machines,where system response time is often degraded by heavy loads. The objective is of course to minimize the interval between starting the program and the start of the desired computations.

2. Wherever possible, shortcuts should be provided in the user query segments, to allow experienced users to bypass extra tutorial information and enter parameters without as much prompting. The loudest complaints

about many interactive programs are frequently from the long-time users who continually encounter additional questions designed to smooth the way for the novice, but which serve mainly as an annoyance to the expert.

3. The functions and options available within the program should be limited in number and specific to a particular task. For example, a set of routines for basic statistics and simple graphical displays such as histograms might be combined into a single program. The user would specify the type of output needed, along with parameters such as titles, names, and scales. More complex applications like factor analysis would logically form a separate package. If many options are truly needed, a good set of default parameters should be defined, to allow creation of output without a great deal of parameter input.

4. Although it is desirable to make a program self-explanatory with optional on-line instructional material, supporting documentation with printed examples of computer sessions is also needed. In situations where some programs are used sporadically, it is more efficient for an occasional user to review a system by reading a manual, than to consume computer resources by scanning lengthy tutorials on a terminal screen.

5. If the application requires extensive calculations, checks should be available to ensure that a reasonable amount of data will be handled. Even if all the above criteria for allowing quick, flexible definition of parameters are met, an analysis cannot be done in a true interactive sense if the user has to sit waiting while computations proceed. It would be advantageous to have an option to switch larger jobs to a background mode. This may require extensive additions to a program, if the computer's operating system does not allow it to be done easily (e.g., different command languages may be needed).

6. Software should be independent of specific display devices, data structures, etc., to minimize the impact of external changes in the computing environment. A modular structure that can be grouped into subsystems is important in distributed processing to insure that appropriate segments of a large system can be run on different machines.

7. Error checks should be as complete as possible, with clear instructions to the user on how to correct the problem. Catch-all messages, or unexpected problems which terminnate the program are frustrating to all users, and discourage the casual user from continuing to use the computer system.

3. Independence from Data Type

The simplest way to store data in a computer file is to leave the data in the form in which it was originally recorded. This allows quick transcription from noncomputer records, and easy comparison of a computer file to its

```
123456789 123456789 123456789 123456789 123456789 123456789 12345

>JAN1980  2.26410  117.958   675.309  38.25682  35.38   378.636
>FEB1980  2.289116 132.362   665.321  35.08500  36.35   390.00
>MAR1980  2.204514 104.602   553.581  24.13333  37.42   393.810
>APR1980  2.209364  93.969   517.410  14.50000  36.35   402.045
>MAY1980  2.302024  92.815   513.820  12.53286  35.38   389.524

          EXCH      COPPER   GOLD     SILVER    ZINC    MERCURY
          (EXCH = exchange rate: $US per pound sterling)
```

FIGURE 5.2. A data file containing metals prices. Only lines preceded by a > are actually in the file.

source. There is a major problem, however, in using such files as input to various programs: each program must be supplied with information on how to read the desired data from the file. This can be built into the program itself, or entered by the user at the time of execution. In the first case, the programs become restricted to a particular type of data. The second method allows a variety of data to be used, but requires knowledge of the structure of particular files. This can be a real job when a variety of data have to be analyzed, since each type will have its own format.

Figure 5.2 shows part of a data file that contains metals prices. To create a histogram for the price of gold, the values coded in columns 28–35 must be read. For other metals, the locations are obviously different. The location of the desired variable is an essential parameter for the program. To run a program which uses several fields (such as a correlation matrix), the user must supply a more detailed format description. This form of input is not only cumbersome, but also error-prone, since there is no way to check that the proper field has been defined: it is easy to produce a graph labelled "price of copper," for what is in fact the price of gold. Such mistakes waste valuable computer time, since the job must be run again. Even worse, if the transposition of data is not noticed immediately, important decisions may be based on invalid data. This can easily happen if the misidentified fields have ranges of values similar to the correct ones.

The solution to this problem is to use "self-documenting" data files. If the description of the data format is contained in the file, along with identifying names for each field, programs can be designed to read data automatically, without external definition. The result is an easier-to-use and more flexible system, since the user is no longer required to know internal details of data structure, and the programs can access a variety of different file types. In addition, the problem of reading the wrong data is eliminated (provided of course that the file description is correct), since fields are accessed by name only.

Another potential problem is the existence of gaps in the data, that is some fields may not be defined in all samples. Missing data are usually coded as some special value (e.g., a blank, −1, 999) which must be known to the programs so that these samples will not be included in analysis of the particular field. This can also be effectively handled by a self-documenting file by the inclusion of the "null" value in the file definition.

Gaps in data files are common in multivariate data, since it is not always possible to record all variables simultaneously. For example, in measuring concentrations of trace elements (for geologic exploration or environmental monitoring, perhaps), minimum sample weights are required. The available samples may not be sufficiently large to allow all desired tests to be performed. Another possibility is instrument malfunction, which may affect only some of the fields involved in automatic recording. Gaps may also result when the data file is prepared by merging independently recorded fields or samples. Various government agencies prepare historical data files on resources in their jurisdiction, but do not necessarily record exactly the same fields. If a number of such data sets are combined for a regional study, it is likely that some of the fields will not be available at all locations.

There are many different ways to implement internal documentation for data files. One simple method is to attach several records to each file, with the file description entered in a fixed form. Any program which uses the data will then read this description before attempting to read the actual data. Much more complex structures are also used, especially for large files, to allow "direct access" to segments of the file. In this case the analysis program does not read the file directly, but calls a utility routine to retrieve the desired data. Software for data management typically includes options for sorting, data selection, data entry and correction, and other features. Applications of these "database systems" are discussed later in this chapter.

4. Effective Forms for Computer Output

Computed results can be presented in a variety of ways. Printed information can be displayed on a terminal screen, or sent to a lineprinter. Graphical forms are often generated using printed characters, or actually drawn on special display devices such as plotters or graphics terminals. Regardless of the medium and format, some general rules can be established for enabling users to extract pertinent information as quickly as possible.

First of all, it is desirable to have complete output, which means that all data required for proper understanding is presented in the same place. In plotting a histogram, it is important to know the total number of samples, the range of values, the basic statistical parameters, and the nature of the variable being plotted. Such parameters are much easier to use if they are printed next to the histogram, rather than in another location.

It is perhaps equally important that the output be compact. One of the main advantages of using a computer is that it can effectively summarize data to reduce the need for manual scanning of printed lists. This often conflicts with the first rule, so a trade-off between these objectives must be established. An acceptable compromise can usually be developed only as a result of experience: with repeated use, the data important to any particular analysis method can be identified, and programs modified to produce only the essential output.

The form of particular displays is also an important factor in minimizing the volume of output. For example, the scatter plots shown in Chapter 4 use a restricted number of cells so that two can be printed on one page. When greater resolution is required, it is necessary to expand the scale, which results in twice as many output pages, each containing one plot. Once again, there are trade-offs to consider in developing programs. Options to display output in a number of sizes can be used in many cases, to allow detailed graphs when necessary, while normal usage produces a more compact form.

It goes without saying that all output must be properly identified. As noted earlier, this can be a problem if data files do not carry names for variables. Another benefit of using self-documenting files is then that all output can be automatically labelled with the correct field names.

COMBINING PROGRAMS: EFFECTIVE ANALYSIS SYSTEMS

When using a number of separate programs that comprise an integrated system, the rules for individual programs must be extended to consider how they interact. This is largely a matter of transferring data files between programs. The basic rule for an effective system of programs then is that all its components must use the same procedures for accessing data. This might involve a fixed format, although as noted earlier a system is then restricted to a particular type of data. If all components are independent of data type, the entire system bcomes adaptable to a variety of analysis problems. The key to this flexibility is then to adopt a data structure in the form described above, with internal definitions of the file contents.

The data structure (and data-handling software) must also allow files to be easily revised and expanded. Many analytical procedures involve adding computed quantities to the existing fields. For example, estimates of given fields derived from trend surface analysis or multiple regression might be saved for statistical calculations or plotting, along with appropriate differences from the original data. If errors are found during analysis, corrections must be applied. New data (either extra fields or additional samples) may be acquired during the analysis, to be added to an existing file. Ratios, differences, or other derived fields are often more diagnostic than the observed quantities.

Another valuable principle is that all programs should have a consistent form of use. This means that a user's experience with any one program is at least partly applicable to other programs, which reduces the learning time for any new procedure. Consistency is largely a matter of setting conventions for defining data files, specifying parameters, etc.: that is, the user's procedures for telling the program what to do should be made as similar as possible. The use of common parameter names, standard names for data fields, and common meanings for parameters are among the items to be considered. In a set of interactive programs, much confusion can be avoided if responses to prompts always have the same rules. For example, yes/no answers might be defined as 0 = NO 1 = YES; use of the opposite code would be prohibited. Similarly, if the input data set is coded by a parameter such as FILE = abc, variations such as INFILE = abc would be counteproductive.

The adoption of an internally documented data structure also helps to ensure use of a consistent style. Each program can call the same routines for locating input data files, selecting specific fields, and creating output. Common routines for handling error situations (e.g., requesting a field that is not in the file) can also be used in this case.

UTILITY OPERATIONS TO SUPPORT DATA ANALYSIS

1. Data Selection

With the great diversity of analytical data, and the basic objective of discerning the interrelationships of the data, a primary requirement of an effective system is the ability to select subsets of data by testing the contents of different fields in a computer file. As we saw in the last chapter, this procedure is used to provide independent statistical analyses of groups of samples distinguished by some descriptive variable. For example, a sociologist may separate population by region, political affiliation, religion, or a variety of other parameters in testing for significant differences in family income. The same method is used to study the behavior of other variables associated with a numeric field that has multiple populations as seen on a histogram, and for clusters of samples observed on two-dimensional scatter plots.

This capability is generally provided by a database software system. Normally a "database" denotes any set of data, while a "data base system" is the program (or set of programs) used to manipulate the information stored in a database. To allow an analysis system to handle all of its I/O operations, it is linked to a database system that does the actual reading and writing of data. The database software uses the internal definitions stored in the database, which fulfills the requirement of being independent of data type. In addition, complete flexibility in retrieval criteria is desirable: that is, it should be possible to use any of the fields to subdivide the data.

Efficiency of data retrieval can often be improved by an ordering of data fields frequently used in data selection. For example, geographically oriented data can be structured so that all samples in a given area (county, state, country, etc.) can retrieved without a complete search through the entire file. Non-numeric variables can often also be used as "key" fields if they can also be logically arranged (e.g., alphabetically) or take only a limited number of values (e.g., political affiliation by party, production status of an oil well). The ordered structure can be achieved by a simple sorting operation when there are only a few key fields. For large databases with many fields used in selection, it is often necessary to have cross-reference tables to allow quick access. If this facility is not provided by the database system, sequential searches through complete file may still be necessary, although the need for complete searches can be reduced by using the primary keys whenever possible.

Data selection takes different forms when numeric or non-numeric data fields are to be considered. When testing non-numeric (i.e., character) data, we are usually interested in selecting records in which character fields match desired values (or lists of values). For example, all data related to a given state can be extracted from a file by selecting only those records with the value NY in the field STATE. Tests on more than one field are often useful as well, for example when locating all producing mines in a given state (say STATE = WA and STATUS = PRODUCER). In some cases, it is convenient to test only part of the name in order to select a number of different values without having to define a complete list. In searching for a given name, we might require only that the name starts with GOLD, so that GOLD HILL, GOLDEN POND, etc., would all pass the test.

As noted in Chapter 4, such tests on character data provide a means for determining if there is a significant relationship between a descriptive variable and the numeric fields. The procedure is to create a number of data sets, each corresponding to a given value, and then to produce statistical summaries of each. Figure 5.3 shows the results of subdividing a set of geochemical measurements according to the type of bedrock in the drainage area where the sample was taken. The statistical summaries for each type show some clear associations of trace element concentrations with particular rock types. For example, the mean value for zinc is 80 parts per million (ppm) in argillite areas, and about 60 ppm for the other types. Similarly, nickel values are higher in dacite, and copper in granite.

(a) Samples associated with Granite

NAME	NDATA	NULLS	MINIMUM	MAXIMUM	MEAN	STD. DEV.
ZN	165	0	16.0000	475.000	57.8182	41.9745
CU	165	0	2.00000	720.000	57.6667	94.0905
PB	165	0	1.00000	365.000	4.47879	28.3387
NI	165	0	1.00000	505.000	26.5091	65.4595

(b) Samples associated with Andesite

NAME	NDATA	NULLS	MINIMUM	MAXIMUM	MEAN	STD. DEV.
ZN	184	0	20.0000	215.000	59.1630	19.3078
CU	184	0	10.0000	190.000	36.2228	18.0158
PB	184	0	1.00000	18.0000	2.43478	2.46419
NI	184	0	3.00000	170.000	26.4239	20.2677

(c) Samples associated with Argillite

NAME	NDATA	NULLS	MINIMUM	MAXIMUM	MEAN	STD. DEV.
ZN	61	0	25.0000	280.000	80.0820	42.3207
CU	61	0	9.00000	68.0000	31.9180	13.8832
PB	61	0	1.00000	14.0000	2.86885	2.46628
NI	61	0	8.00000	54.0000	25.2295	10.4744

(d) Samples associated with Dacite

NAME	NDATA	NULLS	MINIMUM	MAXIMUM	MEAN	STD. DEV.
ZN	73	0	17.0000	135.000	61.7808	18.0148
CU	73	0	12.0000	54.0000	25.4384	9.31842
PB	73	0	1.00000	25.0000	2.41096	3.08147
NI	73	0	7.00000	330.000	45.3699	48.6343

FIGURE 5.3. Selection using descriptive data for statistical comparisons. Example: geochemical samples from areas of different rock type. (*a*) Samples associated with granite; (*b*) samples associated with andesite; (*c*) samples associated with argillite; (*d*) samples associated with dacite.

To confirm that these differences are meaningful, statistical tests are applied to the parameters of the groups. If the data have normal distributions, a confidence interval for the difference of the means may be calculated:

$$\begin{aligned} \text{DL} &= (\text{X1-X2}) \pm [\text{T(M,P/2]} *\text{S12} \\ \text{where S12} &= \text{SQRT}\left(\frac{\text{S1**2}}{\text{N1-1}} + \frac{\text{S2**2}}{\text{N2-1}}\right) \\ \text{and M} &= \text{N1} + \text{N2} - 2 \end{aligned} \qquad 5.1$$

T is the Student's distribution (as in Eq. 3.6), and (X1, S1, N1) and (X2, S2, N2) are the mean, standard deviation, and the number of samples in each group.

Applying the equation to zinc in argillite and andesite, the 95 percent confidence interval for the difference of the means is 9.7 to 32.2. Since 0 is not included, these two groups are indeed different (i.e., we accept the hypothesis that the difference in means is not equal to 0).

A more detailed investigation (e.g., computing correlation coefficients and plotting histograms) would naturally follow this preliminary study. In searching for anomalous values in individual elements, these associations would have to be considered: a zinc value of 100 might be considered near normal for argillite, but would be well above the main part of the distribution for andesite.

To examine possible relationships between a number of descriptive fields, selection is based on one field, followed by counting the discrete entries in the other fields. An alternate method would be to run a number of multifield tests, and to simply store the counts of records which pass each one. Examples of applications would be searching a census file to see if there is a correlation between political and religious affiliation, and finding coincident occurrences of metals in producing mines (e.g., "What percentage of gold mines also contain silver?").

Selection on the basis of on multiple fields may either demand that all fields meet their individual criteria before a record is selected, or only that any field pass, which is a much less restrictive requirement. Both types would be used by a geologist who wanted to compare the number of mines with gold and silver to the total number with either gold or silver, for example. There are many other situations where a primary objective of selection is to indicate the proportion of various subpopulations, as well. A biologist studying the effects of acid rain might select all lakes with either increased acid levels or reduced fish populations. In addition to examining cases where both effects are observed, the instances where only one is noted would also be important. If a significant percentage of reduced populations are not associated with higher acidity, a simple cause and effect relationship could not as easily be supported.

When numeric fields are used in selection, the most common operation is to choose all values within a given range, that is, to test against given minimum and maximum values. As before, several fields can be tested concurrently. This procedure is used to isolate portions of data distributions observed on a histogram plot, for instance eliminating all values at the detection limit, or selecting only those samples in the top 10 percent of the range.

Figure 5.4 contains an example of numeric selection. A set of data containing metals prices is subdivided by choosing all occasions when the price of gold is over $500. The summary statistics for the groups illustrate the well-known fact that other metals tend to follow gold, as the average prices for copper and silver are also much higher in Fig. 5.4*a* than in Fig. 5.4*b*, although they are not in the same ratio. Note however, that mean values

(a) Periods when gold price is over $500

NAME	NDATA	NULLS	MINIMUM	MAXIMUM	MEAN	STD. DEV.
YEAR	13	0	1980.08	1981.08		
CU	13	0	84.7750	132.362	97.9463	13.4176
AU	13	0	513.820	675.309	608.342	57.5424
AG	13	0	12.5329	38.2568	20.1793	7.93948
ZN	13	0	35.3800	37.4200	36.2285	.914481
HG	13	0	363.636	404.773	387.530	12.7172

(b) Periods when gold price is under $500

NAME	NDATA	NULLS	MINIMUM	MAXIMUM	MEAN	STD. DEV.
YEAR	24	0	1981.17	1983.08		
CU	24	0	59.0090	82.6140	72.5509	6.54324
AU	24	0	314.982	499.763	414.412	56.1997
AG	24	0	5.57786	13.0239	9.12408	1.94468
ZN	22	2	36.2900	45.3600	39.8060	3.13364
HG	23	1	331.591	441.667	393.622	29.3507

(c) All data for the time period

NAME	NDATA	NULLS	MINIMUM	MAXIMUM	MEAN	STD. DEV.
YEAR	37	0	1980.08	1983.08		
CU	37	0	59.0090	132.362	81.4736	15.4411
AU	37	0	314.982	675.309	482.550	109.229
AG	37	0	5.57786	38.2568	13.0083	7.21494
ZN	35	2	35.3800	45.3600	38.4772	3.07188
HG	36	1	331.591	441.667	391.422	24.6120

FIGURE 5.4. Selection on numeric fields. Example: Metals prices from 1980 to 1982. (*a*) Periods when gold price is over $500; *b*) periods when gold price is under $500; (*c*) all data for the time period.

for zinc and mercury are essentially the same for the two groups, although both have considerably greater variation in the low gold price group. As the YEAR field indicates, this separation could also have been achieved chronologically. As we shall see in Parts II and III, this type of simple analysis can be more effectively illustrated using computer graphics (plotting all of the values as a function of time), although perhaps not as quickly completed.

A special selection procedure only applicable to numeric data is to consider any two fields as coordinates of a graph, and to select only those values which fall inside (or outside) a polygon drawn on the graph. This provides a simple method for locating samples in discrete clusters on a two-dimensional scatter plot. If the cluster can be isolated inside a rectangle aligned with the axes of the plot, the polygon method is unnecessary: tests on minimum and maximum values will suffice. Tests on two X and Y coordinates are also frequently used to limit data to specific geographic boundaries. As shown in Figure 5.5, the procedure is to draw a polygon around the desired group of data on a two-dimensional plot, and to read off X and Y coordinates for the corners of the polygon. These values are parameters for a selection algorithm, which compares the values of the X and Y fields from each record

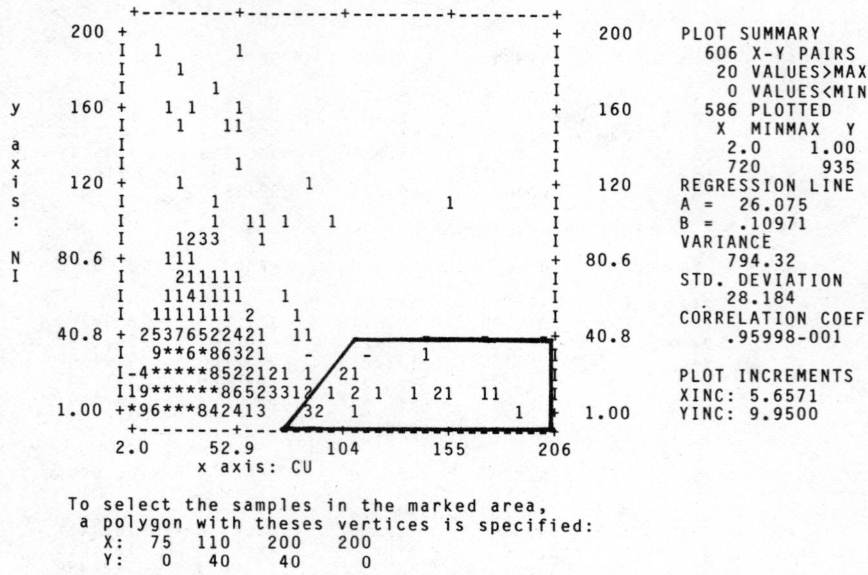

FIGURE 5.5. Selection of data within a polygon using scatter plot of Figure 4.2.

to the boundary of the polygon. It may be possible to define the polygon directly on the X-Y plot if the program is designed to run on a graphics terminal (see Chapter 6). More generally, the coordinate pairs are simply typed on a terminal keyboard, along with other parameters.

In any data selection problem, it is often useful to select records which fail the tests. In some cases, this is the easiest way to define the selection criteria. It can also save computing time if a series of mutually exclusive categories are to be derived from the same data file. In this situation, the second selection test may be applied only to the records rejected by the first, and so on.

Data selection algorithms may be incorporated into larger programs, or be used by themselves to prepare new data files. When selection is an option, it will normally be fairly limited in scope, in order to keep the main program from becoming too complex. For example, a program for producing histogams and scatter plots might be able to limit the value of the variables being plotted, but not to allow extensive tests on several fields. More elaborate subdivisions of the complete data set can be performed by a separate program that creates new files in the database format. These subfiles can then be used as input to the analysis routines.

2. Sorting

Sorting data can be a great help in organizing data files. As noted earlier, complex databases are often ordered by the values of key fields in order to allow quick retrieval of selected values. In the simplest case, this means that records are arranged so values of a given field will fall into sequence. This can apply equally to character or numeric data. Multiple field sorts are also used, requiring a priority order to be established. In this case, all records with a constant value for the primary field are grouped together, their order determined by the values of the secondary sort fields. For example, a database on oil wells might sort first by location, then by production status and amount of production. Alternately, it might be sorted by the name of the owner, location, production, and so on.

When an ordered structure is used, it is not necessary to test all records when selecting data according to the value of the key fields. For a single sorted variable, a commonly used (and easy to implement) method is a binary search. The values of the desired field are considered as an array, with each entry corresponding to one record in the file. The objective of the search is to locate the first and last positions in the array that meet the test condition. The test is whether the data values fall between a defined upper and lower limit (a match to a single value can also be viewed in this way). Note that the test field may be numeric or character. The minimum desired value is considered first so that the start of the sequence can be located. The search begins with a selection of the value at the midpoint in the array. If it is greater than (or equal to) the test value, the desired sequence starts in the first half of the file. If it is smaller than the test value, all desired records must be in the latter half of the file. The next step is to repeat the process, dividing the appropriate part of the array in half again by examining the midpoint of the segment. This continues iteratively until the first record satisfying the test condition is found. The operation is repeated to locate the last record in the sequence, following the same method, but applying the test in the opposite sense. If there is only one selection criterion, all records in the defined range are retrieved. If additional tests are required, only these records need be examined to decide if the record is to be selected. In the oil well example, this approach would allow all information associated with one company to be isolated if the company name was the primary sort field. The same technique is also often applied in locating single entries in a dictionary, as in word-processing programs that check spelling.

Binary searches can be applied to any sorted array. If the array is held in computer memory, sorting is the only requirement. If the array is stored in a file, however, the program using the binary search must be able to read the file in a "direct access" mode. This means that the program can read the *N*th record directly at any time, without having to skip over the preceding *N*-1 records in the file. In most cases, it is necessary to define a special file structure to allow direct access, which may mean that normal utility programs (such as text editors) can no longer be used with the file.

Database systems may use more elaborate schemes to allow rapid selection based on multiple fields. In this case the sorting functions may be automatic. The user is not concerned with the internal arrangement of the file, but may still have to specify sorting fields in preparing subfiles and printed output.

In addition to organizing data files, sorting can be useful in arranging data listings in a convenient form. After preparation of a statistical summary, it is often valuable to examine individual records corresponding to high or low parts of a distribution. The manual effort of reading through a data listing can be greatly reduced by sorting on the value of the particular field before printing the file. For example, commodities prices are normally arranged chronologically, which might make it difficult to quickly identify all periods when a given price is high (when gold is over $500, for instance), although groups of high values are likely to appear together. A listing sorted on gold price isolates the values of interest for quick comparison to other commodities. It may be convenient to sort in descending order, so that high values will be put at the top of the list. The sorting operation can also replace a number of data selections if there are several price ranges to be studied. A simple sorted listing is even more effective when the desired values occur in erratic fashion, and are not strongly influenced by adjacent values. One example is geochemical exploration, where the samples may be collected at widely separated locations, and local effects dominate the measured values. The first step in analysis is to identify the highest values for each element. Another case is the use of residuals (from curve fitting, trend surfaces, or multivariate techniques such as multiple regression) for detection of anomalous samples. Such procedures are likely to produce erratically distributed extreme values (both positive and negative) which will appear at both ends of the sorted list. Computer files with information on earthquakes are likely to be in chronological order, and perhaps geographically separated. To study the effects of very large earthquakes, a sort according to magnitude provides the desired reorganization.

As for data selection, sorting may be invoked as an option in a larger program or may be available as a separate procedure. The same principle applies: that the full range of sorting options should appear only in a "standalone" program that produces new data files in the database structure.

3. Printed Lists of Data Files

The fundamental form of computer output is a printed listing of a data file, whether of original information or computed results. Since this is so common, and all computer systems provide a variety of methods for printing data, it may seem unnecessary to discuss this topic at all. Nonetheless, there are some important considerations in producing printed information that is easy to use, as well as easy to generate. A great deal of time can be wasted in reading through data listings that are not organized properly.

Most utility listing programs simply print an echo of a data file, essentially as it is stored in the computer. As noted in the discussion on sorting, it is often useful to produce listings where the internal arrangement is changed. Not only the sequence of the records, but also the sequence of the fields might be changed. The most convenient form for a comparison of any two fields is to have them printed side by side. As they may not be stored in adjacent positions in the file, a good listing program should be able to rearrange the fields. This often requires an option to print only selected fields when the records are too long to fit on a single line of printed text. The need to reorder printed fields often arises when computed quantities like trend surface residuals are added to a data file. New fields are typically added after all existing data, so we might have the raw data field in columns 20–30, and the corresponding residual in columns 120–130, with many other fields in between.

Another aspect of rearranging the data for printing is to make the text more readable. To save space, the fields in a typical file are compressed into as few characters as possible, often with no intervening blanks. An unmodified printout will again be difficult to read because it may not be immediately clear where one field stops and another starts. The need to conserve disk space often results in the use of binary formats, especially for data which are primarily numeric (since each value takes only four bytes, instead of perhaps eight or nine in character form). In this case, a direct echo cannot be used, so any listing program will necessarily have to translate to a readable form (although perhaps not the most convenient one).

It is also important to have complete headings on each page of the printed output. A simple echo of the data will not usually include field names, so the user must know which columns contain the fields that are of current interest. Once again, an internally defined data structure is helpful so that a proper heading can be created automatically. This also eliminates the problem of misidentification that we saw in considering the need for data independence, and saves time, since the user does not need to refer to another document to find the location of the fields of interest.

A listing program linked to a defined database structure should also account for gaps in numeric fields by printing null values as blanks or nonnumeric characters. This eliminates the need to label the meaning of the null value on the output, which would otherwise be necessary to avoid having such entries interpreted as valid data.

In many cases, it is necessary to know the sequence number of the records in the file in order to make corrections. A listing program should then be able to print this number with each record. An option to print only part of the file (a range of record numbers) can reduce the volume of output when only portions of the data need to be studied in detail.

Data listings are another feature that appear as an option in many programs. Once again it is best to tailor a listing option to the specific function of the main program and to leave the full range of abilities (e.g., printing of any or all fields, extensive reordering) to a single general purpose program that can accept data from any of the available files.

OPERATIONAL PROCEDURES

Efficient use of a computer system is largely dependent on the manual operations involved in running the desired programs. Although software can streamline many procedures, a user can usually save a considerable amount of time by developing consistent practices and documenting particular methods that are used recurrently. This allows an individual user to take full advantage of previous experience, and makes it easy for others to apply the same techniques to their own problems.

1. Naming Conventions

Effective computer use very often depends on an organized system for naming files so they can be found later with a minimum of effort. Even when an elaborate database structure is used, names of individual files are left to the user. A wide variety of files is involved in any project, including original data, programs, parameters, and data dictionaries. As a general rule, names should be as complete as possible under the conventions of the particular computer system. Although shorthand names save typing time, they should not be used for any files that are to be kept for a significant amount of time. Inevitably, the user will forget the precise contents of each file not in active use, and will waste time later finding the file that contains a particular set of data.

As a simple example, consider a project involving three sets of data, say, a geophysical survey, a geochemical sampling, and precious metal assays from drill holes on a mining property. These might simply be called DATA1, DATA2, and DATA3, or perhaps GOLDHILL.GEOPHYSICS, GOLDHILL.GEOCHEM, and GOLDHILL.DRILLHOLES. The latter form makes it clear that these files are associated with the prospect GOLDHILL, and identifies the contents of each. Data analysis might require setting parameters for a statistical summary program, which could be saved in other files. These could equally well be called RUN1, RUN2, and RUN3, or GOLDHILL.STATS.GEOPHYSICS, etc. The computer's operating system may allow a shorter "alias" in place of a full name to save typing, while retaining a fully descriptive name.

2. Use of Standard "Run-Streams"

It is often useful to save parameters for particular jobs in computer files, especially for commonly used programs. Even with interactive parameter setting, many of the same options will be specified when analyzing similar sets of data. The time required to edit an existing "run-stream" to adapt it to a new project will generally be much less than that required for entering the complete set of parameters, particularly for complex programs with many options or procedures where several programs are used together (data selection + statistical summary + listing, perhaps). The editing process can itself be streamlined by using special symbols or parameter names as keywords, so that the portions of the file to be changed can be located automatically. Standard run-streams may be stored in a separate file that will always be available. The variations for a particular project can then be viewed as transient versions which need not be kept after the project is completed. It will also be easier to locate the desired run in such a "master" file, since it will not contain other project-specific data. In the just-cited example, the three STATS run-streams would all have been generated from the same original (called RUNS.STATS, perhaps).

3. Documentation

The next major area for improving efficiency is documentation. This includes detailed instructions on the operating system commands and the applications programs, which are generally the responsibility of the people who develop and maintain the software. In addition to maintaining current versions of program documentation, a user should document his own procedures. The work involved in such an undertaking can be greatly reduced if an organized system for naming files is established, since a record of existing data and run-streams is the major requirement. It is often useful to maintain index files defining the naming conventions and the existing files. In the previous example, we might have a file named PROSPECTS, which contained a list of exploration properties, along with types of data available for each one.

For complex programs accessed by standard run-streams, internal comments in the run-stream file can be used to describe the usual modifications required to adapt the run for a specific project. Definitions of important parameters might also be included, especially if a number of people use the master file. If the files are used by only one person, this might not be as important, although it is still worthwhile for procedures that are applied recurrently, but not often enough for all of the details to be immediately recalled. A run that is used every day does not need as much internal documentation as one that is applied only once a month, for example. The objective of this type of documentation is to guarantee that any useful procedures remain available for other applications, and do not have to be redeveloped on each new project. It is also worthwhile to write a user's guide for common types of analysis. This guide should outline the steps required and list the programs and standard run-streams that will be used. It is essentially an overview of the coordinated use of all the programs needed to complete a given type of study.

4. Other Useful Practices

An important but often neglected peripheral device for any computer user is the wastebasket. The great majority of computer output is needed only once, and should be discarded as soon as possible. It is very easy to fall into the habit of keeping all printouts until a project is completed, and only then search through them to determine which should be kept. This can waste a great deal of time, especially when several sets of output have been created as a result of identifying and correcting errors. It is very useful to have all programs label the date and time on output so that the most recent results can easily be identified.

This principle should also be applied to computer files. In any large project it is likely that a number of temporary files will be created. These files can take up valuable disk space and cause problems when the time comes to consolidate files at the end of the project. It is helpful to establish a distinctive naming convention for short-term files, and to get into the habit of destroying them as soon as they are no longer needed. Some computer systems make this fairly easy by providing an option to create files which will automatically be erased after a stated period of time.

Personal experience with a variety of data analysis problems is essential for efficient use of a computer system. The suggestions in this chapter cannot replace such experience. They are intended to help a new user develop such experience more quickly. The value of an organized and documented approach is that solutions to previous problems remain quickly accessible. Flexibility in applying different programs and analytical techniques is as important as the flexibility of the programs themselves. Perhaps the main lesson to be learned in becoming an effective computer user is that a single approach cannot be applied to all problems: one must be prepared to employ a variety of analytical methods, and to develop the ability to use all of the capabilities of the available software.

PART II

ANALYSIS OF SPATIAL DATA WITH COMPUTER GRAPHICS

Many analytical problems involve spatial data, for which the variables to be analyzed depend on a Cartesian coordinate system. The analysis of such problems is greatly simplified by plotting the data in the given coordinate system to produce a graphical rather than a tabular display.

CHAPTER 6. FUNDAMENTALS OF COMPUTER PLOTTING

This chapter reveiws the requirements for using a computer to plot data. Special output devices, and software to "drive" them, must be added to a computer system to make this possible. In addition, a digitizer for graphical data input, and software packages for coordinate transformations are often needed. Types of computer plots include profile displays, posted and contoured maps, scatter plots, and ternary diagrams.

CHAPTER 7. EFFECTIVE USE OF COMPUTER PLOTTING

This chapter deals largely with characteristics of the plotting system. For data analysis, the most important needs are flexibility and speed, since there is great variety in the types of data to be considered, and in the methods of displaying them. Plotting software should be organized into modular units to allow new programs to use standard functions. Independence from specific types of data is desirable. As in basic analysis, selection of subsets of data will often be required. The ability to display output on multiple devices is another common need. Problems in computer plotting often arise when the data have variable spatial density, and special procedures may be needed for these cases.

CHAPTER 8. COMPUTER PLOTS AS AIDS TO ANALYSIS

When determination of data structure is the problem, profile plots (one spatial dimension) or contour maps (two dimensions) provide an immediate picture. In a search for anomalies, these forms might also be used, after a trend surface is removed. Other techniques for locating anomalies include selecting data by minimum-maximum limits from a histogram, or within a polygon on a scatter plot. Posted maps using different symbols for different classes of data are also effective in many cases.

CHAPTER 9. ENCHANCED DISPLAY TECHNIQUES

In many cases the plots produced for analysis are considered working copies only, and may not require embellishment for final use. A number of simple techniques can make computer maps more effective for the analyst, and more aesthetically pleasing as well. For example, plotting background grid lines and reference coordinate ticks aids the analyst in locating specific points, and gives more of the appearance of a published map. Complete preparation of maps on a computer should be left to a computer-aided design (CAD) system.

CHAPTER 6

FUNDAMENTALS OF COMPUTER PLOTTING

Many types of data analysis involve geographic data, that is, samples which are associated with a specific location. This can be expressed in a variety of coordinate systems, including position on the earth's surface, vertical cross sections in the earth, location inside a test chamber (e.g., a wind tunnel), and the angular measures used to locate astronomical objects. A major part of the analysis of such data is to determine the spatial characteristics of the variables, which usually requires drawing a number of maps. Here a "map" is taken to mean any two-dimensional diagram that displays locations of samples and values of particular variables associated with each sample. One great benefit of using a computer is that the map-making process can be extensively automated, which saves a great deal of time in data preparation. A computer may also be used to create many other types of plots used in data analysis: graphical displays are virtually indispensable in studying data with several variables and/or a great number of samples.

One of the fastest growing areas in computer technology is computer graphics, which can be defined as the use of computer hardware and software to create visual displays. Special devices must be added to a computer system to provide a plotting capability: hardcopy plotters and interactive graphics terminals (these categories can be further subdivided by whether or not there is a capability for color shading). Special software must also be available, which frequently demands very complex programs. Areas of possible application are essentially unlimited. They include statistical charts and graphs, topographic mapping, automated drafting and design, and satellite image analysis. In this chapter, the basic principles for plotting data with a computer will be reviewed. Following chapters will use this background to study particular plotting applications.

COMPONENTS OF A PLOTTING SYSTEM

As the examples in Chapters 3 and 4 indicate, a normal printer can create a variety of graphical displays using character codes to represent points and lines. Many types of "plots" have been produced this way, including contour maps, areal shaded maps, scatter diagrams, and profile plots. The great advantage of printer output is that it is fast and inexpensive, since no special devices or extensive computation are required. There are major drawbacks, however. The resolution of a printer plot is poor: typically there are only ten characters per inch horizontally, and six or eight lines per inch for the vertical dimension. The limited size of printer paper requires large plots to be created in segments, which must be spliced together manually. Lines must be represented by printed characters, so it is difficult to produce a readable display when several features must be overplotted on the same map. In this book, we do not consider printer output to be true computer graphics, but reserve the term rather for the special devices that actually draw lines and symbols in the style of a manually drafted plot. Printer plots are a very useful tool, however, and should be considered in any case where quick output is an important consideration, and detailed resolution is not essential.

1. Plotters

Automated plotting facilities were first developed as an extension of strip-chart recorders, with a computer controlling the movement of pen on paper. The basic functions of a pen plotter are simple: to move to a defined position on the paper either with the pen down (to draw a line), or up (to move up the start of a new line). All plotted lines, symbols, and shading patterns can be reduced to this simple form. The mechanical implementation can take many forms, however. In a "drum" plotter, the pen moves along a fixed bar in one dimension only, while the paper rolls back and forth to give movement in the other direction. Various widths of paper are used, in some cases on continuous rolls, or on pre-cut sheets. A "flatbed" plotter uses fixed sizes of paper attached to a table, with the pen on a moveable gantry. These may range in size from desk-top units that plot on letter-size paper, to machines capable of drawing very large maps (perhaps four by six feet) equivalent to those produced by a skilled draftsman. For either type, the capacity (i.e., the number of plots that can be done in a given time) is largely dependent on the maximum pen speed. Resolution is usually expressed in terms of a "step-size," the smallest distance of movement along either axis. It is difficult (and expensive) to provide both high speed and resolution, so a great range of capabilities is available.

A plotter may be controlled directly by a central computer, or have its own small computer that reads plot instructions from a magnetic tape created on the main system. These configurations are called "on-line" and "off-line." An on-line plotter will generally require a special interface device on the main computer, and associated software for sending output to that device. An off-line setup does not impact the main system in this way, but requires more computer operator work, since the plotted data cannot be automatically transferred to the plotter. Plotters used with a personal computer are in the on-line mode, although some manual switching of connecting cables may be involved.

In either case, the actions of the plotter are controlled by the data it receives. Normally the plot instructions are coded as a series of "vectors," each consisting of a pair of numbers defining a unique position on the plot, plus a code for the action required. The X-Y position is given in inches (or centimeters) from the physical origin of the plot (usually the lower left corner). The plotter moves from the current position to point defined by X-Y, where it performs the designated action. In addition to the basic pen up/down command, the code may signal a change of pens (for drawing lines of different thickness or color), or command that a given symbol be drawn at the defined location. If the plotter can internally generate plotted symbols, the plot vector will also include the size of the symbol and an angle of rotation relative to the horizontal axis. This greatly reduces the volume of data that must be sent to the plotter, since a series of vectors defining all of the line segments in the symbol would be required otherwise. Sophisticated plotting devices may also perform such operations as generating dashed lines, areal shading, and rescaling the plot. Such capabilities reduce the workload on the main computer and speed up data transmission.

A second major class of plotters employs a completely different technology than pen plotters, which simply mimic manual methods for drawing lines and symbols. Electrostatic plotters treat the entire plot as a series of dots, which can be either black or white. The plot is created by a line of finely spaced electrodes, which place an electric charge on special paper. The paper is fed continuously past the electrodes from a roll, with each electrode turned on or off as required at each line. After charging the black areas, the paper passes through a chemical "toner" containing carbon particles, which are attracted to the charged portion of the paper. A final stage is to dry off the toner and fix the carbon particles to avoid smearing. Typically, the density of dots is 200 per inch in either dimension (i.e., 40,000 per square inch), which is just barely detectable to the naked eye. As with pen plotters, there is a tradeoff of resolution and speed, as finer dot spacing allows greater detail, but takes longer to plot (and is more expensive to generate).

Data organized in this matrix fashion are called "raster," and "rasterizing" is the process of computing the dot matrix from data in a vector form. The vector data are again the X, Y, CODE plot instructions for the line segments of the plot. Given the density of the raster data, this may demand extensive calculations and require a powerful computer. The volume of raster data can also be enormous, and may pose serious problems in data transfer to an offline plotter, or to one at a remote site. Rather than send the complete raster file, it is often possible to compress it by using a code that defines the points where the dots switch color. For example, a vertical line on a 36-inch plot requires 7200 raster points (at 200 dots per inch). Instead of the full 7200 bits, the line could be expressed by two numbers (say 0 and 7200) defining the start and end of the black segment. A raster scan containing a number of black segments would be coded as a longer series. Eventually, the coded form might require more space than the original form. A variety of other compression schemes might also be used. The plotting device must be able to translate the compressed instructions into the full raster form for each line, of course.

A more complete solution to these data transfer problems is to use a special plotter "controller," which has a microprocessor capable of performing a complete raster conversion. In this case, the central computer has less work to do, and the plot instructions could be sent in the much more compact vector format. Once again, if the controller performs such operations as generating symbols, the size of the plot file is further reduced.

The great benefit of electrostatic plotters is their speed. A detailed contour map might take an hour or more on even a fast pen plotter, while an electrostatic plotter would complete it in less than a minute. This speed is not free, of course: it assumes either that the main computer has done a great deal of work to prepare a raster file, or that an expensive extra component is attached to the plotter. Still, where plotter volume is high, electrostatic plotters have an overwhelming advantage.

The limitations of electrostatic plotters are primarily associated with the plotting media. As noted above, special papers are required to take the electric charge. Standard paper is somewhat flimsy and not suitable for manually drafted enhancements. Clear film can be used but is quite expensive. Unlike a pen plotter, which can use multicolored pens on any paper, electrostatics are limited to black and white, although shades of gray and variable line widths are available to distinguish different plotted information. In 1983, however, an electrostatic plotter with color capability was announced (for delivery in early 1984). The process is similar to that of a black and white electrostatic except that multiple passes over the electrodes are required for the different colors. Due to the large size (42 inches wide), and corresponding high price, this type of plotter will likely find only specialized applications in the near future. It is almost certain that the technology will be adapted to smaller plotters, however, making color "hard-copy" much more widely available.

In many data analysis problems, the majority of plots are only working copies, so some of these limitations are not a serious concern. In large organizations, it is common to use electrostatic plotters for most output, with a drafting-quality pen plotter available for plots which will be stored permanently.

Many small printers used with microcomputers employ a dot matrix to generate characters, and can be adapted to allow true graphics. Once again this involves a raster conversion, although in this case it is manageable on a small computer, given the limited size of the paper, and fairly low resolution. Additional hardware in the microcomputer is usually required as well. Such improvements in small computer technology have opened the use of computer graphics to a much larger user group than before.

The use of color can be very effective for multivariate problems. Color in effect adds an extra dimension to a map, as one additional variable can be displayed by color coding existing lines or symbols. Color plotting can be achieved by any pen plotter that allows multiple pens. Full color shading is desirable when displaying variables over an area, rather than just at a sample point (e.g., political zones, types of vegetation, and surface geology). This can also be done with a pen plotter by tracing a line pattern throughout the area. It is usually not practical for large plots, however, because of their slow speed. As a result, special color plotters have been developed. The raster concept is applied, except that the raster data are not simply 0 and 1, but contain a color code. Color is usually defined as a mixing ratio of three primary colors, with range of perhaps 0–16 for each. A basic set of eight colors are often provided to simplify the task of assigning colors. A raster file for color plotting, then, is very much larger than a raster file for black and white, and the problems of computation and data transfer are correspondingly worse. There are relatively few color plotters on the market, and their maximum plot sizes generally are much smaller than for pen or electrostatic devices.

Most color plotters use three ink jets to transfer the raster data onto paper. At each raster point, each jet is turned on or off, depending on whether the associated primary color is required. Intermediate shades are produced by a secondary pattern of perhaps 25 dots. Color "hard-copy" is also often produced directly from color graphics terminals, using special "cameras" to make slides or prints (up to eight by ten inches).

Plots can also be produced on microfilm, using a modified CRT that focuses its electron beam on photographic film. Microfilm plotters use vector data, but are much faster than pen plotters since no mechanical motion is involved. Microfilm output is very compact, and thus is often used when many plots are to be permanently stored.

2. Graphical Displays on a Computer Terminal

A natural outgrowth of computer plotting is interactive graphics, where plotted output is displayed on a CRT screen for immediate evaluation by the user. These special devices are called "graphics terminals." Plotting at a terminal provides much faster turnaround, and is of great advantage for iterative procedures (e.g., comparing a computed model to real data). In experimenting with the format of a particular type of plot, trial efforts may be previewed at the terminal to save the expense of a hard-copy plot that might be immediately discarded as unacceptable.

Graphics terminals can operate in a vector or raster mode. Vector terminals use an electron beam to trace lines between any two points on the screen, and thus can produce high-resolution drawings. To prevent a flickering image, all of the vectors need to be redrawn frequently (at least 30 times a second). This "refresh" operation requires that all of the plot vectors be stored in the terminal, which must accordingly contain a fairly powerful microprocessor. The memory available in the terminal necessarily places limits on the number of vectors contained in any one drawing.

To avoid the problem of storing and redrawing many vectors, a "storage tube" can be used. The vectors are drawn the same way, but the drawing stays on the screen until erased. This allows a considerable savings in computer resources over a refresh system, since there is no need to store and redraw the plot vectors. As a result, storage terminals are considerably cheaper, although limited in application to "static" types of drawings, since new images cannot be drawn fast enough to give the illusion of motion. To offset the slower speed, some storage terminals incorporate additional memory to retain portions of the plot that are redrawn frequently. The cost advantage is then reduced, although this configuration is still considerably cheaper than a complete refresh system.

As noted earlier, the raster approach is to treat the graphic image as an array of dots (called "pixels"). A raster terminal operates like a normal televison set, continually redisplaying a series of horizontal lines. This is a simpler process than the moving beam of a vector display, and employs widely-used technology. Raster terminals are therefore generally the least expensive type of terminal display.

Like a refresh vector system, the raster terminal must have a considerable amount of memory to store the large array of points. This limitation, along with restrictions on the number of "scan lines" in the image, means that a raster display is normally of lower resolution than a vector display. This is most evident when drawing slanted lines, which show a characteristic stair-step pattern (called the "jaggies"). The resolution of a vector display is also finite, since the screen is considered as a fixed array of "addressable points" where the electron beam can be focussed. Currently the highest resolution commonly available on vector terminals is 4096 by 4096 points, on a screen of about 12 by 15 inches. Raster displays may use as few as 256 by 256 pixels, with a current practical limit of about 1024 by 1024.

Raster displays have their own advantages. A raster image can be redrawn virtually instantly, without regard to the complexity of the image, while a vector drawing must be completely retraced. As with raster plotters, this plotting speed requires considerable extra computation, to prepare the raster data. A raster terminal can easily produce full-color images if a multiphosphor screen, equivalent to a color TV, is used. Areal shading (or color fill) imposes no extra burden on a raster terminal, but is generally not practical for vector displays. Raster displays are thus the standard form for computer animation and other applications where areal shading is a requirement.

Rapid changes in technology are always a factor in computer graphics, so it is difficult to determine which type of display will dominate. It appears clear, however, that increasingly powerful microprocessors will enable raster terminals to greatly improve resolution, without becoming prohibitively expensive. Storage tubes will likely decline in popularity, since they cannot compete in terms of speed, and are unsuitable for animation and other dynamic displays.

For many types of data display, resolution on the terminal is not a critical factor, since only the basic characteristics of the data are required. It is usually easier to study fine detail on a "hard copy." Where large plots are required, it may be faster to produce a full-size hard copy than to selectively view portions of the display on a small screen. If plotting scale is important, for comparison to other maps, for example, a plotter must be used.

After viewing transient images on a terminal screen, a permanent copy is often needed for more detailed study, or for archival purposes. Copiers attached directly to the terminal can supply a page-size copy of the screen display very quickly. For color terminals, these devices can be quite expensive, and simple alternatives like mounting a conventional camera on a frame in front of the screen can produce a copy suitable for most purposes. If a larger plotter is available, the same display can always be redrawn at full scale, of course.

The small image on a graphics terminal can also be displayed on a large screen using a projector attached to the terminal. This provides a convenient way of demonstrating interactive applications to a large audience, or of presenting data at a meeting without resorting to hard copies.

Additional components can be attached to a graphics terminal to allow graphic input, that is, to mark points or lines on the screen. This capability is useful in pointing to items on a menu, outlining a cluster of data for selection, or free-form drawing. The device may be a light pen, which points directly at the screen, a digitizing tablet (see Section 4 below), a joystick or thumbwheels to move a cross-hair, or a "mouse" which can be moved around on any surface near the terminal.

3. Plotting Software

Display devices cannot produce useful output by themselves: this is a function of software. Plotting software must create the plot instructions needed to create the desired drawings, and code the instructions in the form expected by the particular plotting device used to display the drawing. It is then possible to consider applications plotting programs and system plotting software as two separate categories.

The system plotting software is provided by the plotter (or terminal) manufacturer, as it must be intimately linked to the physical characteristics of the hardware. Its main function is to encode plot vectors in the format assumed by the plotting device. If the device is on-line, the data must also be sent to the proper output channel, with appropriate checks that it is ready to accept more data. For off-line plotters, the data are written to a magnetic tape. For raster devices, the system software will also provide the vector-to-raster algorithm, unless this function is performed by a dedicated microprocessor attached to the plotting device itself. For output to a pen plotter, the system software may also include routines to rearrange the plot vectors to minimize unnecessary pen moves. For example, a series of random points may be sorted into small blocks to avoid the need to move back and forth across the entire plot area.

Programs for specific plotting applications have an almost infinite variety of forms, to accommodate the many types of drawings that may be created with a computer. There are three types of operations involved:

1. reading the data to be plotted
2. computing plot vectors by appropriate transformations of the data (scaling, rotation, etc.)

3. calling the system routines to encode the plot instructions in the required form

The link between the applications programs and the plotting system routines is a set of simple commands which control the basic functions of the plotting device. All of these can be reduced to an instruction to move to a given location, with pen up or down. A number of higher level operations are usually available through system commands as well, for example, plotting a given symbol or string of characters, plotting a line from an array of X-Y coordinates, changing pen (or line thickness), and redefining the origin of the plot.

Although the plotting system routines are specific to a particular device, the plot commands which must be used in the applications program are very often in a fairly standard form, which allows easy conversion of output to different devices. The first major plotter manufacturer was Calcomp, and their FORTRAN commands are very widely used as the link to the plotting system. Some examples of the commands are:

CALL PLOT(X,Y,CODE) move to X,Y, with action determined by CODE (2 = pen down, 3 = pen up, etc.)

CALL SYMBOL(X,Y,SIZE,N,ANGLE,CODE)
plot symbol N with size SIZE at location X,Y. ANGLE defines a rotation from horizontal, CODE indicates whether N is a character string, or a reference number to a table of symbols

Note that the use of Calcomp-style commands does not restrict the output to Calcomp plotters, since system routines from other manufacturers generally use this form, as well. Additional commands may be provided, depending on the capabilities of the plotter. Shading an area enclosed within a polygon in a given pattern or color may, for example, be possible.

For graphics terminals, there is also an effective "standard" in the format of the plot instructions. Most manufacturers provide an option to use the form developed by Tektronix, the leading company in the field. This allows a variety of different graphics terminals to be used with the same system software.

Standards for graphics software are aimed at providing "device independence": applications programs do not need to be modified when a new output device is used. In the next chapter, the advantages of device independence will be considered in discussing the effective use of computer graphics. This goal has not been fully realized, although most available software can be adapted to a variety of output devices without a major effort. A formal definition of graphics standards is incorporated into the "Core" system developed by SIGGRAPH (the Special Interest Group on Graphics of the Association for Computing Machinery). A similar system used in Europe is the GKS (Graphical Kernel System). These systems will likely be integrated into an internationally accepted composite. They are defined in several levels, to accommodate the full range of graphics devices, from those which accept only basic commands to the sophisticated plotters and terminals that can generate many graphical operations internally. While preparing to display output on a particular device, the plotting system software can determine which operations must be done in the main computer, and which can be passed off to the display device.

4. Digitizers

The hardware and software discussed above provide a means of producing graphical displays of data in computer files. In many cases, the data are originally in a graphical form, and must be converted to the "digital" representation required by a computer. This requires a special input device called a digitizer (or digitizing "tablet"), which produces an array of X-Y coordinates to define a continuous line on a map as a series of straight line segments. It is also used to get coordinates for randomly located points on a map, and to associate other data with that location.

The most common type of digitizer has a large tabular surface over a finely spaced grid of wires. The desired position is marked by a moveable "cursor" with cross hairs (or a pen), which induces an electric field in the grid by passing a current through a loop centered on the cross hairs. Variations in the induced field allow the location of the cursor to be determined electronically, to within an accuracy of 0.001 inches in some models. The cursor position is sent to the controlling computer by depressing a switch (for point locations), or at regular intervals for tracing a line. Alternate methods can be used for sensing the cursor location, such as mounting it on a gantry (as for a flatbed plotter), and monitoring the motions along the two axes of the table.

To digitize a map, it is fastened to the table, and reference coordinate points are entered. The map coordinates of these points are also provided to the program that reads the digitized locations, to establish a transformation from a position on the table (normally in inches from the lower left corner) to the map coordinate system. Lines are entered by typing in an identifying number (e.g., the contour value from a topographic map), and tracing the line with the cursor. Point data (e.g., locations of towns) are entered simply by placing the cursor at the point marked on the map. Associated data may be typed on a keyboard or from a numeric pad attached to the cursor.

Digitizers are used extensively in many mapping applications, particularly when historical data must be merged with newly acquired information. Maps are often the only permanent record of spatial data like surface topography, geologic boundaries, and sample locations. These may include observed data for point locations, as well (e.g., the concentration of gold in rock samples might be labeled beside a location symbol). Digitizing is a time consuming and error-prone process, even on a computer, so detailed checks on the quality of the data are essential.

More automatic digitizing devices can be used for applications where the basic requirement is to "capture" the original picture for computer reproduction. These "scanners" pass a laser across the entire drawing to determine the intensity of a finely spaced array of points. Special programs are used to examine this raster image and determine the positions of lines (by testing for similar "grey levels" in adjacent pixels). Since the output is simply the line locations, and does not contain associated numeric or textual information, these devices cannot be applied in most analysis problems. This is a major research and deveopment area, so it is possible that fully automatic digitizing will become a reality in the future.

COORDINATE SYSTEMS

All maps are based on a two-dimensional, orthogonal coordinate system: that is, the position of any point on the map is related to two perpendicular axes. Before any map can be drawn on a computer, then, it is necessary to have the coordinates of all data to be included on the map in a computer file. Coordinates can be recorded automatically with the analytical data, but frequently must be entered independently, to be merged with other information. As we saw in Chapter 2, this operation is subject to error, and the merged result must be checked to guarantee that the coordinates and data are properly matched.

If the available coordinates are in an orthogonal system, they can be used directly for plotting. This is usually the case when the locations are measured directly from a reference grid on a planar surface. For maps representing part of the earth's surface, orthogonality can be assumed when the coordinates are surveyed directly as offsets from a baseline or reference point. When the mapped area becomes large, the curvature of the surface becomes a problem, and a transformation reducing the curved surface to a plane must be applied.

1. Position on the Earth's Surface: The UTM System

True position on the earth is defined by the angular measures of latitude and longitude. Since these coordinates are not orthogonal (lines of longitude converge towards the poles), and are not equidistant (the distance equal to one degree of longitude depends on the latitude), they do not meet the requirements for accurate plotting on a two-dimensional surface. To solve this problem, a variety of map projections have been developed to convert latitude and longitude to X and Y coordinates in an orthogonal system. No projection can adequately serve to display the entire world on a single map (consider the well-known high-latitude exaggeration of the common Mercator projection, for example). Different projections are suited to maps which display parts of the globe—sterographic projections are used for polar regions, and the Lambert conic conformal projection is frequently used for maps of large longitudinal extent (e.g., the contiguous United States). A full discussion of this subject is beyond the scope of this book; interested readers should consult an introductory text on cartography for more details (see References).

One particular map projection is worthy of further discussion. The Universal Tranverse Mercator (UTM) system is used for the standard topographic maps of many countries, including Canada and the United States. Like a normal Mercator map, the X-Y coordinates are considered as projections from positions on a spherical surface onto a cylinder. In this case, the cylinder touches the surface along a given meridian of longitude, rather than the equator (hence the term "transverse"). To preserve accuracy, the range of longitudes is limited. This requires that the coordinates be separately computed in a number of zones. In the UTM system, there are 60 zones, each encompassing six degrees of longitude about a "central meridian" (Fig. 6.1*a*). The zones are numbered from west to east, with zone 1 at 174 to 180 degrees west, zones 30 and 31 bracketing 0 degrees, and zone 60 at 174 to 180 degrees east. The central meridians are thus at 177, 171, . . ., 3 degrees (east and west).

A map drawn in UTM coordinates has the central meridian as a straight vertical line, with all other lines of longitude curved to account for convergence. The parallels of latitude also appear as curved lines, which means that the direction to north varies with position in the zone (with the greatest departure from vertical at the zone boundary). To reduce distortion at the edges of the zone, the cylinder cuts the surface at either side of the central meridian. The accuracy is within 4 parts in 10,000 for latitudes less than 84 degrees (other types of projections are more suited to polar regions).

The X and Y (or easting and northing) coordinates are given in meters. The X coordinate of the central meridian is arbitrarily set at 500,000, so

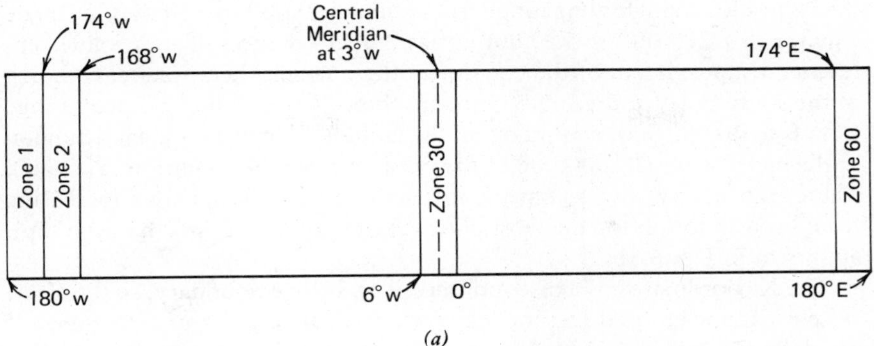

(a)

y = 10,000,000
North Pole
84°
Northern
Hemisphere
x <
500,000
x >
500,000
3°
3°
Equator
y = 0
x = 500,000
Central Meridian

Central Meridian
x = 500,000
Equator
y = 10,000,000
3°
3°
Southern
Hemisphere
84°
South Pole
y = 0
y
x

(b)

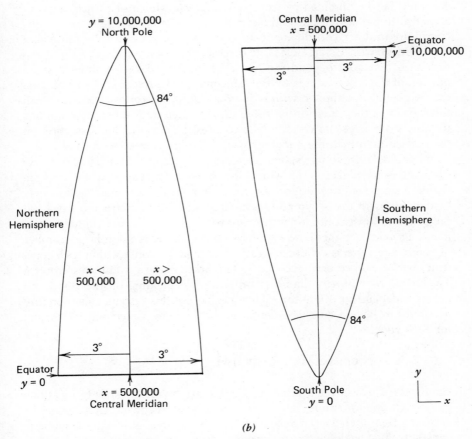

FIGURE 6.1. The UTM (Universal Transverse Mercator) coordinate system. (*a*) Arrangement of UTM "zones." (*b*) Coordinates within any UTM zone.

the values for a single zone range from about 160,000 to 840,000 (near the equator), or 280,000 to 720,000 at latitude 50 degrees. The Y value represents distance north of the equator in the northern hemisphere, or north of the south pole for the southern hemisphere. The Y value then may range from 0 to 10,000,000, depending on the latitude (since the original definition of the meter was 1/10,000,000 of the distance from the equator to the pole). These conventions always have X increasing to the right, and Y increasing from bottom to top for the normal orientation of a map (north at the top), as shown in Fig. 6.1b.

The X coordinate has a discontinuity at each zone boundary, so the UTM system cannot be used to plot maps which include parts of two zones. If the desired range of longitude is less than six degrees, a map of equivalent accuracy can be obtained by using a Transverse Mercator projection with a central meridian within the boundaries of the map. There is also a discontinuity in the Y coordinate at the equator, which again rules out use of the UTM system. If some cases, it is desirable to plot a map in UTM coordinates that goes beyond the normal zone boundary (to show a small portion of the adjacent area on the same map, for instance). The projection can be extended, although with reduced accuracy (distortion increases with distance from the center of the zone). This procedure is most often applied to large scale maps, however, which reduces the effect of the distortion on the plotted map (i.e., the apparent size of the location error is small).

While the UTM zoning system provides a simple way of defining accurate coordinates anywhere in the world, it is often inconvenient when working within a single political region. In this case, a local coordinate system may be defined, with the origin and boundaries specific to the region (to avoid the problem of discontinuities at arbitrary locations). In the United States, many agencies use the State Plane system, which is really a large number of coordinate systems defined for each state (and for zones within each state, if necessary, to preserve accuracy). The State Plane system uses either a Transverse Mercator or Lambert projection, depending on the state, and has an independent origin for each zone. To use this system, it is therefore necessary to have a complete definition of the map projection parameters for each zone.

2. Coordinate Transformations

Databases which cover a large geographic area typically specify locations by latitude and longitude, so it is often necessary to convert these values to an X-Y system. Relatively simple formulae are required, although the numeric constants must be defined to many significant figures to ensure the accuracy of the result. Many of the government agencies which use maps employing the UTM system release the required programs for public use. Software for other commonly used projection systems is also available. Note than a program to calculate UTM coordinates can also give any Transverse Mercator projection by simply replacing the standard central meridian with the appropriate value.

Reverse transformations, from orthogonal systems to latitude and longitude, may also be required in some situations. If a detabase contains UTM coordinates, and a large scale map is to be drawn using a Lambert Conic Conformal projection, the procedure is to compute latitude and longitude from the UTM values, and then calculate the Lambert projection. In other words, latitude and longitude are the link between the various coordinate systems. This type of problem may arise when large scale composite maps are to be drawn using data assembled within separate smaller areas (e.g., when plotting all the mines in a state or province, with locations derived from standard topographic maps).

Transformations betweeen different coordinate systems are often required on a more local scale. In laying out a sample collection program, locations can be measured relative to a local grid system (perhaps defined specifically for the program, or already available as a local network of survey posts, roads, etc). If more than one grid is involved, all coordinates must be expressed in the same system before a map can be drawn. A coordinate conversion is needed if the maps are to be drawn in another system, perhaps in UTM for comparison to existing topographic maps.

Transformations between two orthogonal coordinate systems can be achieved by rotation and scaling, as shown in Fig. 6.2. The coordinates of any two points (given in both systems) are sufficient to define the conversion formula. Alternately, if the rotation angle and scale factor are known, we require only one common point (which might be the origin of either system). Any point may then be transformed using simple trigonometry:

$$x = \mathrm{SCALE} * [\ \mathrm{XX} * \mathrm{COS}\ (\theta) + \mathrm{YY} * \mathrm{SIN}(\theta)\ ] + x_1 \qquad 6.1$$

$$y = \mathrm{SCALE} * [\ \mathrm{YY} * \mathrm{COS}(\theta) - \mathrm{XX} * \mathrm{SIN}(\theta)\ ] + y_1 \qquad 6.2$$

where XX = X − X1 and YY = Y − Y1. Coordinates in the original system are given by X and Y, and the corresponding values in the new system are x and y. Note that the rotation is applied first, and requires that the two sets of coordinates be measured from a common origin (the common point (x1,y1), (X1,Y1). The offset of this reference point from the absolute

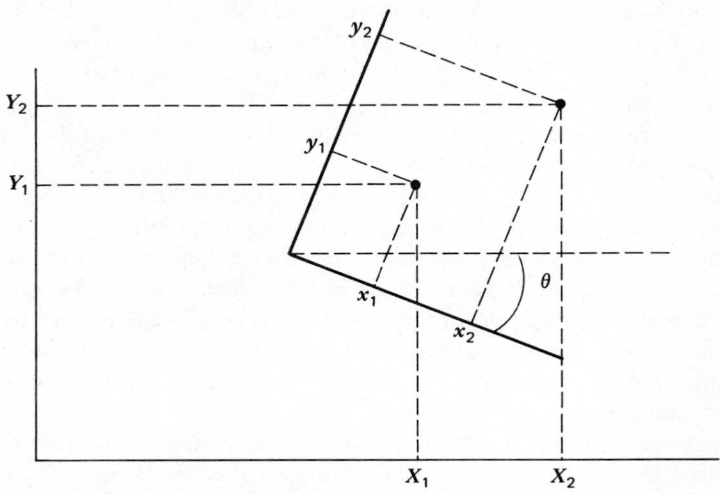

FIGURE 6.2. Transformation of coordinate systems by translation and rotation. Two common points (expressed in both systems) are sufficient to define the transformation.

origin is added after rotation and scaling. The factor SCALE allows for differences in the units of the two systems (feet and meters, for example).

Given two common points, the rotation angle and scale can be computed:

$$\text{SCALE} = \text{LEN1} \;/\; \text{LEN2} \qquad 6.3$$

where LEN 1 = SQRT [(x2 − x1)**2 + (y2 − y1)**2]
LEN 2 = SQRT [(X2 − X1)**2 + (Y2 − Y1)**2]

$$\theta = \text{ANGLE2} - \text{ANGLE1} \qquad 6.4$$

where ANGLE1 = ARCSIN [(y2 − y1) / LEN1]
ANGLE2 = ARCSIN [(Y2 − Y1) / LEN2]

These equations can be simplified somewhat if the common points are chosen to lie on the axes of one of the coordinate systems.

This procedure can be applied to a variety of problems in preparing data for plotting. As noted above, a number of independent local coordinate grids can be used for collecting data, and require conversion to a common system. In digitizing existing maps, a translation between the coordinate system of the digitizer table and the attached map is required. Using a translation and rotation algorithm means that the map can be fixed to the table in any position without special alignment procedures. Cross-section plots can be constructed by selecting data along lines which are not aligned with the coordinate grid of the standard maps. This requires choosing data within a rectangle, and computing "in-line" coordinates for plotting the cross section. A coordinate rotation fills both needs, as the converted X coordinate can be used as an in-line distance, and the Y value can be tested to select only those data within a prescribed distance of the section line.

To allow these operations to be used routinely, they should be part of the database system used by the plotting programs. As we noted in Chapter 5, it is desirable to add converted coordinates as additional fields in the data file, while retaining the normal ability to use them in data selection, and to retrieve the values easily whenever necessary.

3. Coordinate Systems Used in Plotting

The instructions for a plotting device are expressed in actual distances from a physical origin point: the coordinates of the plot vectors are usually given in inches (or centimeters). The size of the plotting area dictates maximum allowable values for X and Y. A major task of the software is then to convert the coordinates of the data to the X-Y values required by the device.

The first step in defining a map (or any other type of two-dimensional drawing) is to set the coordinates which mark the borders. That is, set the minimum and maximum X and Y values to be included on the plot (in map units). Next the scale of the map is defined, perhaps in terms of map units per inch (e.g., 400 feet = 1 inch). An alternate and more flexible form is a natural ratio, which is independent of measurement unts. For example, a scale of 1:50,000 means a distance of 50,000 units (meters, feet, etc.) in the original system has a length of 1 unit on the map. If the X and Y coordinates are not in the same units, two scale values are needed, one for each axis. This is necessary in plotting profiles (e.g. gravity readings along one line) or scatter plots, for example. In this case, the variables may not represent a distance, so a natural ratio scale cannot be used.

Once the X-Y limits and scale have been set, the size of the plot is known. Plotting programs often include an option to automatically segment the display into pieces if the size is greater than the physical limits of the plotting device. To calculate position on the plot for any point, a simple translation and scaling is required:

$$\begin{aligned} \text{XPLOT} &= (\text{X} - \text{XMIN}) * \text{XSCALE} \\ \text{YPLOT} &= (\text{X} - \text{YMIN}) * \text{YSCALE} \end{aligned} \qquad 6.5$$

This assumes that the plot origin is at XMIN, YMIN; if not, an additional displacement is required. XSCALE and YSCALE convert map units to plotter units at the desired scale. Note that these parameters are dependent on the units of both the map and plot coordinates, although they can sometimes be computed internally from a natural ratio.

The other components of the plot vectors are set according to the desired form of the final display. If a continuous line is to be drawn (e.g., a coastline, river, or political boundary), the first vector defines a move with pen up to the first X-Y position, followed by a series of moves with pen down to all succeeding points. To plot a sample location, the code for the desired location symbol is included in the vector, along with its size and orientation. A string of text annotation is generated in a similar fashion, by a series of vectors with appropriate symbol codes, and offsets to the X and Y coordinates for proper positioning.

TYPES OF COMPUTER PLOTS

Virtually any graphical display that can be drawn manually can also be plotted with a computer. It is impossible to create a complete list of the possibilities, since the variety of forms is essentially infinite. In this section, a number of commonly used plotted displays will be described. More detailed examination will follow in the next three chapters. Several examples are shown in Fig. 6.3 through 6.9.

1. Line Maps

The basic feature of any map is a set of lines which represent geographic features such as coastlines, lakes, and rivers. Man-made alterations to the earth's surface can also be drawn as lines, for example, roads, rail lines, and pipelines. There may also be theoretical subdivisions which do not correspond to a physical feature, for example, political boundaries, and lines of latitude and longitude. Standard routes for air and sea travel are in a similar category. In drawing maps for data analysis, not all of these are required, of course, although the major geographic and cultural features are very useful for orientation and for comparison to other maps.

2. Posted Maps

In addition to the basic lines, identifying text must be written ("posted") on the map, to name the features marked by the lines. Posting also facilitates inspection of spatial patterns, by labeling data values at the sample locations. Comparisons of several variables may also be possible, provided there is

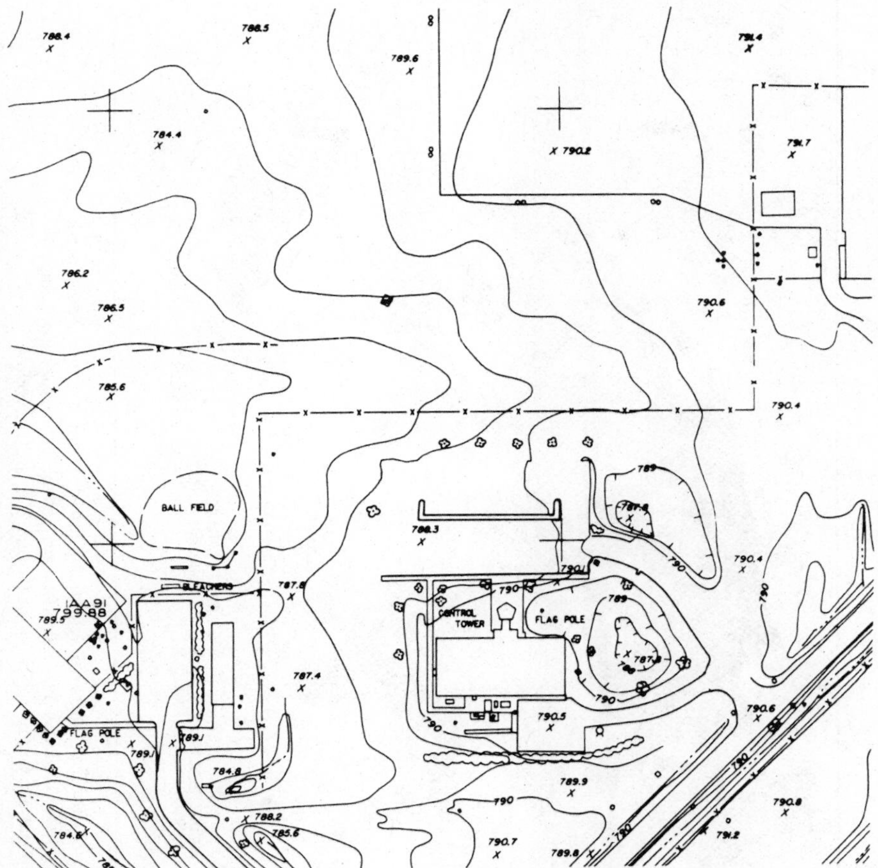

FIGURE 6.3. A complex computer-drawn map. This example shows line outlines of roads and land units, identifying text, contours, and posting of data values at point locations. (Reproduced from "An Automated Approach to Large-Scale Mapping", by B. A. Meyer, in *Computer Graphics World*, February 1981, by permission of the publisher, Pennwell Publishing Co.)

sufficent room for labeling all of the desired values on the same plot. Rather than actually labeling the data values, different symbols may be plotted at the locations, each representing a unique value (or range of values).

3. Contour Maps

A contour map consists of a series of continuous lines that connect points of equal elevation, as in topographic maps. Such maps are the most common method for displaying the shape of a three dimensional surface (e.g., the

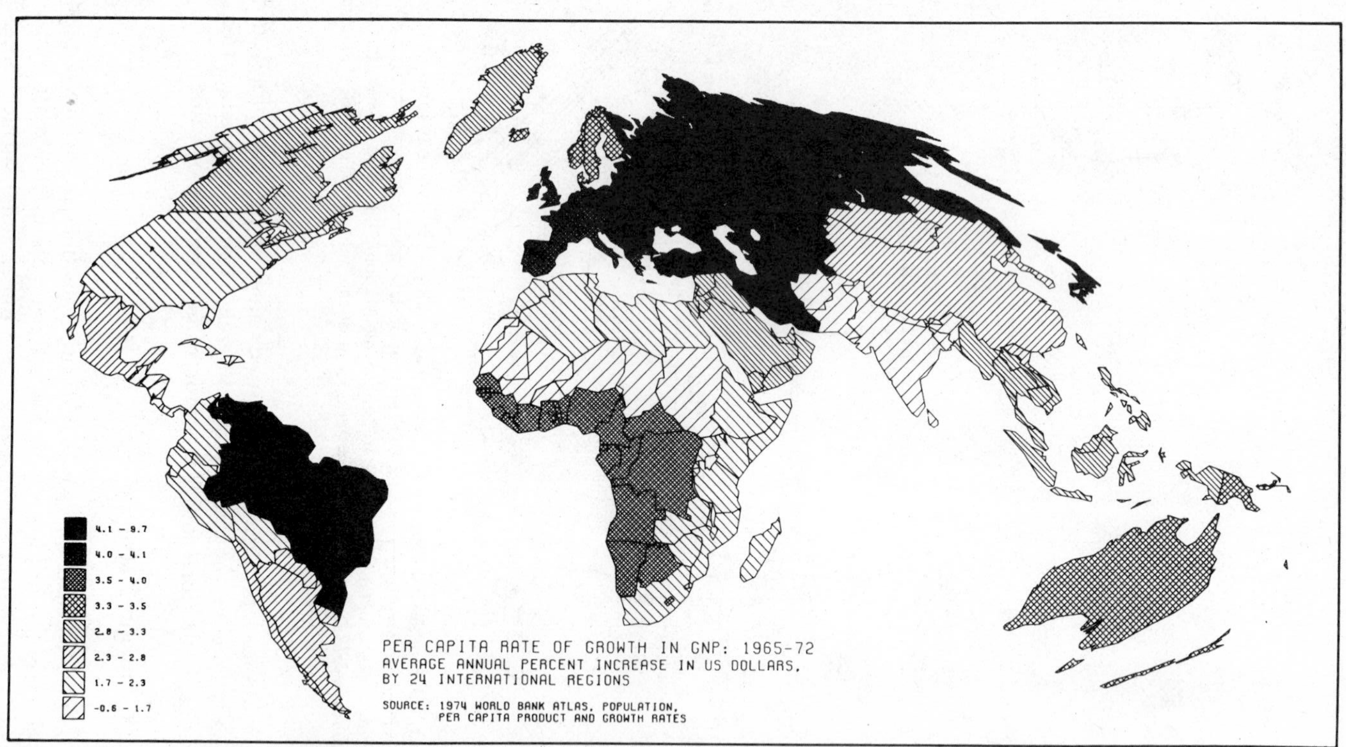

FIGURE 6.4. A choropleth map. The shading patterns for each country might be replaced by colors if a color plotting device is available. (Courtesy of the Laboratory for Computer Graphics and Spatial Analysis, Graduate School of Design, Harvard University).

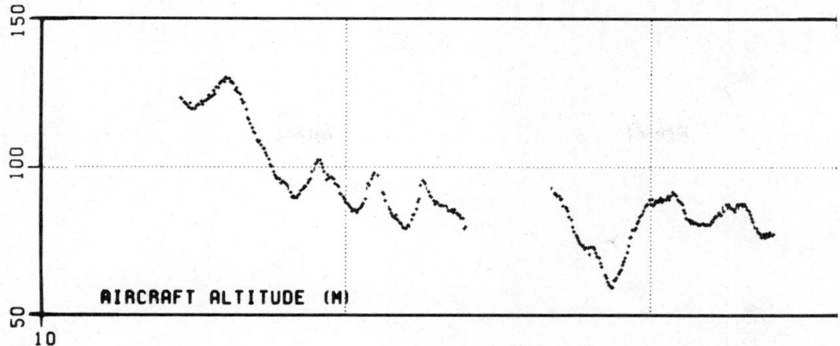

FIGURE 6.5. A profile plot. The unlabeled horizontal axis represents distance along a flight line in a geophysical survey.

earth's surface, or the top of a structure in the earth's crust). This kind of map can also be used to represent other variables. The term "contour" is often still applied to maps of other variables, although the alternate terms "isoline" or "isopleth" are preferred in some disciplines. Specific names are also used for particular variables, for example, isobar and isotherm are used for weather maps (denoting lines of equal barometric pressure and temperature, respectively). In this book, a broad definition of "contour" is used which includes isolines of any numeric variables, and not just elevations.

Drawing contours requires an implicit assumption that the mapped variable is a continuous function of the spatial coordinates. This may require the contours to be computed in restricted geographic areas if there are discontinuities in the data value (i.e., the distribution is "piecewise" continuous). For example, demographic variables are likely to show abrupt changes across national boundaries, and geologic data are often strongly controlled by the type of bedrock, and so may be quite different on either side of a contact line such as a geologic fault.

4. Choropleth Maps

A choropleth map is used to display single data values within arbitrary geographic boundaries by shading with color or line patterns to fill the different regions. Demographic studies provide countless examples: maps of population density, average income, political affiliation within counties or states, etc. Choropleth maps are also used to display discrete variables (e.g., types of land cover) that may be associated with numeric data (e.g., concentrations of trace elements, or densities of animal populations). Combined displays (e.g., areal shading with overplotted points or contours) allow direct comparisons of the variables.

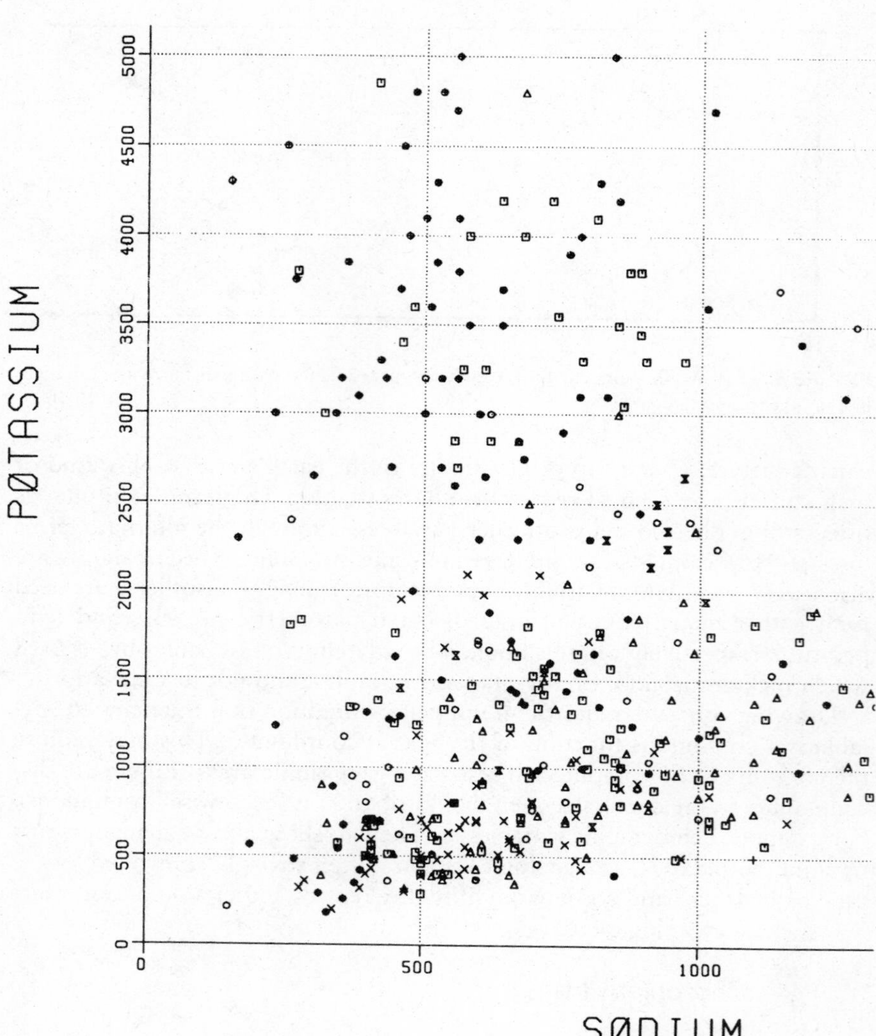

FIGURE 6.6. A scatter plot. The points on the plot define levels of sodium and potassium in a collection of rock samples, while the plotted symbol denotes the type of rock for each sample.

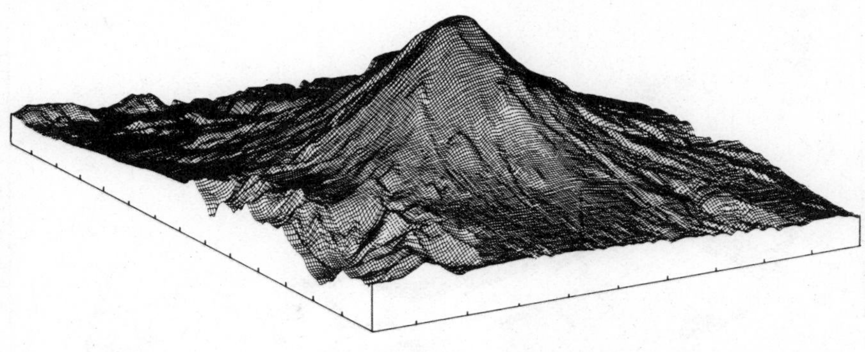

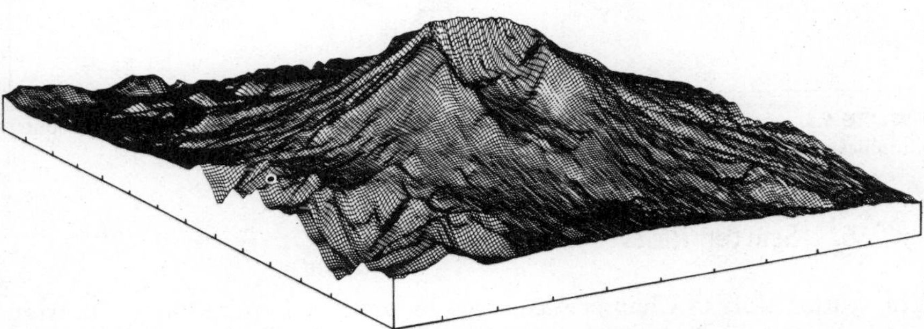

FIGURE 6.7. A computer portrait of Mt. St. Helens. (Reproduced from "Mt. St. Helens Before and After", by D. Golde and M. Higgins, in *Computer Graphics World,* March 1981, by permission of the publisher, Pennwell Publishing Co.)

5. Profile Plots

A recorded sample can be studied as a function of a single coordinate (e.g., time, or position along a highway). This means that any variable can be plotted on a two-dimensional graph with the X axis representing the coordinate, and the Y axis the data value for each sample. An example was presented in Chapter 4 where a lineprinter graph was used for a time series of the price of gold. With true computer graphics, a number of variables can be simultaneously compared by plotting a number of different lines on the same graph. In this case, different line widths, colors, or dashed lines are used to distinguish the items shown on the graph.

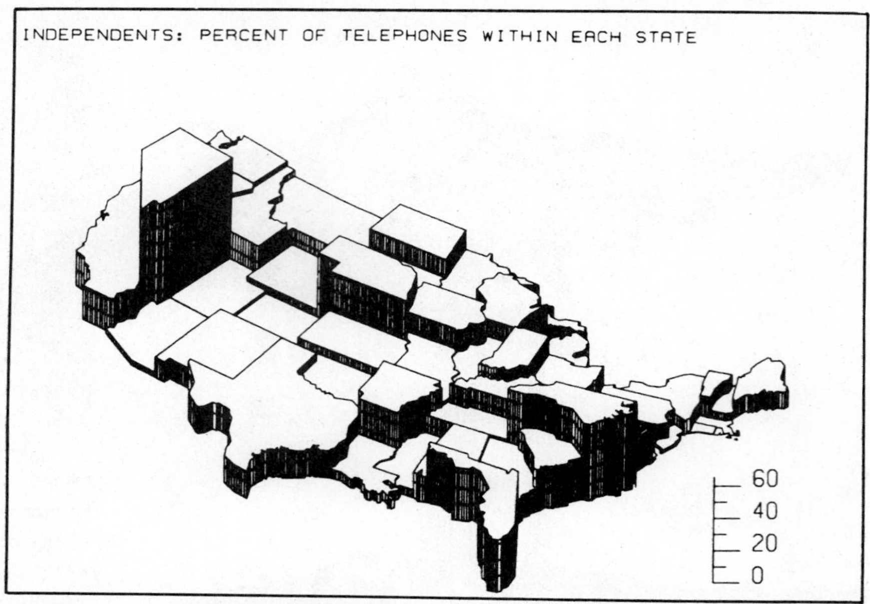

FIGURE 6.8. A three-dimensional choropleth plot. (Courtesy of the Laboratory for Computer Graphics and Spatial Analysis, Graduate School of Design, Harvard University).

6. Scatter Plots

The scatter plots in Chapter 4 can also be produced on a plotter, allowing much greater precision in locating the points. In addition, a third variable can also be displayed by using different symbols for each point (e.g, by coding the symbol for a plot of gold vs. silver by the type of rock). In a printer plot, this is usually not possible since the limited resolution means that there are many overplotted points, and the print character is required to indicate the density of data.

7. Histograms

Instead of the printed form used in Chapter 3, plotted histograms are often used for aesthetic reasons, since the addition of features such as of color or shading patterns makes a more effective presentation. It is also easier to display a number of histograms together for comparing different data, since the resolution of a plotter allows each one to be drawn smaller than is practical on a printer. Alternately, the histogram bars for each variable can be plotted together using color or patterns for identification.

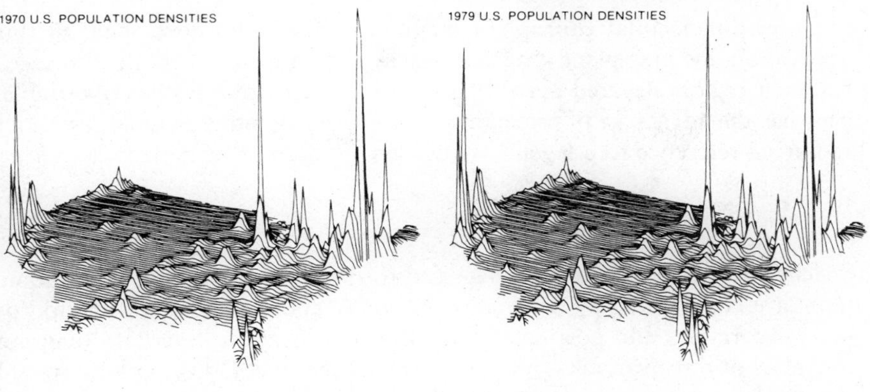

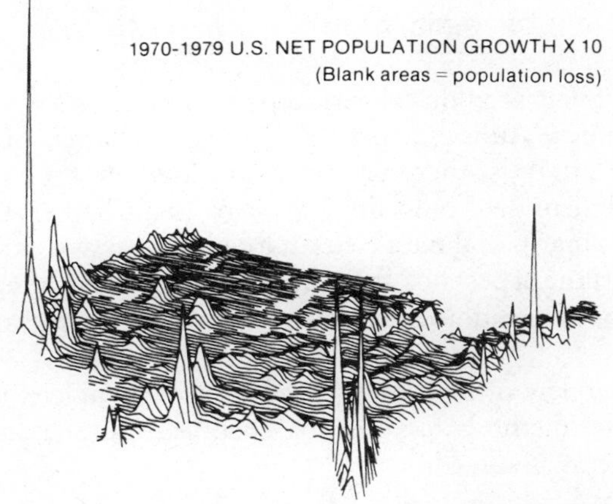

1970-1979 U.S. NET POPULATION GROWTH X 10
(Blank areas = population loss)

FIGURE 6.9. A perspective view of demographic data. (Courtesy of the Laboratory for Computer Graphics and Spatial Analysis, Graduate School of Design, Harvard University).

8. Three-Dimensional Views

An apparent three-dimensional view can be created using an isometric projection. Here the map plane is the base of the figure, while the data values are used to set the vertical offset from the plane. While this form is not generally useful for quantitative interpretation, it can give a much more immediate view of the gross structural behavior than a corresponding contour map. As for contours, perspective plots can also be used on variables other than elevation, although this application is not as common.

Three-dimensional choropleth maps have also been developed. In this application, the map plane is again show in isometric view, with the "surface" for each region elevated according to the value of the displayed variable. This has the advantage of presenting the relative magnitudes visually, without requiring reference to a legend (as needed for a color or pattern code.)

9. Multivariate Displays

Special procedures are sometimes used to display mulitvariate data. Some plots are constructed by calculating X and Y coordinates as a function of several variables and posting a symbol at that location (a ternary diagram for ratios of three variables, for example). Another method is to plot a special figure, the shape of which is controlled by the data values. Some examples will be presented in Chapter 10.

10. Computer Animation

Many special effects seen on television or in movies today are created with computer graphics. Although the use of such dynamic displays is rather limited in data analysis, there are some areas where they can be quite effective. Three-dimensional modeling problems (see Chapter 12), and displays of rapidly changing spatial data (see Chapter 11) are two examples. Perhaps the most important aspects of these applications is that they provide much of the stimulus for technological advances in computer graphics.

With this overview of plotting procedures now complete, the next chapter will examine the methods for creating graphical output, and consider the practical problems involved.

CHAPTER 7

EFFECTIVE USE OF COMPUTER PLOTTING

As we saw in Part I, having a set of programs which perform certain tasks does not guarantee that it will be easy to perform those tasks on a computer. There are many considerations involved in organizing programs and operating procedures for effective use. This is especially true with computer graphics, since additional hardware is employed, and the options available to the user are usually extensive (necessarily so, to provide the wide range of display formats useful in data analysis). In this chapter, we examine the problems involved in using computer graphics, and consider methods for reducing their impact. All of the general rules given in Chapter 5 apply equally well here, and should be the foundation of any software system.

ORGANIZATION OF PLOTTING PROGRAMS

Although graphic displays are created by special types of hardware, the form of the display (and thus its value) is totally controlled by software. Since there are so many kinds of useful plots, a great deal of software is required. Plotting software is notoriously difficult to develop as a result of the complexity of the output, and the delays inherent in actually plotting a result after the plot instructions have been completed. In addition, new options and modifications are frequently required to accommodate requests for embellishments of the drawings. It is therefore very important that a plotting program be organized with flexibility and future expansion in mind.

1. Input of Data and Parameters

Before a plot can be created, the program must receive all data to be plotted and the parameters defining particular options. These operations are not unique to computer graphics, of course, but are a general requirement in all types of data processing. The principles outlined in Chapter 5 should be restated: flexibility in parameter specification, and independence from data type are desirable goals.

A map-drawing program typically has many parameters, to allow for the many different kinds of maps. This can make the setting of parameter values a severe problem, requiring extensive documentation and user training (for an "expert" style program), or complex interactive routines to aid the user. If an interactive form is used, it is almost mandatory that the program provide reasonable default values for most parameters, to prevent lengthy sessions which can only discourage use. The need for shortcuts for the experienced user takes on extra importance for the same reason. It is often necessary to remove some options from a complex plotting program in developing an interactive preliminary phase. It may still be possible to leave these options available to the experienced user by allowing the prepared parameters to be edited before actually running the plotting phase.

These problems must also be considered for other types of plotting besides maps. Profile plots, scatter plots, charts, and graphs can all be created with a computer, and all require parameters for setting scales, labeling supporting information, changing pens or colors, etc.

As was the case in basic analysis, plotting programs must also be easily adaptable to a variety of data types. In analyzing spatial relationships, a simple map of the various data is often the most useful tool for interpretation, so we must be able to plot any of the recorded data on a map. The plotting programs should use the same data structure as the analysis routines, so that interesting features noted in basic analysis can immediately be plotted on a map. There is an additional requirement for plotting: the coordinates of each sample must be included in the file. This can lead to problems in merging and delays in spatial analysis, if the coordinates are entered separately from the analytic data.

The self-documenting type of data file described in Chapter 5 is also of great value in computer graphics. It enables a plotting program to accept a wide variety of different data, and to automatically label the plot with identifying information. Existing data selection facilities can easily be integrated with plotting programs to produce location maps for subsets of data. In essence, the plotting programs are considered as part of an overall system, with the data structure as the link to the other components.

2. Standard Plotting Functions

As briefly outlined in Chapter 6, computer graphics software can be classed as system software or as applications software. System plotting routines provide the basic functions from simple calls to standard subroutines. The applications programs may be considerably streamlined as a result, since the fundamental elements of the plot do not have to be explicitly created. For example, to plot a line of text, the applications program passes the text to a system routine, along with a starting location and size, and does not have to compute the position for each character in the string.

As a general rule, the more functions that can be created by calling existing routines, the easier it will be to write a new plotting program. The library of functions received with the hardware may be quite limited (perhaps consisting of basic line and symbol plotting only), or very extensive (with areal shading with patterns or color, automatic plotting of large blocks of text, etc.). At many computer installations, plotting routines are developed to perform common tasks suited to local requirements. If all maps are drawn with the same style of title block and border, each plotting program can draw the frame of the map with a single command. Automatic plotting of reference grid lines, creation date, and user identification are other such routines.

The development of an extensive function library not only speeds up software development, it encourages consistency of form for the plots. While individual variations are often necessary, a standard style of data presentation can save time in interpreting the results. A data legend might always be plotted in the same corner of the map, for example, and a standard set of symbols defined for various classes of data.

3. Output of Plotted Data

The third major function of a plotting program is to encode plot instructions in the particular form required by the device that actually produces the plot. It is now very common to have a variety of plotting devices available, and ideally it should be possible to display any plot on any device. This "device independence" is achieved by having the plot vectors stored in an intermediate file (sometimes called a "metafile") by the plotting programs. Displaying the plot is a second step, performed by an independent program that reads the metafile and has options to convert the plot instructions to the formats used by each plotting device.

Although this two step procedure involves more I/O than having the applications programs create output for a single device, there are considerable benefits to be gained. If a graphics terminal is used for previewing, a hardcopy can be produced later by another reformatting of the metafile, without a recomputation of the plot vectors. This can be a major savings for complex displays like detailed contour maps. Similarly, a working copy from an electrostatic plotter can be redrawn on a large flatbed plotter. It may be possible to "edit" a plotfile to correct minor errors introduced by the applications program (for example, to remove contour lines that move into a title block). This editing might also involve adding extra titles and legends when preparing a final map from a work copy.

Another distinct advantage is that the plotting programs need not be modified when new plotting equipment is introduced. An additional option is simply added to the reformatting program. This may result in a different split of the workload between the main computer and the plotting device. For example, the reformatting program would generate all of the vectors to draw a symbol only when output is to a device which does not have this capability. If a new plotter or graphics terminal has extensive new capabilities, changes in the applications programs may still be desirable, however. For example, a color plotter enables plots to have full areal shading, a function that will probably not be present in plotting programs designed originally for a line drawing device.

PLOTTING REQUIREMENTS FOR DATA ANALYSIS

Effective use of graphics for data analysis involves hardware, as well as the complex software outlined above. The capabilities of the available plotting devices may impose severe constraints on the use of graphics. If the demand for plotting is greater than the capacity of the system, it will be necessary to restrict usage or accept long delays. If many requested plots are larger than the physical size of the plotter, a considerable manual effort will be required to splice segments of plots together.

Although economic considerations may dictate that only one plotter be available, multiple devices can be a great asset. A graphics terminal can be used for previewing plots, which can save a great deal of plotting time on a large plotter by allowing unacceptable plots to be discarded immediately. In many applications, a low resolution (i.e., inexpensive) terminal is adequate, since the basic form and layout of the plot is all that is checked in the preview. Detailed examination is generally more practical on a full scale plot, anyway, since the display must be broken into many smaller pieces on a terminal screen.

Where volume warrants, additional plotters can be installed. Since many plots will be considered working copies, a fast electrostatic plotter is often used for the bulk of the plots, and a drafting quality pen plotter for final copies only (e.g., basemaps, contour maps to be included in an engineering report, etc.). If color is needed in some applications, a color device can be dedicated to those jobs, while other output is created in black and white on conventional plotters. As we saw earlier, when multiple devices are installed, it is important that the software provide the flexibility for any plot to be sent to any device.

In data analysis, the most important requirement of the plotting system is speed: it is essential to produce plots quickly, to allow an analyst to experiment with different mathematical procedures, display formats, etc. When pen plotters are used, this requirement becomes a problem if several people use the system, or if a large number of plots are needed. In general, the limited speed of pen plotters mean they cannot be effectively used for analysis of large volumes of data unless a number of plotters are provided and operated continuously. The great speed of electrostatic plotters provides the solution: depending on the complexity of the plot, an electrostatic plotter might produce 10 to 100 times the output volume of a fast pen plotter. Recall that this speed requires additional computing, however, as the plot vectors must be converted to a dot-matrix form. While this may demand a fair amount of CPU time, the elapsed time between running a plotting program and seeing the result is short (which is what is important to the user).

Even greater speed can be supplied by a graphics terminal, although this may not always be the ideal solution. To begin with, each user must have convenient access to a terminal, whereas many users can easily be supported by one electrostatic plotter. Many plots require fairly detailed study, which is not practical on a screen (especially if it ties up a terminal shared by other users). In addition, it may be necessary to work with a specific scale hardcopy, which demands output to a plotter. For example, a computer map showing pollution levels might be compared to a map showing cities and towns to locate critical areas. Complex plots are often run in batch mode since they may take a long time, so there is little advantage to interactive viewing anyway (except perhaps to decide on whether the result is usable). As we noted in Chapter 5, true interactive programs are generally much more difficult to write than batch-oriented versions. When the many options in a typical graphics program are considered, it may prove impractical to create an interactive version even if the calculation time would be short.

The majority of computer plots (like all computer output) are working copies, for short-term use by the person who created them. As such, they do not generally require as much "window-dressing" (external frames, title blocks, etc.) as a permanent map, although such embellishments can be useful for clearly identifying the contents of the plot. For the same reason, aesthetic enhancements (fancy lettering styles, color shading, etc.) may not be necessary. As mentioned above, it may be possible to add such features only when a final copy is created. This can speed up the analytical process considerably, since many of the plotting options are ignored in generating the display of the basic data. It also means that extremely high-resolution drawings are not required for working copies, so that faster plotting devices can be used.

COMMON PROBLEMS IN PLOTTING DATA

1. Data Availability

We have already mentioned that sample coordinates must be entered into a computer's files before a plot can be created. This often demands an extensive effort in digitizing locations and merging with the analytical data, especially for historical data whose locations are known only from a manually posted map. A scientist collecting samples in the field may record a location by marking a detailed topographic map, so that these coordinates must be determined later, independent of any laboratory measurements performed on the samples.

A potentially much larger problem arises when the data must be related to surface features like topography, type of rock, vegetation, etc. Most data of this type are available only in map form, although government agencies have long-term projects underway to provide the information in digital form. Once again, digitizing is necessary and typically requires a much greater time than a sample location map because of the sheer volume of data. A digitized version of a detailed topographic map may contain 50,000 or more "points," and represent many hours of work. If a large study area is involved, many such maps must be digitized. The large volumes of data can also create problems in processing and display if the plotting programs have not been designed to accommodate large datasets.

Some types of spatial data (e.g., bedrock type and land cover) generally have a constant value over large areas. The contact lines between different categories are digitized, which usually requires fewer points than topography. To define each zone, an enclosing polygon is constructed from the contact lines, either with the manual digitizing procedure or with software. In either event, care must be taken to prevent overlaps and undefined zones.

In plotting a variety of data on the same map, it may be necessary to apply coordinate transformations to some of the files in order to have all locations in the same system. This need might arise when samples collected on a local grid are plotted on an topographic map drawn with UTM coordinates, for example. This is generally not a serious problem, provided the required conversion algorithms are already included in the software library.

2. Contour Maps and Grid Interpolation

Plotting contours with a computer can be a time-consuming and error-ridden process, demanding complex software and a relatively large computer. Since each contour line is actually a series of straight-line segments, a vast number of plot vectors can be produced, leading to difficulties in storing the plot instructions, and long plotting times (if a vector device is used to create the plot).

Machine-drawn contours can be produced as a direct echo of a digitized map: the plotting program simply reads through an array of X-Y coordinates and moves the pen from point to point. This requires computation only for converting to plot coordinates and checking for a code indicating interruptions in the line, and perhaps for generating labeling text at periodic intervals. This procedure is used extensively in automated mapping, where extensive files of topography, cultural features, etc. have previously been digitized and stored in a compact form on a special "drafting" computer system.

In many cases, the positions of the contour lines must be calculated as a function of data values at randomly located samples. This is a much more difficult problem than simple re-tracing, since an exact solution does not exist: the contour lines fall in "uncontrolled" areas (i.e., between samples), and thus can only be estimated. Many different mathematical procedures are used in contouring, although none is universally successful. The particular method which best suits a given set of data cannot be predetermined, although experience with similar types of data is very often useful in choosing a "standard" procedure. In all contouring applications it is important to check the quality of the result (how well the contours fit the original data), and to experiment with alternate methods.

Most automatic contouring programs assume that the data values lie on a regular "grid," that is, that the locations occur at regular intervals of the X and Y coordinates. The tracing of any contour line then involves searching through a two-dimensional array where the rows represent lines parallel to the X-axis, and the columns represent lines parallel to the Y-axis. The basic procedure is to test all adjacent pairs of data values to see if the desired contour passes between the corresponding points on the coordinate grid. The actual crossing point is determined by interpolation, often using a low-order fit to a small group of grid values to allow for curvature of the contoured "surface."

When gridded data are used, the major problem is no longer the actual tracing of the contours, but the calculations of the data values at the grid locations. This requires interpolation between a number of randomly positioned samples—a very difficult computational problem. Ideally, all available data might be used in calculating each value, but this is not practical even for the largest computers. In drawing a contour map, there is an implicit assumption that the variable is continuous, so that the grid value will match the original data when the locations are coincident. This also means that the grid value is controlled mostly by the nearest samples, so that it will be possible to select data within a finite distance of the grid point to estimate the grid data value.

The first phase in computing any grid value, then, is to select a number of samples in the vicinity of the grid point. This can in itself be time-consuming, especially when there are a large number of samples available. Since the process must be repeated for each cell, it is important to have an efficient data selection algorithm. To avoid continual complete searches through the data, the samples may be sorted according to their X and Y coordinates, so that a fast access procedure (such as a binary search) can be used. This reorganization of the input data is typically incorporated as a preliminary step, automatically performed by the grid interpolation program.

For accurate estimation of the variable, the samples selected for grid interpolation should be radially scattered about the grid point, to allow for possible directional trends (see Fig. 7.1). Instead of simply finding the nearest N samples, the search should divide the area into sectors (usually octants) and select the nearest *M* points in each sector. This prevents the computation of a grid value from samples that are all on one side of the grid point. If the grid is extrapolated beyond the limits of the sampled area, this situation is unavoidable, however (and as a result extrapolated values are much more likely to "blow up," that is, to be far outside the range of the sample values).

Many different algorithms can be applied to compute the grid value from the selected samples. A least-squares procedure can be used to compute the equation of a plane or a low-order surface that "fits" the selected data. The grid vlaue is then obtained by simply evaluating the equation for the appropriate X and Y values. The fitting procedure usually involves a distance weighting, so the samples closest to the grid point have a larger contribution. Inverse distance or inverse distance squared are common examples (the data value is divided by its distance from the grid point before applying the least-squares procedure). Another possibility is to estimate the gradient of the surface, or to use measured gradients, to project from each sample to the

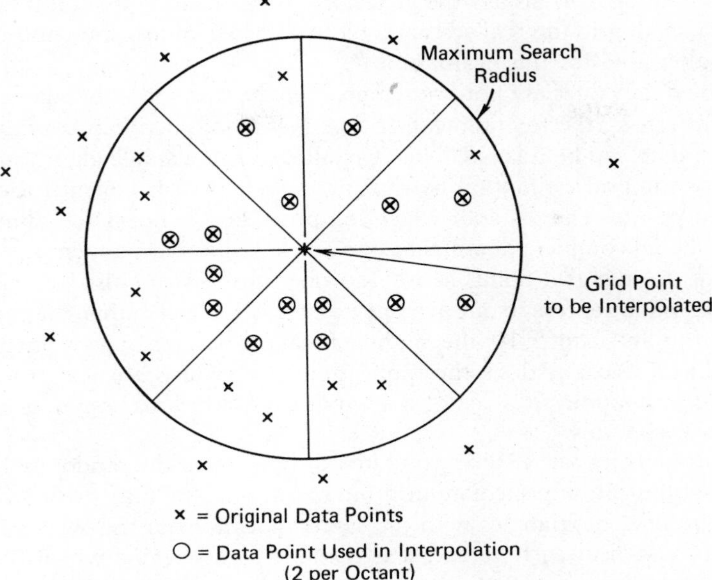

FIGURE 7.1. Selection of data points for grid interpolation.

grid point. The grid value is the average of a number of projected values in this case. Once again, distance weighting can be applied to increase the relative importance of the closest samples.

As this discussion indicates, a number of parameters are involved in using a gridding program. The selection of samples to use in interpolation involves a maximum search distance and the number of values to be used. A number of interpolation algorithms may be provided, perhaps with different distance weighting options. The size of a grid cell is very important, since it controls the level of detail which can be preserved as well as the amount of computer time that will be required. Note that the number of cells has a inverse square relationship to the size (i.e., cutting the cell dimensions in half means four times as many cells). There is thus a marked tradeoff between cost and resolution, and additional constraints might also have to be considered (e.g., a maximum number of cells allowed as a program limitation).

The success of such interpolations may be very data dependent, and cannot be guaranteed in advance. Normally, the quality of the result is judged by how well the grid values agree with the original data. If the grid interval is large relative to the average sample spacing (i.e., if many samples lie within one grid cell), this is necessarily a statistical decision. If the intent of gridding and contouring is to display the behavior of individual samples, it is essential to set a small grid interval so that a plot of posted values and contours can be reliably used for this evaluation.

If the data values are not known precisely because of unavoidable measurement errors, the requirement of a perfect match between contours and original data can be relaxed. This may allow a more stable algorithm to be used for the grid estimation by making greater use of the statistics of the selected points. The distance-weighting procedure is normally adjusted as well to avoid complete dominance of a single point that happens to be very near (or on) the grid point. More rigorous statistics can also be applied if the grid value represents an average value for the cell rather than a point estimation. In Chapter 10, the mathematical procedures of geostatistics will be outlined. Geostatistics is the application of rigorous statistical procedures for grid estimation, in place of the empirical algorithms common in most gridding programs.

Contour plots can also be generated directly from the randomly located data, without an intermediate grid interpolation. The map area is divided into a number of triangles with the sample locations at the vertices. From the data values at each vertex, it is possible to determine which triangles will contain a given contour line. Points on the contour are calculated by interpolating along the sides of the triangle.

Estimated values on a grid are often needed for more than just plotting contours, however, which is a potential drawback of a triangulation contouring program. Comparisons of several variables measured at different locations first demands interpolation to common points. For example, a geophysicist might wish to study a possible correlation between the magnetic field measured from an aircraft and the topography of the land below. A wildlife biologist might compare patterns in population density for different species that were derived from separate sampling surveys. Volumetric calculations usually involve gridded data, as do graphical displays like isometric projections of a surface and profiles along arbitrary lines.

Whether the approach is gridding or triangulation, the contours are drawn by connecting the calculated points with straight lines. To give a smooth curved appearance, it may be necessary to generate a number of additional points between the calculated line intersections. The algorithm used for this step is typically a polynomial fit to a number of adjacent points (e.g., a bicubic spline) allowing the contour to bend gradually. The data value corresponding to each contour must be periodically labeled on the plot for identification. A number of other options can be incorporated in a contouring program to improve the visual impact of the map: some contours can be highlighted with heavier lines, color, or dashes; local highs and lows of the surface can be highlighted; some contours in high-gradient areas (where the lines become very close) can be suppressed; and "hash" marks can be used to indicate the slope direction. A variety of methods can be provided to specify the particular contour levels to be drawn. The contours can be drawn at regular increments of the data value (e.g., elevations contoured every 20 meters), or perhaps at arbitrary intervals (e.g., bathymetry at 0, 10, 50, 100, and 1000 meters). For data with skewed distributions, contouring at logarithmic intervals may be useful (either by a specific program option, or by a list of desired values).

3. Variable Data Density

In collecting point samples to estimate the properties of a continuous variable, a random sampling pattern is theoretically best, since it should not introduce a bias into the data. Random sampling implies that the average density of samples is approximately constant throughout the mapped region (here "density" means the number of samples per unit area). In practice, there are many reasons why random patterns cannot be used, so we must often deal with data sets where the sample distribution is not random. This can lead to difficulty in plotting posted and contoured maps, and in interpolating values onto a grid.

A major reason why random sampling is infrequently used is cost: it is much more economical to collect samples along existing access routes than to locate a truly random pattern. If the sampling procedure requires land clearing (as in seismic prospecting for oil), land-use regulations as well as cost dictate that the affected area be minimized, normally by clearing a limited number of straight lines. In developed areas, access may be limited to public land (e.g., road allowances). Logistical problems may also be a factor. It is common to drill several wells from a single offshore platform, for example, because of the great cost of moving to a new location. If heavy equipment is needed, it may not be usable in all kinds of terrain. Geography can also be a controlling influence. If land is covered by water, ice, or swamp, it is very difficult to determine its geologic characteristics, which might be readily observable elsewhere where the bedrock outcrops at the surface.

There is often a tendency to collect more samples in some areas than others on the basis of prior knowledge of a region. This results in a biased distribution with a disproportionate number of samples in regions that may have characteristics that are different from those of the surrounding areas. If this effect is not accounted for, misleading results may be obtained in computing the statistical parameters of the entire set of data. For example, there are many more oil wells drilled in known producing areas than elsewhere. In geologic exploration it is customary to collect additional samples only in areas that look promising in preliminary investigation. Air pollution

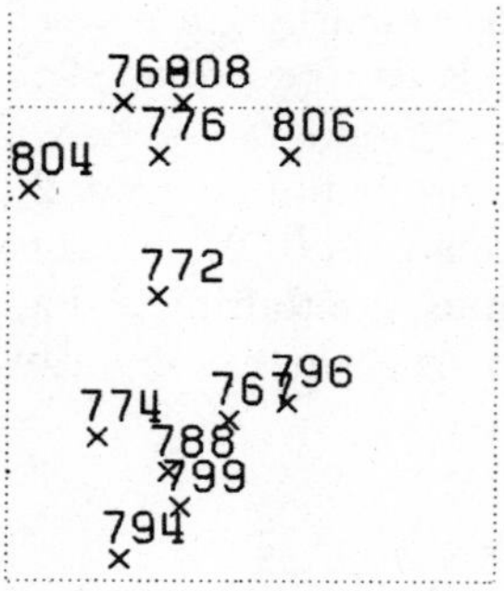

FIGURE 7.2. An example of overposting.

studies are likely to be much more detailed in the vicinity of industrial plants than in a remote wilderness.

Plotting a simple posted map can become a difficult task when the samples occur in such clusters. Depending on the scale, many samples might appear so close together that they cannot be easily distinguished. The effect is compounded when the plot includes annotated data as well as a location symbol. Figure 7.2 shows a portion of a map with "overpostings." With a close examination it is possible to read annotation that is partly obscured, but in very dense areas the appearance may be simply a dark cloud.

There is no magic solution to the problem of overposting, although measures can be taken to reduce its impact. It often occurs that the clusters are in restricted areas, so that detailed maps (i.e., maps at a larger scale) can be drawn for those regions. The scale change increases the distance between the plotted points, creating more room for text and location symbols, as shown in Fig. 7.3.

If it is necessary to use a particular scale, though, alternate methods will be required. If the annotated information can be grouped into classes, different symbols can be plotted at each location, thus avoiding the need to post additional text. This eliminates the possibility of using the symbol to describe another variable, of course. If the map shows a numeric data field, it may be possible to display the average value in a block for the dense areas (i.e., to do a grid interpolation). If several fields are posted simultaneously, it may be necessary to plot more than one map, with less annotated text on each one.

Theoretically the answer lies in having a program that automatically checks for overposting and moves some of the annotations into open spaces, with a trailing line to the sample location. Such programs would divide the plotting area into small cells, and keep track of any cells which contained plotted information. In very dense areas it may prove impossible to find a reasonably close position for some text, so a list of samples that are not

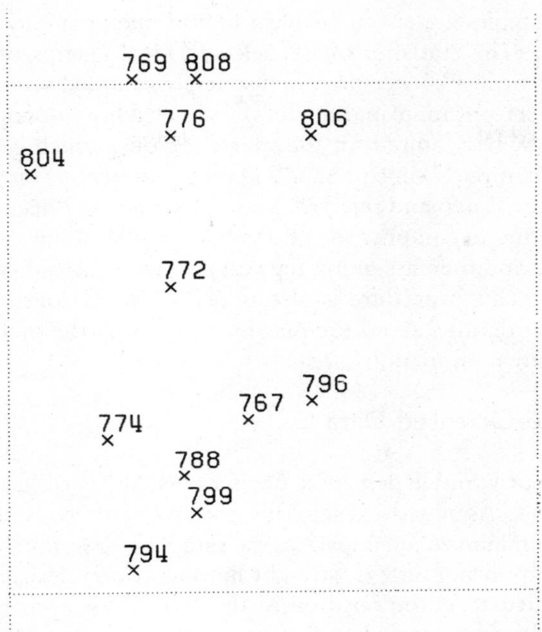

FIGURE 7.3. Overposting removed by plotting the same data at an expanded scale.

plotted must be created as well. The success of the program depends in large part on the size of the cells, and on the number of alternate posting locations it tests before deciding the text cannot be plotted. There is a lower limit to the size of a posted symbol beyond which it cannot clearly be distinguished. The map cannot be simply divided into cells of this size (perhaps 0.04 to 0.06 inches), since the locations may fall anywhere on the plot. It is desirable for aesthetic reasons to have the text appear in the same position relative to the sample location. For this and other reasons, no program has yet been developed to provide a completely satisfactory suppression of overposting for all types of plotting. Quite effective programs have been developed for particular kinds of maps, however.

As we shall see in Chapter 9, overposting can be corrected with the aid of a computerized drafting system. This involves editing a computer plot by displaying it on a graphics terminal, and employing the special features of a CAD (computer-aided design) system to move strings of text, adjust sizes, line weights, etc. The interaction of a human operator is required, yet this technique provides greater adaptability to different sets of data than is practical in a completely automatic process.

Clustered samples are also a problem in grid interpolation (for contouring or other uses). The statistics of the selected local groups of data may be quite different near a cluster than in a sparsely sampled area, which makes it difficult to set optimum parameters for a gridding alogorithm. A large search area may be required for the sparse regions, which can result in excessive use of computer time in handling the dense areas, since many distant samples must be tested and rejected. One solution is to "decluster" the data before attempting to compute the grid values by first doing a simple average within blocks, and then assigning the value to the centroid of the locations in each block. This procedure is also useful in computing statistics of the complete set of data to avoid the bias introduced by the inclusion of extra samples in known anomalous areas.

4. Line-Oriented Data

A special case of variable density is having all samples collected along a set of straight lines. As noted earlier, this pattern is often used for logistical reasons and to minimize the impact of the sampling procedure on the surface. In aerial or shipborne surveys, straight lines are often desirable to ease the problem of calculating the position of the vehicle for each reading. Coordinates are obtained by recording the time of each sample and taking periodic location "fixes" (from onshore beacons, satellites, or aerial photographs). Sample locations are later derived by straight line interpolation between the fixed points (as a function of time). Many types of geologic and geophysical data are acquired using drill holes into the earth's crust, which appear as lines (or a series of straight-line segments) in plotting cross-sections along surface traverses.

Line-oriented surveys typically have a much finer sample spacing along the lines than the distance between the lines. For example, an airborne geophysical survey might have flight lines 1 or 2 km apart with readings taken every 100 meters. A drilling program in mining exploration might use holes at a 50 meter spacing with the drill "core" broken into samples 1 meter long. Like the general problem of clusters, this can create problems in plotting contours and in posting individual data values.

Even when the plot scale allows sufficient space for posting, overposts can occur because of the orientation of the lines. When the survey employs a grid of lines in two directions (e.g., N-S and E-W), it is almost inevitable that the values at the intersections will interfere. In addition, special care is required in placing the annotation, to avoid overwriting adjacent samples. To minimize the space required, the annotated text should be oriented in a direction away from the survey lines. In the case of a N-S, E-W grid, the text may be written at 45 degrees from horizontal. When several line di-

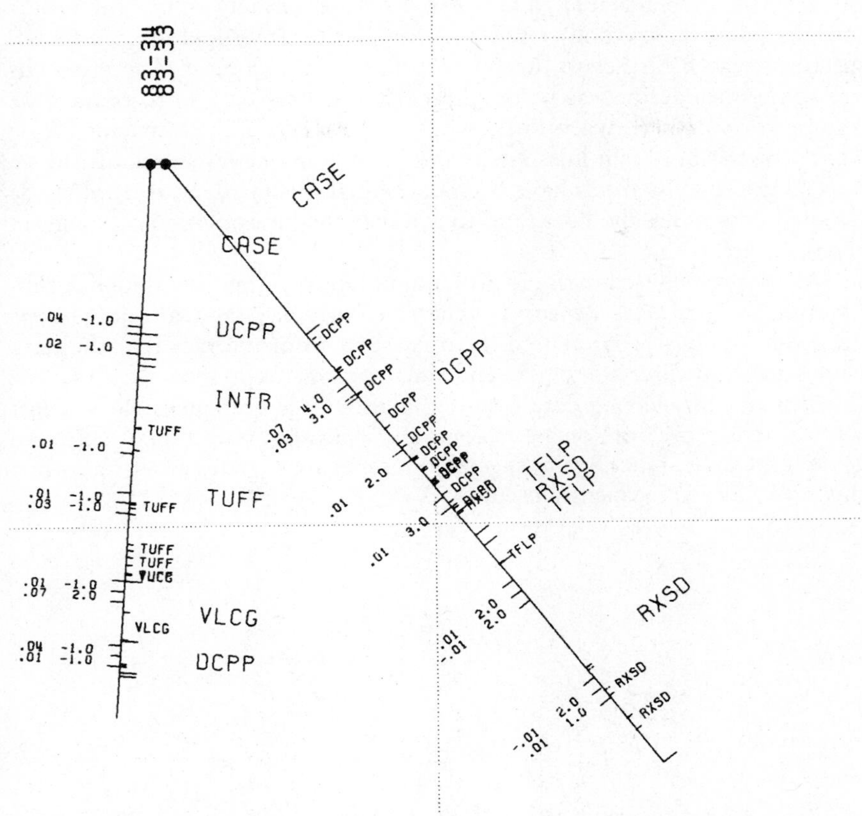

FIGURE 7.4. "Tracking." Annotation is aligned perpendicular to the direction of a survey line.

rections are involved, this simple procedure is inadequate. A better solution is to align each text string perpendicular to the local direction of the sample line. Such a "tracking" algorithm can be incorporated directly into the posting program or applied in advance by storing the line direction for each sample in the data file. An example plot is shown in Fig. 7.4. This strategy may still fail where the lines cross, of course.

Conventional gridding methods often have difficulty with line oriented data, particularly in the open areas between the lines. This is in part a problem of inadequate sampling, although the mathematical method used for gridding can have a strong influence. Algorithms involving projection of gradients often fail, since it is very difficult to compute the component of the gradient perpendicular to the survey lines accurately. When the grid is fairly regular, the method of selecting samples for interpolation can be adjusted to search farther to the sides of a line than along it. The grid cells are sometimes defined as rectangular (rather than square) to reduce the number of values between lines, while maintaining a close spacing along lines. This assumes that lines are predominantly in one direction, of course. Special gridding methods have been developed for line data, to exploit the detailed data along the lines, and to stabilize the interpolation of values in the open areas.

Similar problems can arise in grid interpolation of digitized data like topographical data. Data density is generally fairly constant, and large gaps need not be considered. The difficulties stem from the fact that the data values take on discrete values, and thus may not represent a continuous distribution. In selecting data for interpolation, it is quite possible to select samples that come from only two contours, which can lead to poor estimates of the grid value. Once again, special programs are sometimes written when this procedure is frequently used.

CHAPTER 8

COMPUTER PLOTS AS AIDS TO DATA ANALYSIS

Computer graphics are an invaluable, and in many areas, virtually indispensable aid to data analysis. Graphical presentations can quickly reduce overwhelming volumes of data to an easily interpreted and greatly compressed form, allowing an analyst to examine a much broader array of information than would otherwise be possible. With plotted displays, a variety of different variables can be examined concurrently. This avoids the awkward manual procedures needed when the data are stored in different locations and formats, and cannot be easily listed on the same page.

In the previous two chapters, the principles of plotting data with a computer were outlined, along with the requirements for an effective graphics system. We now examine a number of particular applications, to illustrate the benefits gained from incorporating plotting into a complete analysis system. The discussion concentrates on map-oriented data, although some other types of displays will also be considered. Special techniques for plotting multivariate data will be outlined in Chapter 10.

POSTED LOCATION MAPS

A great deal of information can be obtained from a map that simply shows the locations of the samples to be analyzed. To begin with, such a posted map is necessary to verify the accuracy of the coordinates stored in the file.

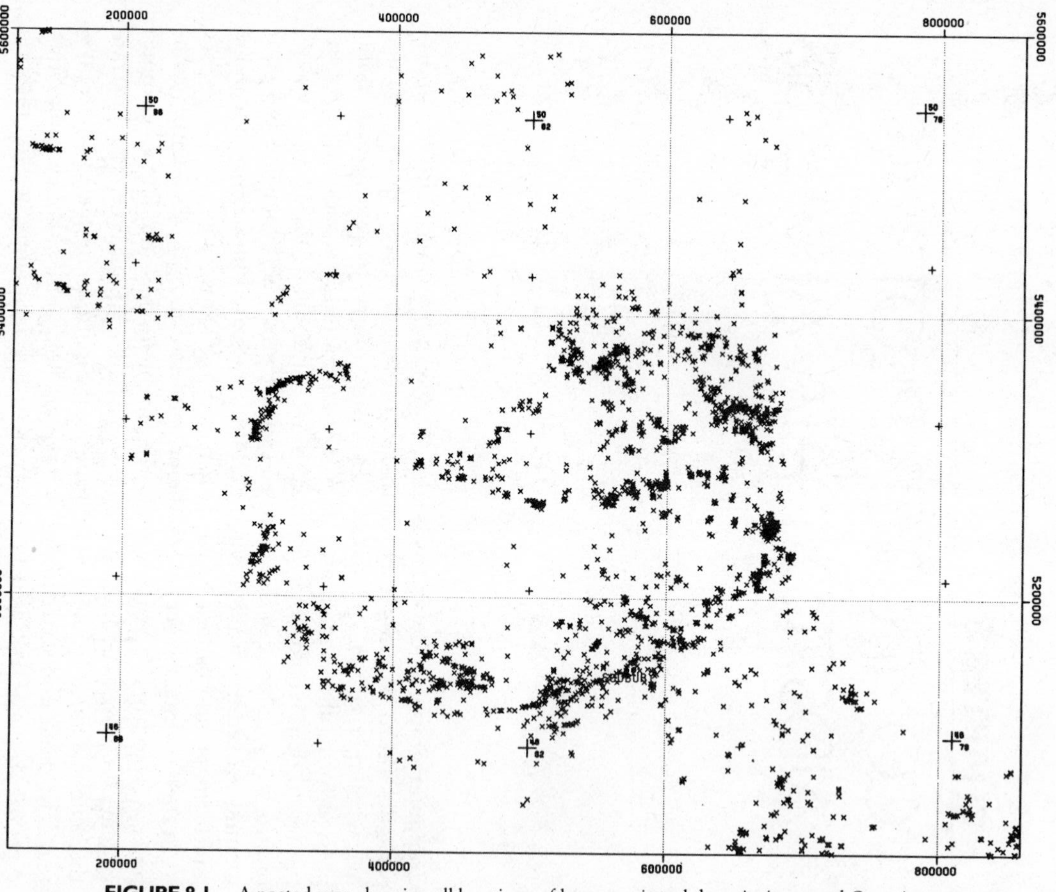

FIGURE 8.1. A posted map showing all locations of known mineral deposits in central Ontario.

If the coordinates were digitized from an existing map, the usual procedure is to create a posted map at the same scale and then to overlay it on the original to check that the points are coincident. If coordinates are recorded automatically (e.g., surveys taken from a ship or airplane), a location plot provides confirmation that the survey points were taken in the desired locations and correctly interpolated to the sample points.

Posted maps are also used when the locations of a particular subset of samples are of intrinsic interest. For example, a geologist may use a computer file of mineral deposits to determine where certain combinations of metals have been found in the past. The locations are an unknown quantity that must be extracted from a file and plotted on a map. It may be possible to identify clusters of points, and derive associations with other data (such as surface geology) by a quick visual comparison. An example is Fig. 8.1, which shows mineral deposits in central Ontario. Note the massive oval pattern, which includes the rich nickel deposits of Sudbury. This mineralized trend is undoubtedly related to the geology of the region, although a proper description is beyond the scope of this book, as it involves complex structural features created over a billion years ago, and extensively modified since.

Location maps for specific subsets of data may also prove interesting. Figure 8.2 is derived from the same data as Fig. 8.1, showing this time only those deposits containing iron. It is clear that this element is neither pervasive throughout the area, nor controlled by the main structure. A proper understanding of these observed distribution patterns would obviously require additional information, by comparing the maps to such existing data as a geologic map.

While this example is drawn from geology, the technique can be applied in a great variety of fields. Market researchers might plot locations of a particular type of store in a large urban area for comparison to mean family income. Many studies of demographic data require visual comparisons of various classes of the population—average years of education in a district versus voting pattern, for example.

Instead of manually overlaying maps, it may be possible to produce a combined plot showing more than one type of data. This requires that the separate types be distinguished (normally by different symbols), and that the scale be sufficiently large so that most points do not interfere with adjacent samples. For example, known mineral deposits might be plotted on a map showing geochemical analyses of rock samples, to see if high readings correspond to known bodies of ore (Fig. 8.3). This procedure can be applied to any type of data, as it depends solely on having common coordinates. As another example, population density might be plotted on the same maps as the locations of major earthquakes, as a first step in evaluating the risk of earthquake damage.

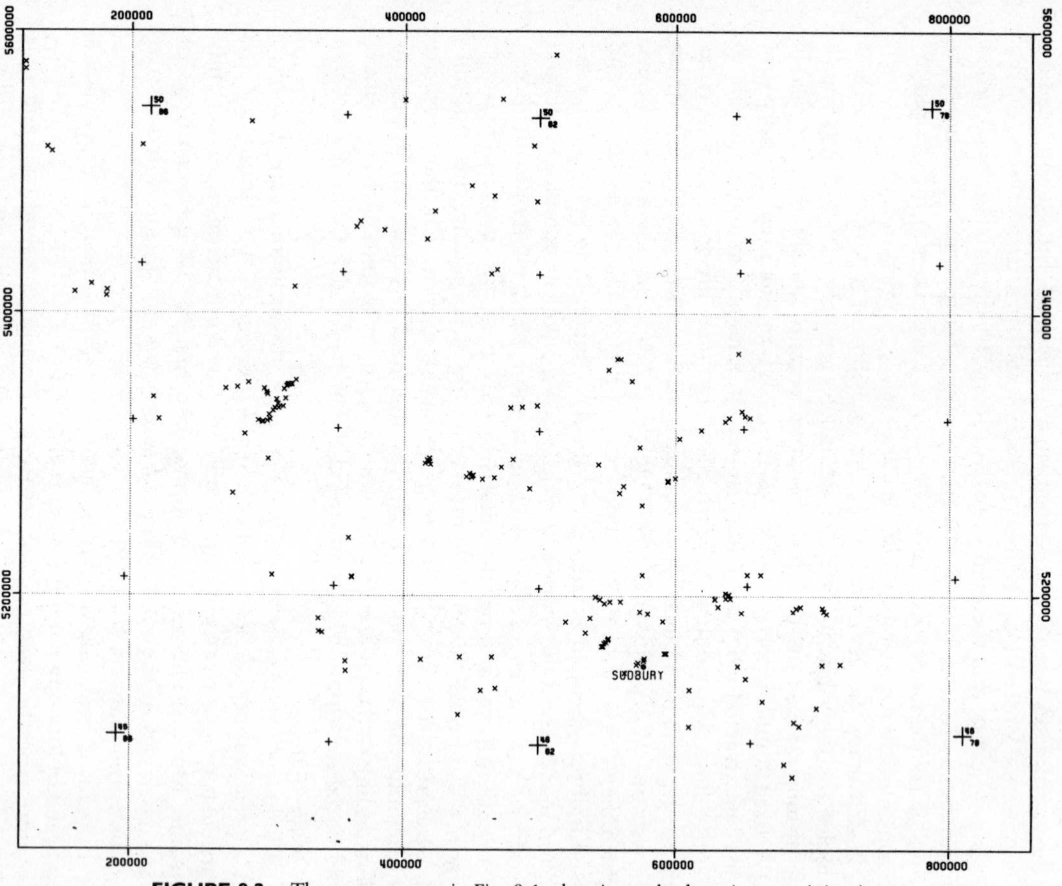

FIGURE 8.2. The same area as in Fig. 8.1, showing only deposits containing iron.

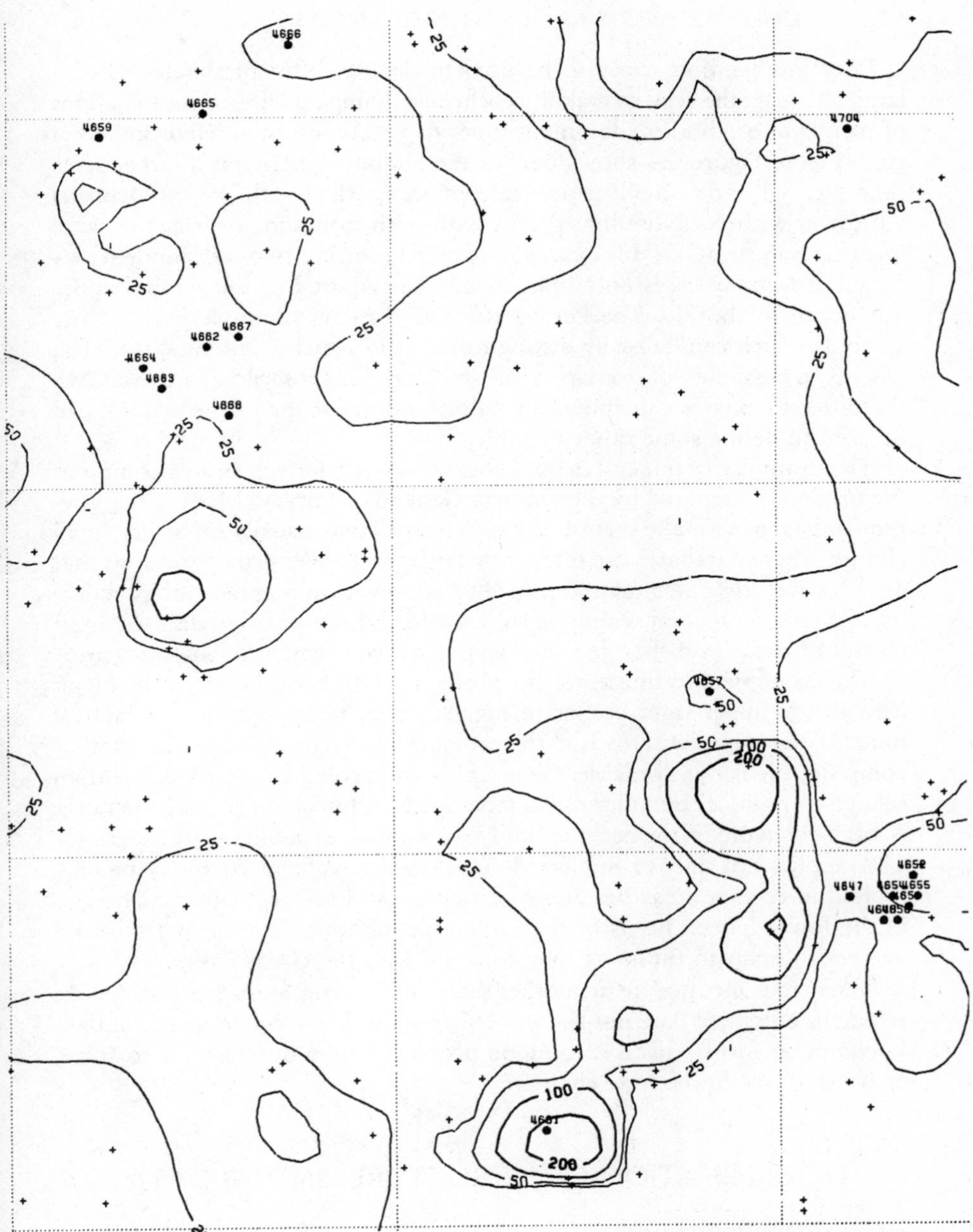

FIGURE 8.3. Combining independent sets of data on the same map. The contours show the copper concentrations found in a regional geochemical survey, while the posted points (solid circles) show known mineral deposits containing copper. Note that many, but not all, of the copper deposits are enclosed by contours (i.e., in areas with concentration levels above the regional background).

Location symbols can also be used to denote different subclasses of a large file, (e.g., the type of rock in geochemical samples, various combinations of metals in ore bodies, dominant types of vegetation in an environmental study, etc.). Figure 8.4 shows part of the Sudbury district at a larger scale than Fig. 8.1 and 8.2. Silver occurrences are marked with +, and deposits with iron with ×. Note that points with both iron and silver at the same location appear as *. This example involved plotting two independent sets of data: in many cases only one set may be required, if the symbol codes are stored in the file. The key to effective displays of this type is to use symbols which can be easily distinguished (and which combine effectively, where the possibility of overlap exists). If color plotting facilities are available, the different classes can shown by color, and the shape of the symbol can be used to define some other variable.

The examples of mineral deposit locations were derived from a computer file originally prepared by the Ontario Geological Survey. Many other government agencies make their data publicly available, usually for a very small charge. These databases are often very large, and cover broad areas, so that an effective computer mapping facility is almost imperative for practical use. As this very simple example shows, the ability to easily select different classes of data from the file is an important requirement of the software.

This example also illustrates the problem of data availability. The blank area in the upper right corner of Fig. 8.1 does not result from a lack of mineral deposits: that area is in the province of Quebec, for which a similar computer file is not available. Geographic and geologic features are seldom related to political boundaries, so incomplete defintion of physical features is often unavoidable when the study area involves multiple jurisdictions. This applies not only to published data, since private surveys may be prohibited in certain areas because of different land-use regulations. The gap in the lower left corner is of the same type, although certain parts would be very difficult to fill in, as they coincide with the Great Lakes.

The map is incomplete in another sense: main geographic features (lakes, rivers, borders, etc.) are not shown. Once again this is due to a lack of data in computer form. This is a common problem, and a difficult one to solve, as we shall see in the next chapter.

DETERMINATION OF "STRUCTURE" IN THE DATA

A primary question in studying spatial data is whether there is a structural component, that is, whether the data value is at least partially dependent on its position. Although a number of mathematical procedures can be used for this evaluation, maps showing the data values at various locations allow an immediate visual determination (although necessarily a subjective one).

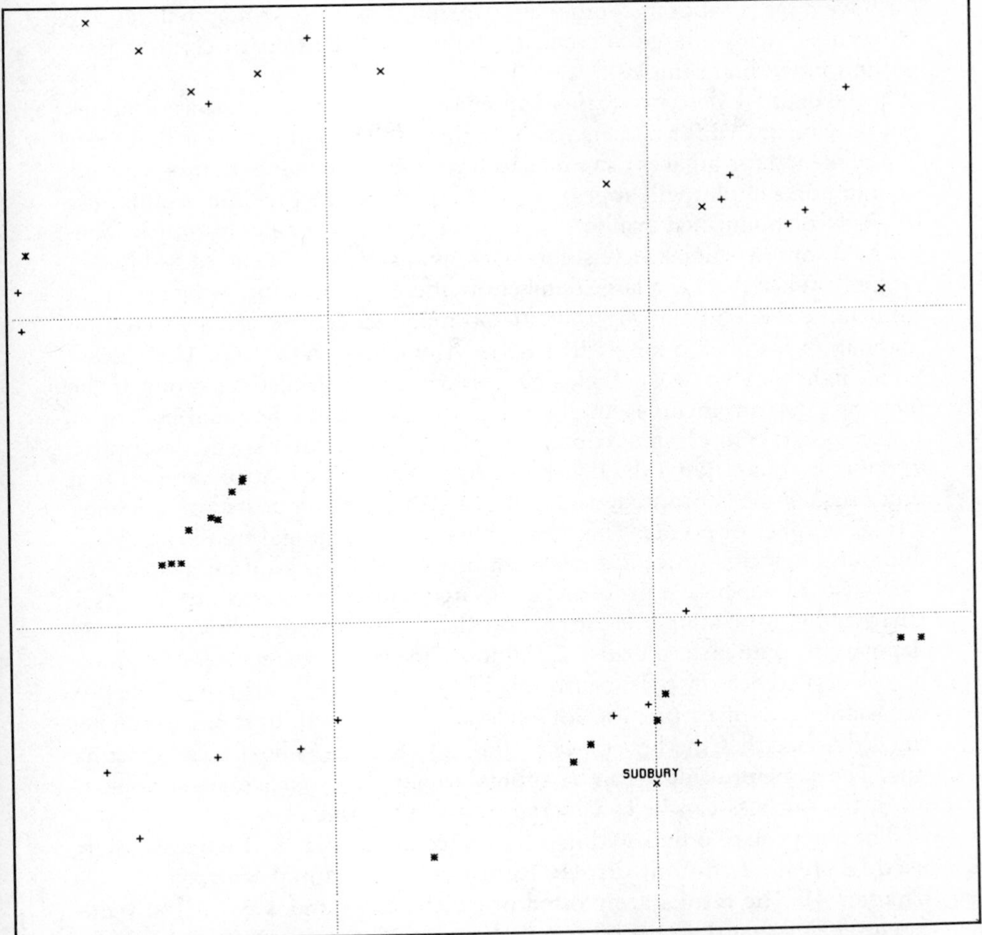

FIGURE 8.4. Use of symbols to distinguish classes of data. Mineral deposits with silver are marked by +, those with iron by ×, and those with both by *. Many other classes could also be shown, providing distinct symbols could be assigned to each.

If there is no structure, the data will be essentially random, and will not be influenced by adjacent samples.

1. Display Methods

The basic display can be a posted map, with the data value annotated beside the sample location, or a contour plot. An implicit assumption of continuity (hence structure) is made in drawing a contour line. If the data are random (or have a large random component), the plotted contour map will tend to "blow up," with a large number of "bulls-eyes" (clusters of contour lines around individual samples).

If the data are descriptive, the map must be in posted form, since contours can only be drawn for numeric data. In this case, structure means that there is a tendency for adjacent samples to have the same value, that is, clusters of common samples will appear on the map. As in the previous section, use of easily distinguished symbols or distinct colors is the key to quick identification of any spatial segregation (each unique value is assigned a different symbol). When there is a large number of different classes, it may be necessary to group some of them together. If too many categories are displayed on the map, it may be no longer be easy to visually separate them. The plotted map might also show an enclosing polygon for each distinct group if the plotting program includes an algorithm for picking the boundaries.

It is possible to create a contour display for maps of a single descriptive variable by quantifying the density of occurrence. A count of samples in a unit area can be contoured, as an alternate display to a posted map having a large number of points. The contour lines make regional trends more visible, although this procedure may not always be successful because of the various data-dependent problems associated with computer contouring (see Chapter 7). An example is Fig. 8.5, which shows the distribution of gold deposits in southeastern British Columbia. The contours represent the number of occurrences in cells measuring 10 km on a side. This type of map is occasionally used to prepare for regional geologic exploration, following the old adage that the best place to find a new mine is next to an existing one. The same procedure can be applied to any occurrence map, so long as all of the samples can be considered part of the same class.

The counting of points within cells is a technique that is also occasionally used to create a contour display for a two-dimensional scatter plot (see Chapter 4). The results are plotted in exactly the same way, the only difference being that this type of "map" does not relate to geographic location. It may be necessary to use different scales for the X and Y axes to allow for large differences in the range of the two variables. Preliminary scaling of the data values will be required if the contouring software does not provide this option.

Three-dimensional views which display the variable as a continuous surface can be very effective, since they give a more immediate impression of shape than a contour map (Fig. 8.6). If the purpose of the plot is to precisely locate structural features, conventional maps are more useful, however, since exact positions can be scaled directly from the map. In addition, a great deal of other information is already presented in map form, and can be most easily compared by plotting the data at the same scale.

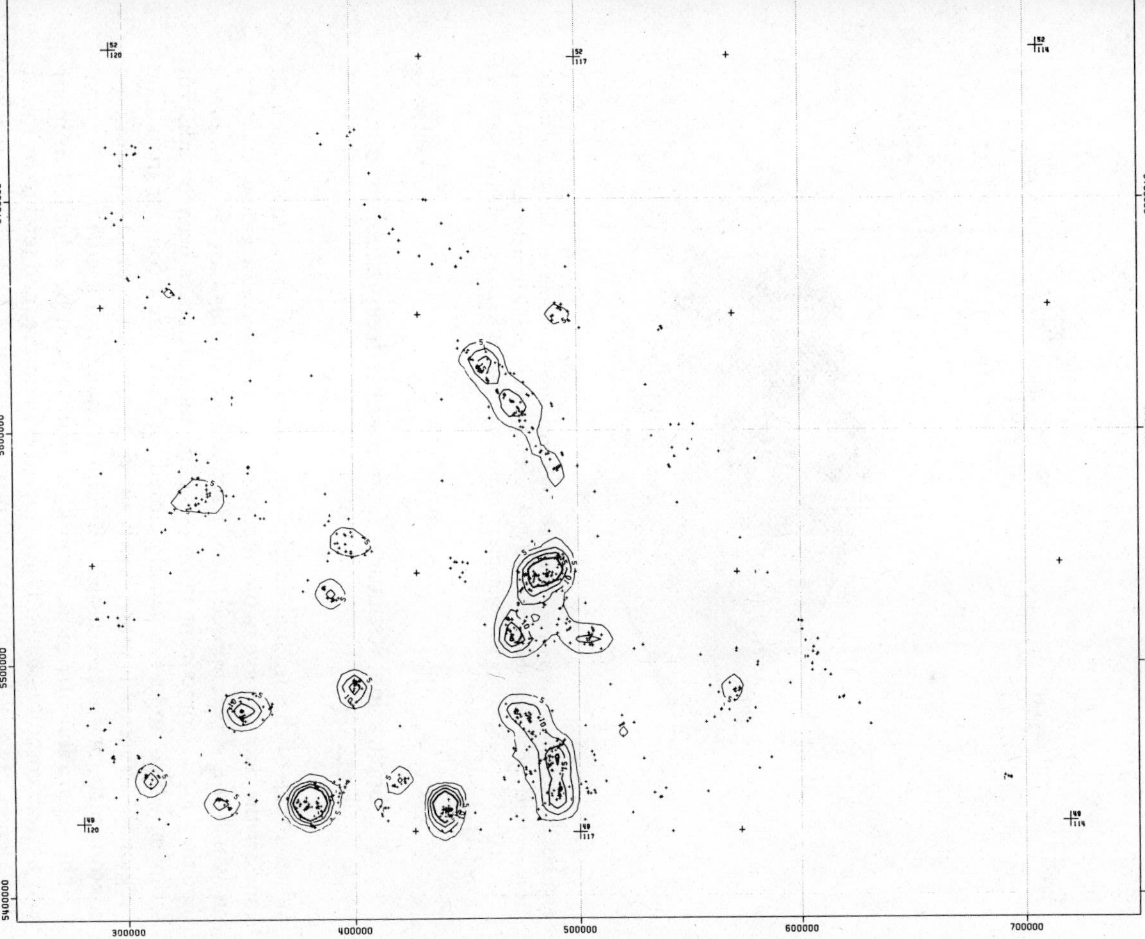

FIGURE 8.5. A contour map representing the "density" of occurences. The location points (+) represent known occurences of gold in southeastern British Columbia. The contours are drawn by counting the number of locations in each 10 km by 10 km area.

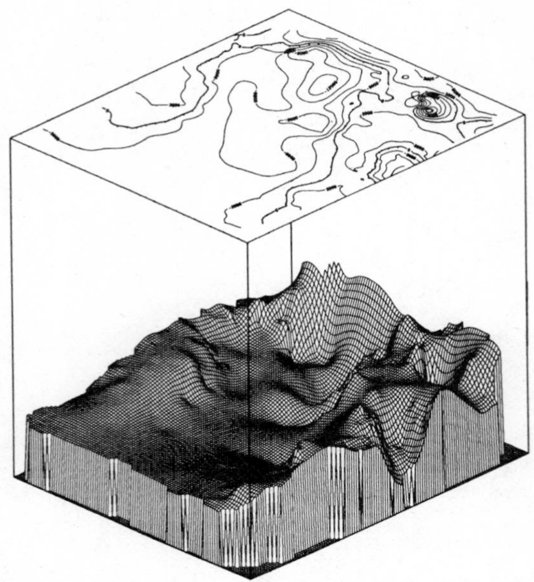

FIGURE 8.6. A three-dimensional view of a contoured variable. Note that "highs" and "lows" are immediately obvious in the perspective view, but that precise position on the map is obscured. (Courtesy of the Laboratory for Computer Graphics and Spatial Analysis, Graduate School of Design, Harvard University.)

2. Separating Structural Components from the Complete Data

When a map of the original data exhibits strong local variations, we might consider the data to have two components: a well-behaved regional structure, on which are superimposed local fluctuations. In this case, it is assumed that the "local" component imposes significant differences between adjacent samples, which appear as small "closed" features on a contour map. The "regional" structure is more slowly varying, appears as large features on a contour map, and is not subject to sudden changes of gradient.

The separation of regional and local features can be achieved in many ways. Most common methods are empirical in nature, and tend to be rather data dependent, so that a universal procedure cannot be applied. A variety of approaches may be required, with evaluation of the result demanding considerable knowledge of the characteristics of the particular type of data. This is much like the situation with grid interpolation and machine contouring that was discussed in the last chapter.

a. Smoothing the Data

The simplest procedure for separating components is to average a number of adjacent data together to reduce the effect of individual variations. This can be done with the original data prior to grid interpolation, or to the grid values. Like the gridding process itself, the individual values are often weighted according to their distance from the central point in order to avoid abrupt changes between data points. When averaging (or "smoothing") is applied to gridded data, a considerable amount of computer time can be saved, since the complex searching process involved in grid calculation need not be repeated. If the local variations are extreme, and have led to problems in gridding, this approach may not be adequate, however. For example, if some grid values are far outside the range of the raw data, a simple smoothing operation will not restore realistic values. When the samples are obtained along lines, the data can be smoothed along the lines prior to gridding, which does not require a lengthy search so long as the data file is structured according to position along the survey lines. At the same time, the density along the line can be reduced to produce a more uniform spatial distribution.

The effect of smoothing on local variations depends on the degree of smoothing applied, that is, on the areal extent of the averaging function. At one extreme, the smoothing "operator" may encompass all available data, and simply produce an average value for the map. The other extreme is an operator that is very small, and normally takes in only a single data value: smoothing then has no effect. Neither of these cases would be used in practice, of course. Short smoothing operators are often applied to suppress "noise" in the data (random fluctuations of each sample). The actual size needed to produce an acceptable display is dependent on the relative magnitude of the noise (termed the signal-to-noise ratio): the higher the noise level, the more samples must be averaged to reduce its effect.

Smoothing may also be used to detect large scale ("regional") features in a map. This involves a large smoothing operator, since it is assumed that the regional structure is slowly varying across the extent of the map. The size of the operator is directly related to the size of the features that will be retained in the smoothed map. This process may suppress many smaller scale real structures, in addition to any random variations in the data.

A series of examples are shown in Fig. 8.7. The basic contour map (Fig. 8.7*a*) was derived from an aerial magnetic survey, and shows a number of small closures around individual samples. A light smoothing operation has been applied in Fig. 8.7*b*, to suppress these small features, and make the larger structures more evident. In Fig. 8.7*c* the original map has been greatly smoothed to leave only very large features.

As can be seen from the location ticks on these maps, the magnetic readings were taken along a number of lines. In raw form, there is a great disparity

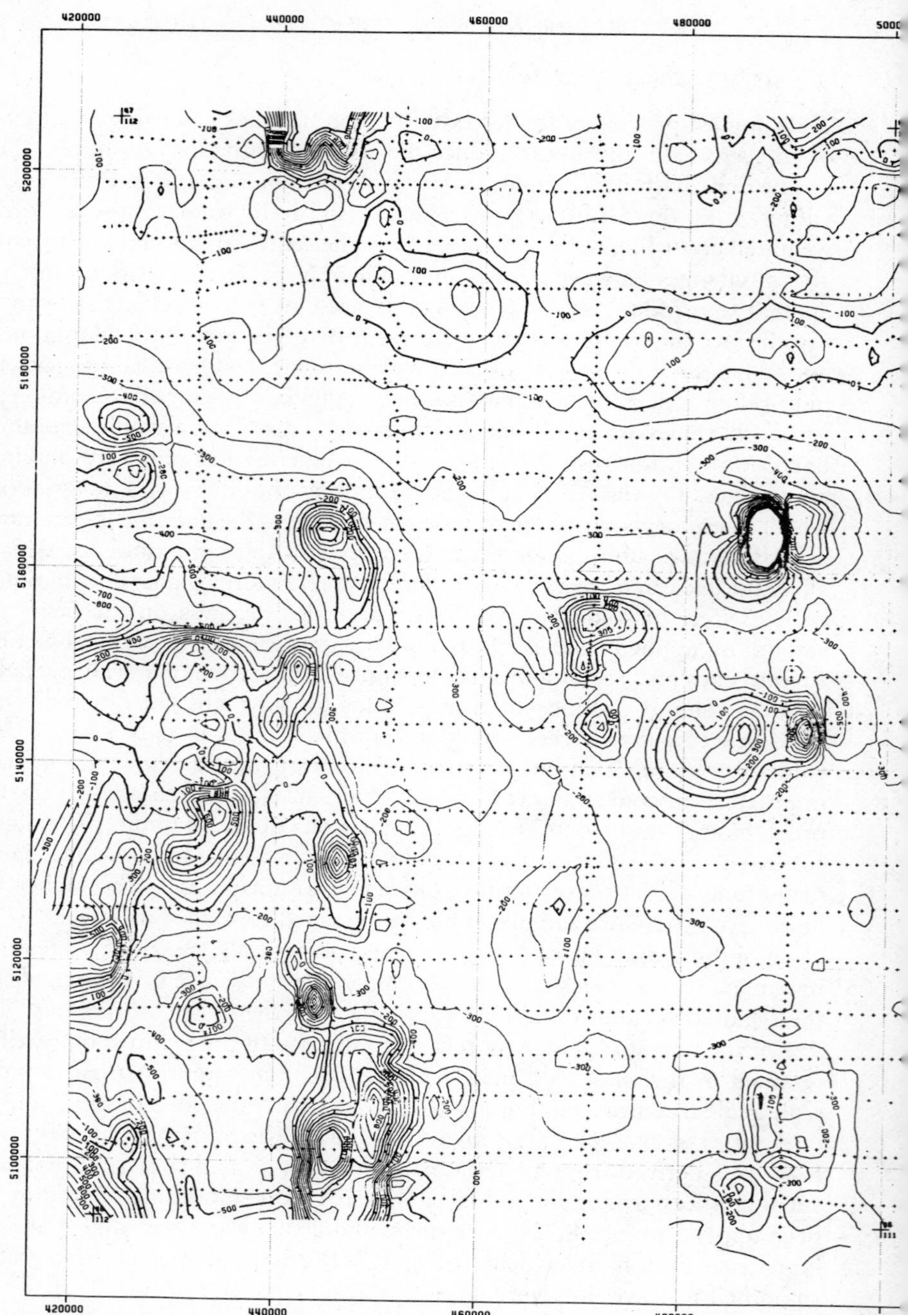

FIGURE 8.7. "Smoothing" a contour map. (*a*) Original contour map from a aeromagnetic survey. Note the complex form, and the many small closed contours. The blank areas within densely contoured closures are due to an upper limit on the requested contour levels.

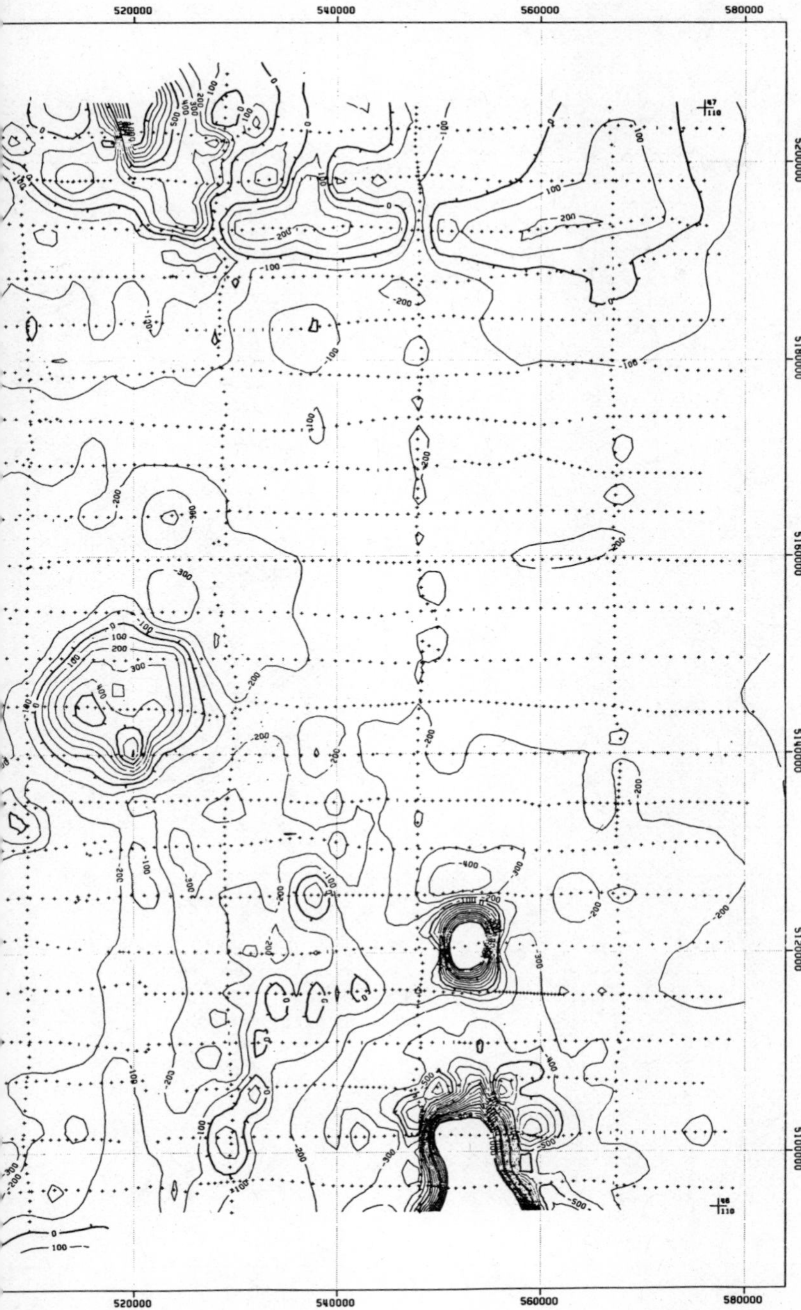
520000
540000
560000
580000
5200000
5180000
5160000
5140000
5120000
5100000

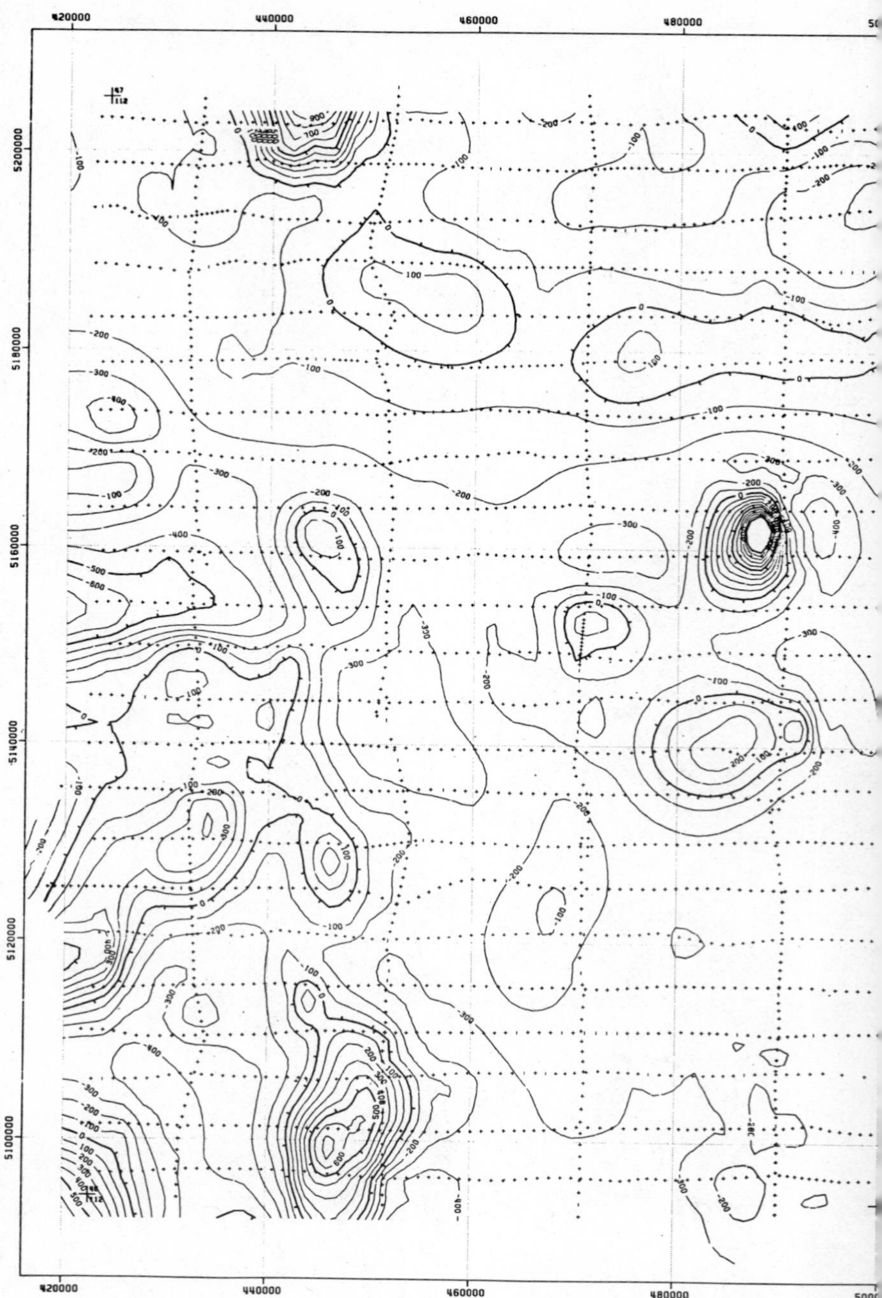

FIGURE 8.7. (*b*) The same data as in Fig. 8.7*a*, with one pass of ad smoothing operator on the grid values. Most small closures are gone, and the larger structures have a simpler shape.

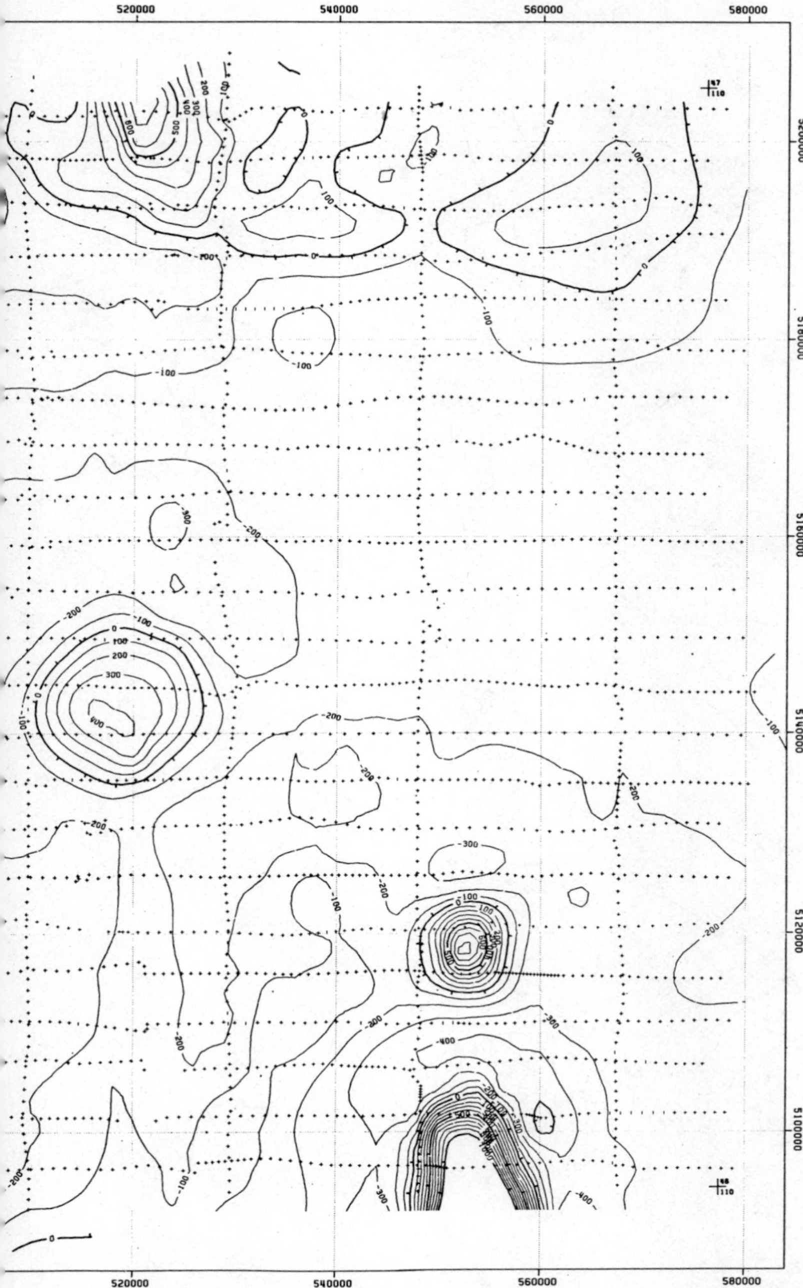
520000
540000
560000
580000
5200000
5180000
5160000
5140000
5120000
5100000

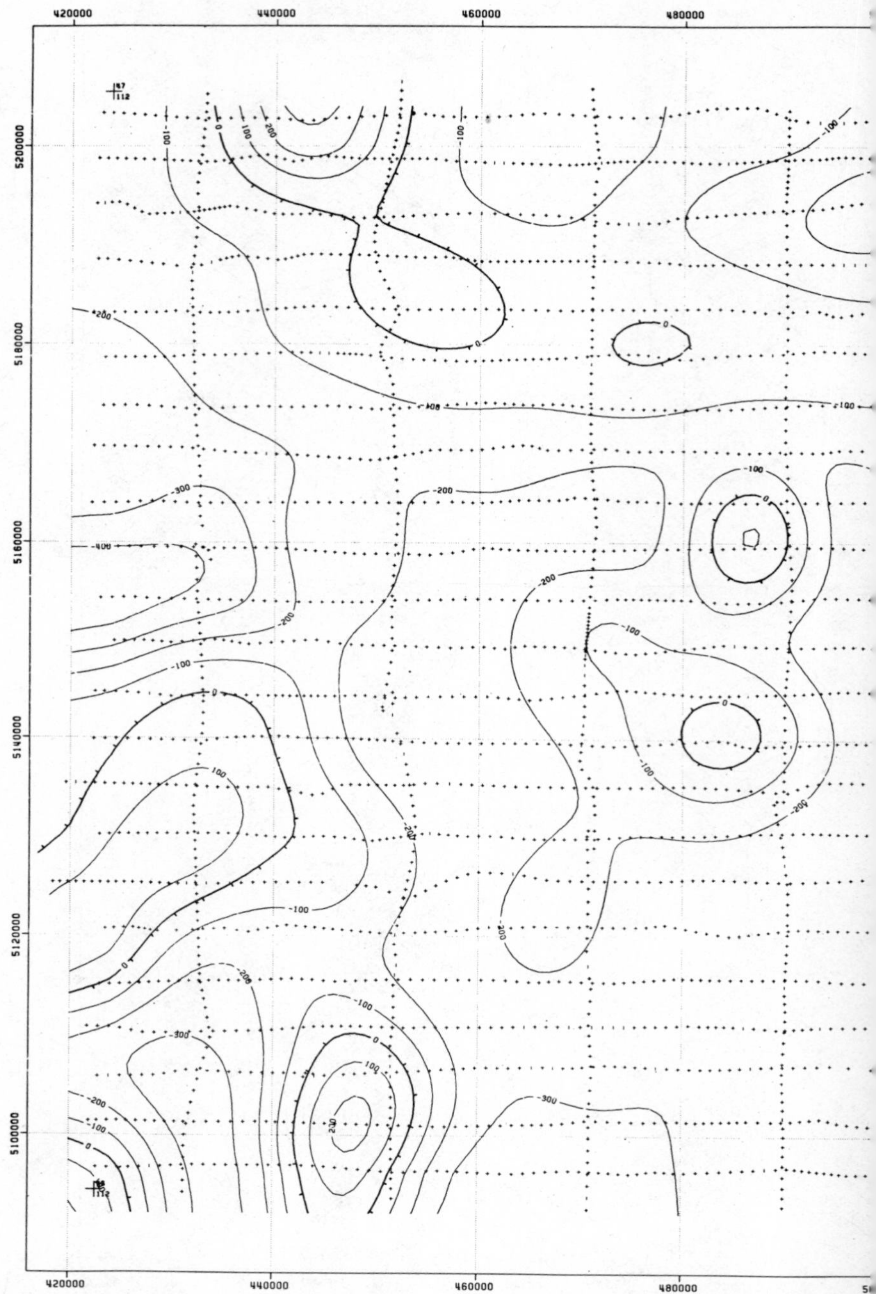

FIGURE 8.7. (*c*) The same data as in Figs. 8.7*a* and 8.7*b*, with five smoothing passes. Only very large features are left, and the range of values has been greatly suppressed.

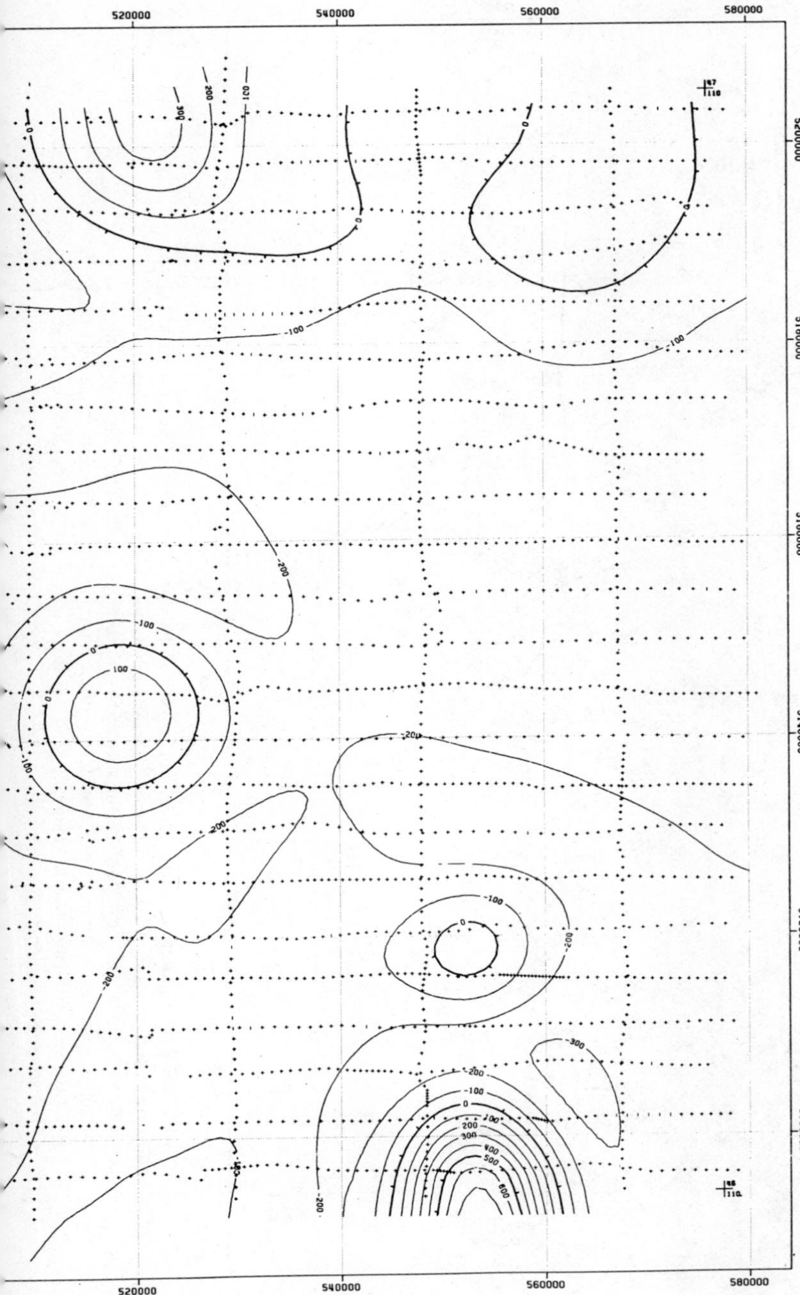

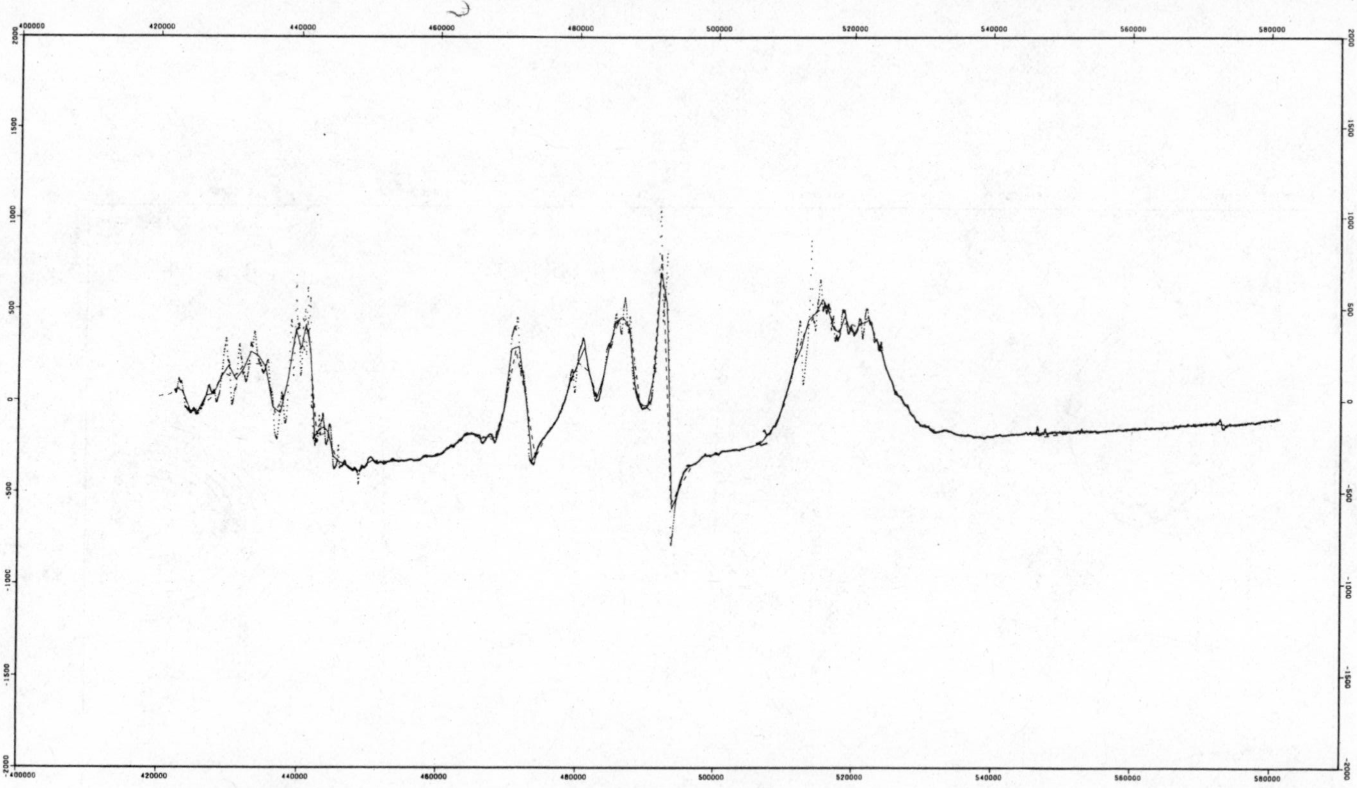

FIGURE 8.8. Smoothing along a line. This is one of the survey lines in the raw data used for the contour maps of Fig. 8.7. The original data points are shown as +, but are generally so close together that they appear as lines. Note that in some places the smoothed value (the continuous line) has completely suppressed some of the rapid variations. The dotted line which is occasionally visible is the grid value closest to this flight line, which in general is very close to the smoothed value.

in sample spacing, and in fact the contour map was derived from data already smoothed along the lines. In Fig. 8.8, the effect of this initial operation is shown. The original data contain many rapid flucuations, which have been greatly reduced by the smoothing process (25 points were averaged into one). The level of detail is obviously reduced, although it would not have been possible to produce a readable contour map of the original data. To use the individual closely spaced samples, a profile plot (such as Fig. 8.8) is used directly, since the rapid variations can be plotted without concern for potential problems in grid interpolation.

b. Trend Surface Analysis

An alternate procedure for determining large scale structure is to compute a "trend surface" from the data values. An estimated data value is calculated as a function of the X and Y coordinates. Normally the function is a low-order polynomial, the coefficients of which are derived by a least-squares fitting procedure analogous to that outlined in Chapter 4 for the two-dimensional case. (Although a map is a two-dimensional display, contouring and trend surface calculations may be considered as three-dimensional problems, with the data value as the third variable.) Different orders of the trend surface can be tested by computing a series of grids from subsets of the polynomial coefficients. Note that all coefficients (up to some maximum order) can be computed with one pass through the raw data, so that additional contour maps do not require as much computer time as the first one.

Trend surfaces quickly become unstable as higher orders are used, as the polynomial function produces an increasing number of local high and low points in the surface. For this reason, they are usually restricted to quite simple functions (perhaps a maximum of fourth or fifth order). As such, they are very useful for removing strong regional gradients which are relatively uniform over the map area, and for quantifying such gradients in mathematical terms. Averaging techniques are generally more stable when smoothing out local effects, while allowing a considerable amount of variation across the map. These two procedures may be considered as complementary to each other, rather than as alternate approaches to the same problem.

Figure 8.9 shows trend surfaces corresponding to the original data in Fig. 8.7. None of the closed structures are visible, and a strong regional gradient is not evident. Note also that the contours extend beyond the limits of the data, and that artificial gradients begin to show along the edge in the fifth-order surface. These effects are unavoidable consequences of using a mathematical formula to compute grid values.

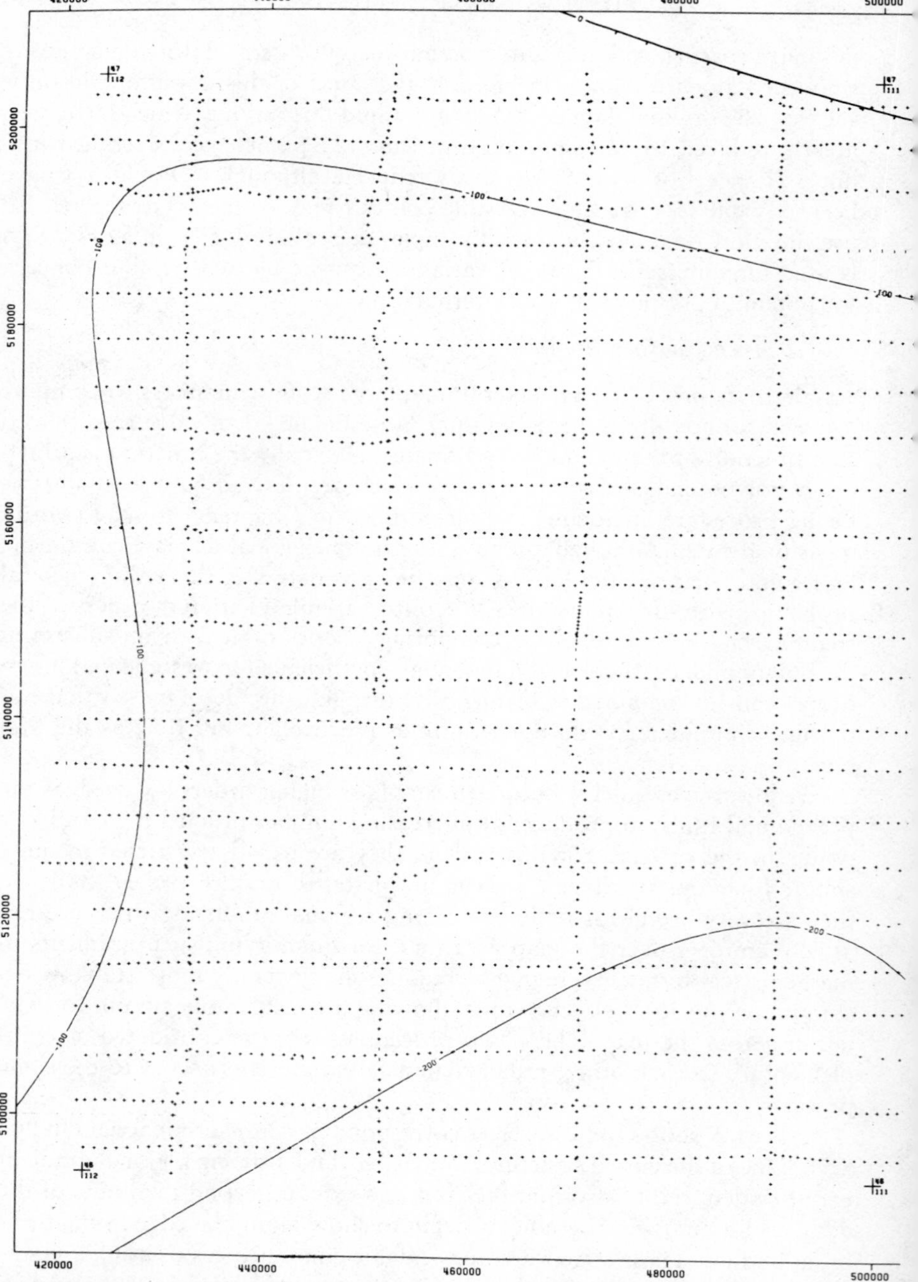

FIGURE 8.9a. Trend surfaces for the data in Fig. 8.7. A third-order fit is shown in (*a*), and a fifth order fit in (*b*). Note that there is little evidence of regional gradient, other than a gentle slope from north to south. Some edge instability is evident in (*b*).

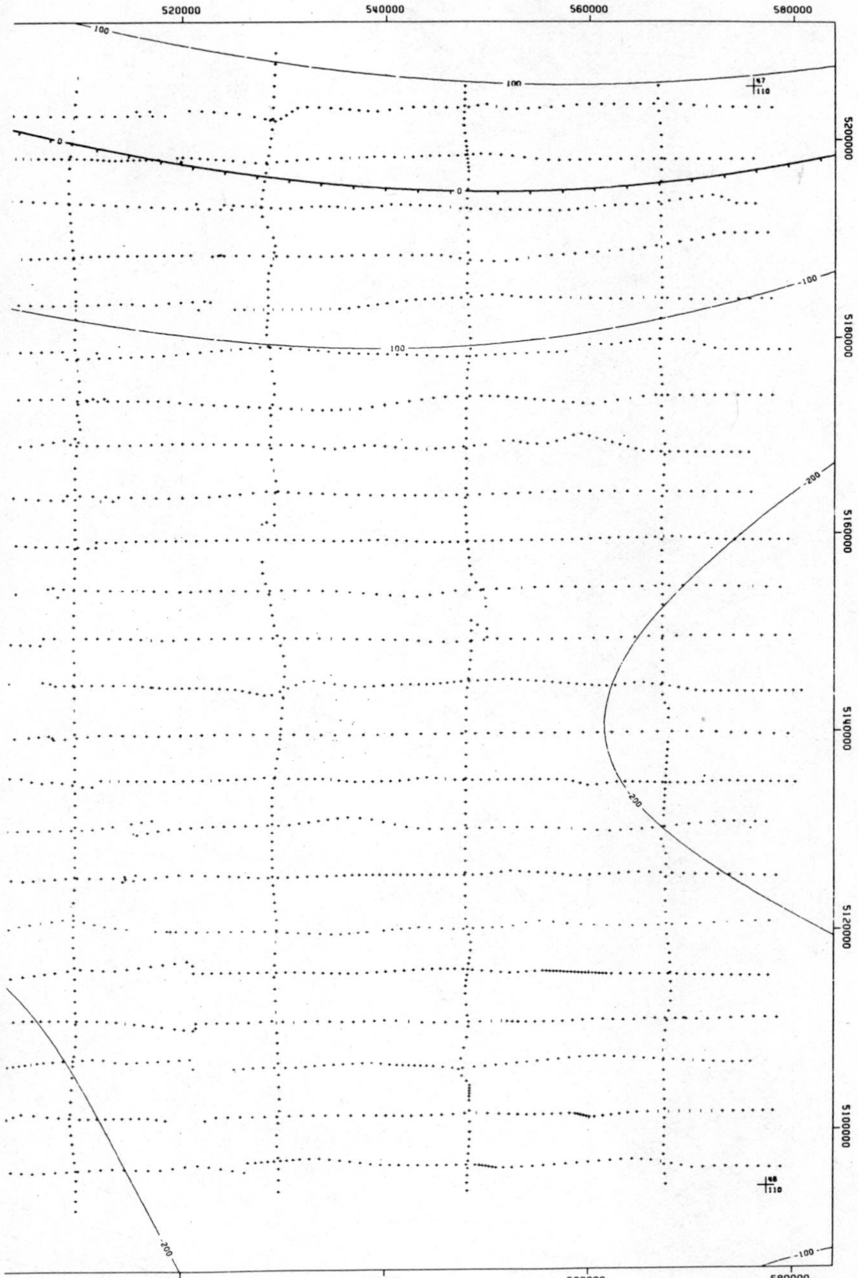
520000
540000
560000
580000
5200000
5180000
5160000
5140000
5120000
5100000
100
0
-100
-200
47
110
48
110

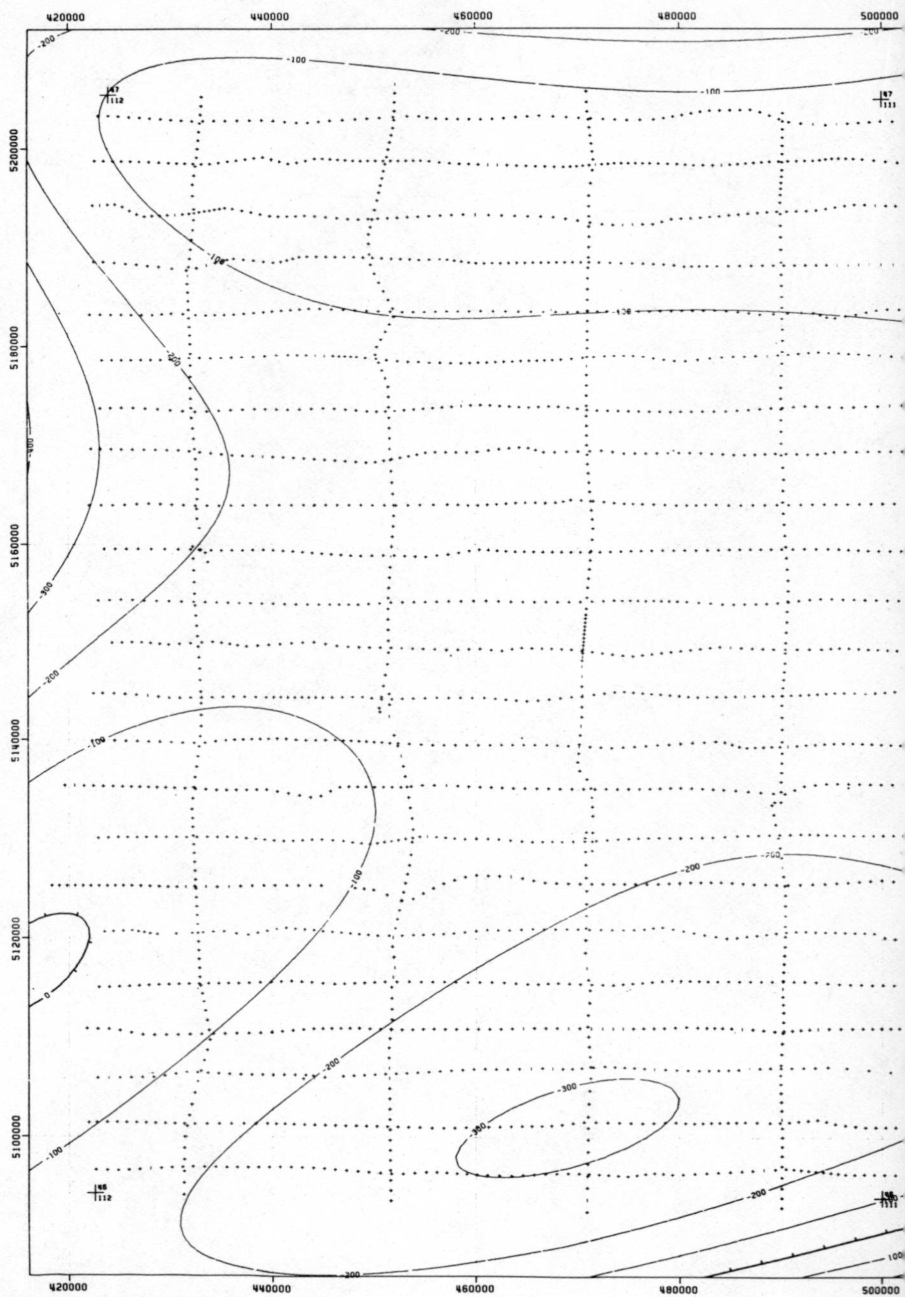

420000
440000
460000
480000
500000
5200000
5180000
5160000
5140000
5120000
5100000
-100
-200
-300
0

FIGURE 8.9b.

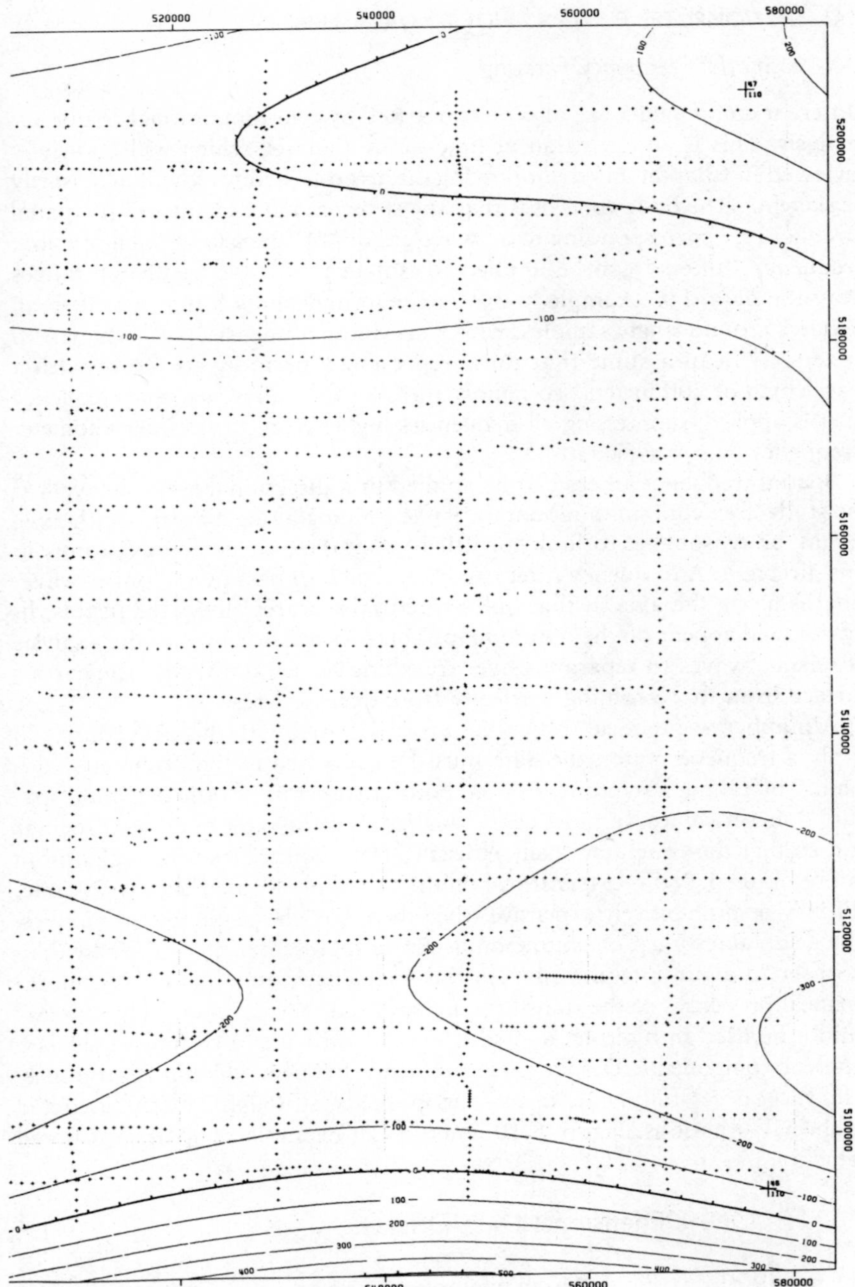

520000
540000
560000
580000
5100000
5120000
5140000
5160000
5180000
5200000
-100
0
100
200
-200
-300
300
400
500

c. Spatial Frequency Filtering

Different components can also be segregated by two-dimensional frequency analysis. This is an extension of time-series analysis, which will be briefly reviewed in Chapter 11 (the following discussion, therefore, will necessarily be sketchy). The basic concept is that any structure has a characteristic spatial "frequency," corresponding to a "wavelength" of a recurring phenomenon. Frequency "filters" can be applied to isolate particular frequency ranges from the data. For example, a contour map may show a number of small closures around single samples, with a maximum dimension of perhaps 100 meters. We can assume that these represent a periodic structure with a wavelength of 200 meters. To remove these local features, a spatial frequency filter is applied, suppressing all frequencies higher than 5 cycles per kilometer (frequency = 1/wavelength).

Spatial frequency filters can be applied in a directional sense, as well. If the study area contains a mountain range running along a north-south axis, it may be reasonable to look for other geographic or geologic features in this direction. A frequency filter can be designed to pass much longer wavelengths along the axis so that only structural features elongated in this direction will appear on the output map. This procedure is used in the analysis of seismic waves to separate waves travelling horizontally near the earth's surface from those coming vertically from deep sources.

A number of practical difficulties are associated with this procedure. To apply a frequency filter, the data must be expressed in the "frequency domain," by taking a two-dimensional Fourier transform of the original "spatial" domain values. In most cases, this requires the data to be on a regular grid so that the computationally efficient "fast" Fourier transform algorithm can be applied. A direct transform on the randomly located data is possible, but may be prohibitively expensive when there are a large number of samples. The grid values must constitute an accurate representation of the raw data in order to avoid introducing spurious frequency components. The mathematical properties of the transform are such that abrupt frequency "cutoffs" cannot be used in filtering, and so it may be difficult to completely isolate different components. Despite these problems, frequency filtering is routinely (and very successfully) used in a variety of fields, although it is still restricted to special situations. Figure 8.10 contains an example of spatially filtered data.

3. One-Dimensional Data Displays

The profile plot in Fig. 8.8 is an example of a one-dimensional data display. Structure in this case has the same basic meaning as before, except that there is only one spatial coordinate instead of two. The averaging and trend fitting

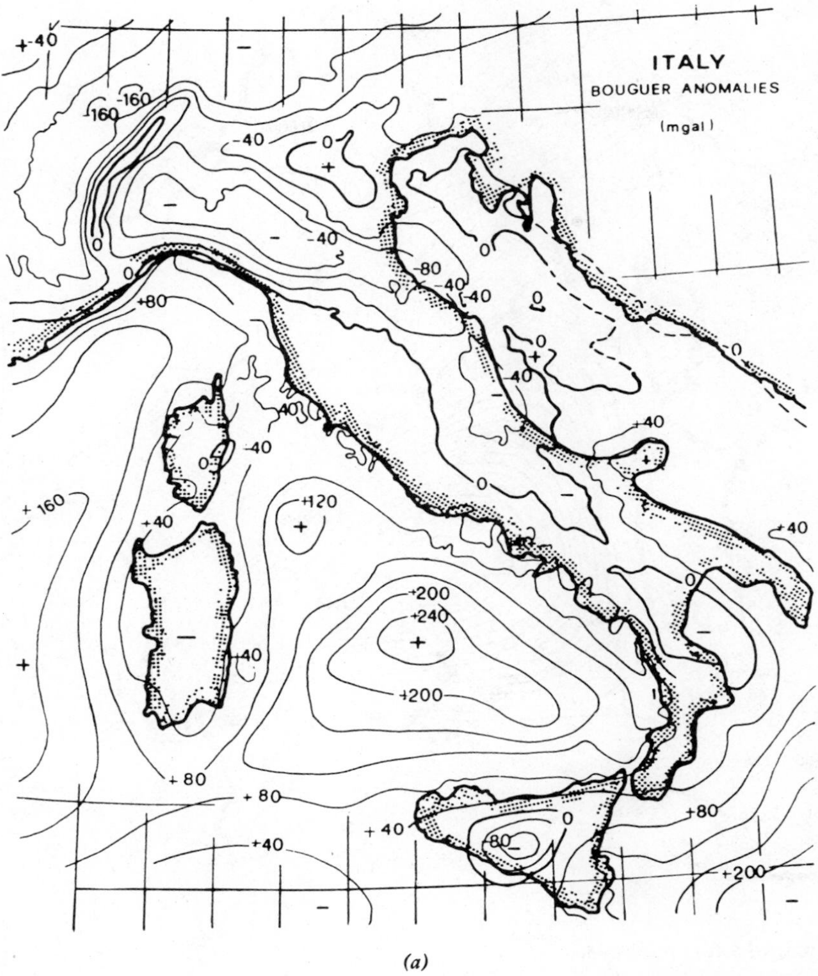

(a)

FIGURE 8.10. Spatial filtering. (*a*) Regional gravity over Italy and the Mediterranean; (*b*) filtered map, in which only large scale features were retained (wavelengths greater than 215 km); (*c*) filtered map displaying medium scale features (wavelengths between 100 km and 215 km). (Reproduced from "Some Aspects of the Interpretation of Gravity Data for the Study of Regional and Local Structures", by A. Rapolla, in *The Solution of the Inverse Problem in Geophysical Interpretation,* copyright New York; Plenum Press, 1981, by permission of the publisher).

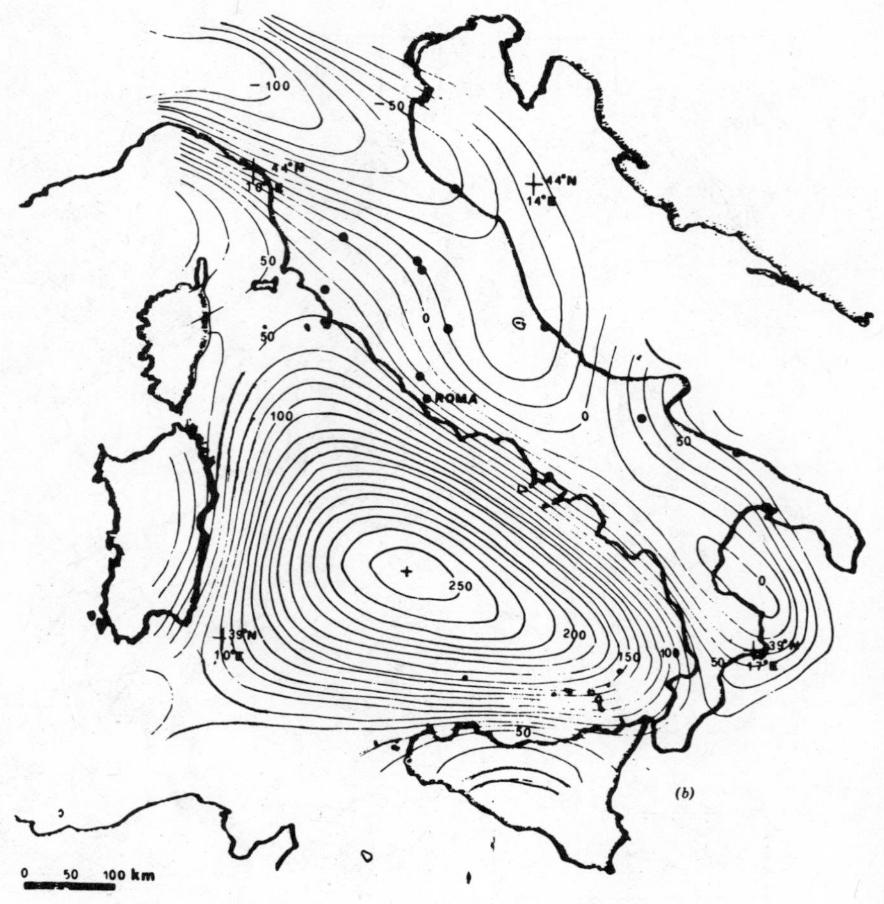

FIGURE 8.10. *(Continued)*

procedures can still be applied, using the appropriate one-dimensional algorithms. In plotting the results, the raw data can be plotted as points superimposed on the trend (or smoothed) line, to give an immediate impression of the variability of the data. This is usually not possible in plotting maps, since different sets of contour lines tend to interfere with each other. As we shall see in Chapter 10, this form of display can also be used to display mulitvariate data by plotting a number of lines representing different variables. If the lines cross on portions of the plot, different colors, dashed patterns, or line thicknesses can be used to avoid confusion.

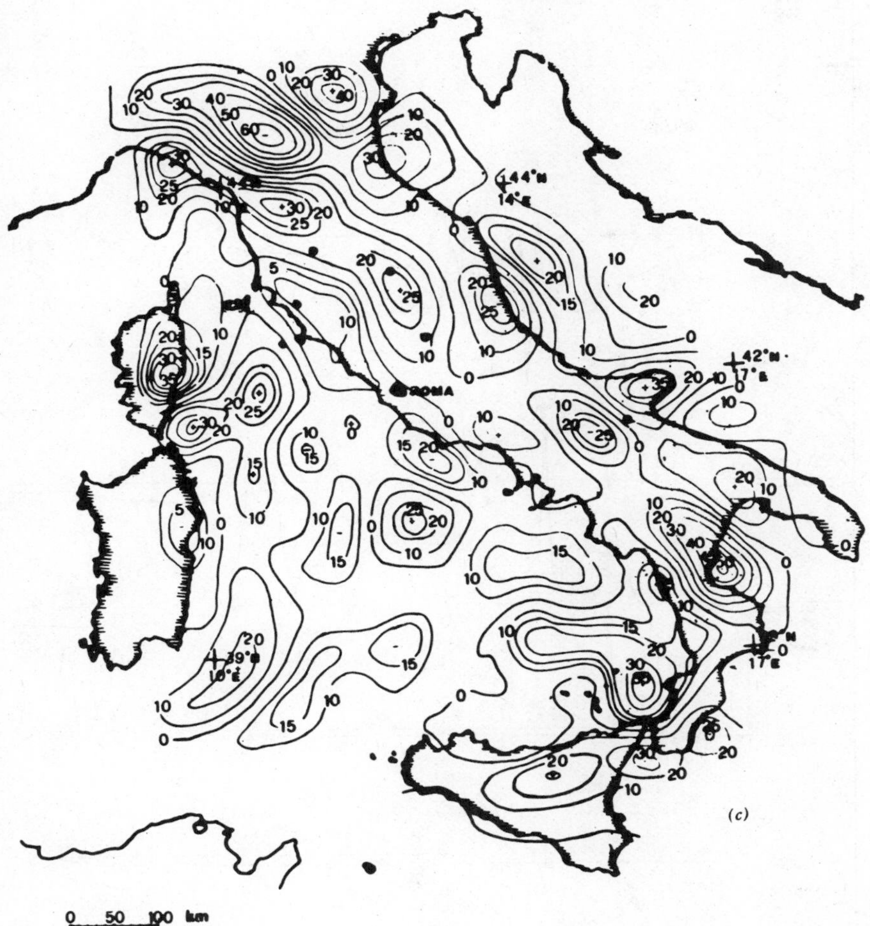

FIGURE 8.10. *(Continued)*

As we saw in the previous chapter, variable data density is often a problem for data collected along a series of lines. Conventional maps (postings or contours) cannot display the level of detail along a line that can be achieved with a profile plot. Map views are important in studying spatial relationships, however. A composite form can be used in this situation: all of the lines are plotted in map view, with the data values for each line plotted as a profile offset from the line location (that is, the track of the line forms the X-axis of the profile plot). An example of such a "stacked profile" map is shown in Fig. 8.11. A similar form is often used to plot cross-sections, where

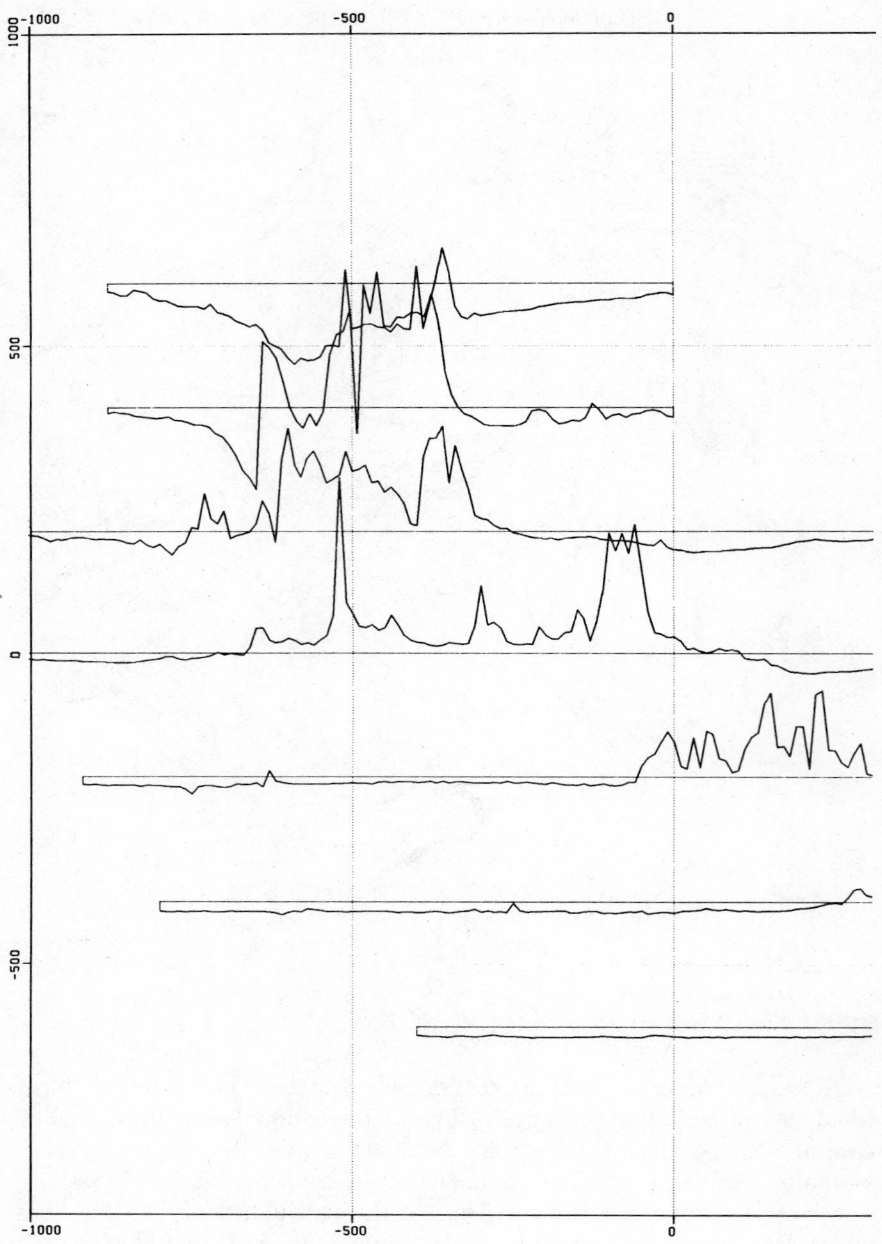

FIGURE 8.11. A "stacked profile" map. Profile plots for multiple survey lines are plotted in map view by calculating an offset from the line position according to data value (in this case, magnetometer readings).

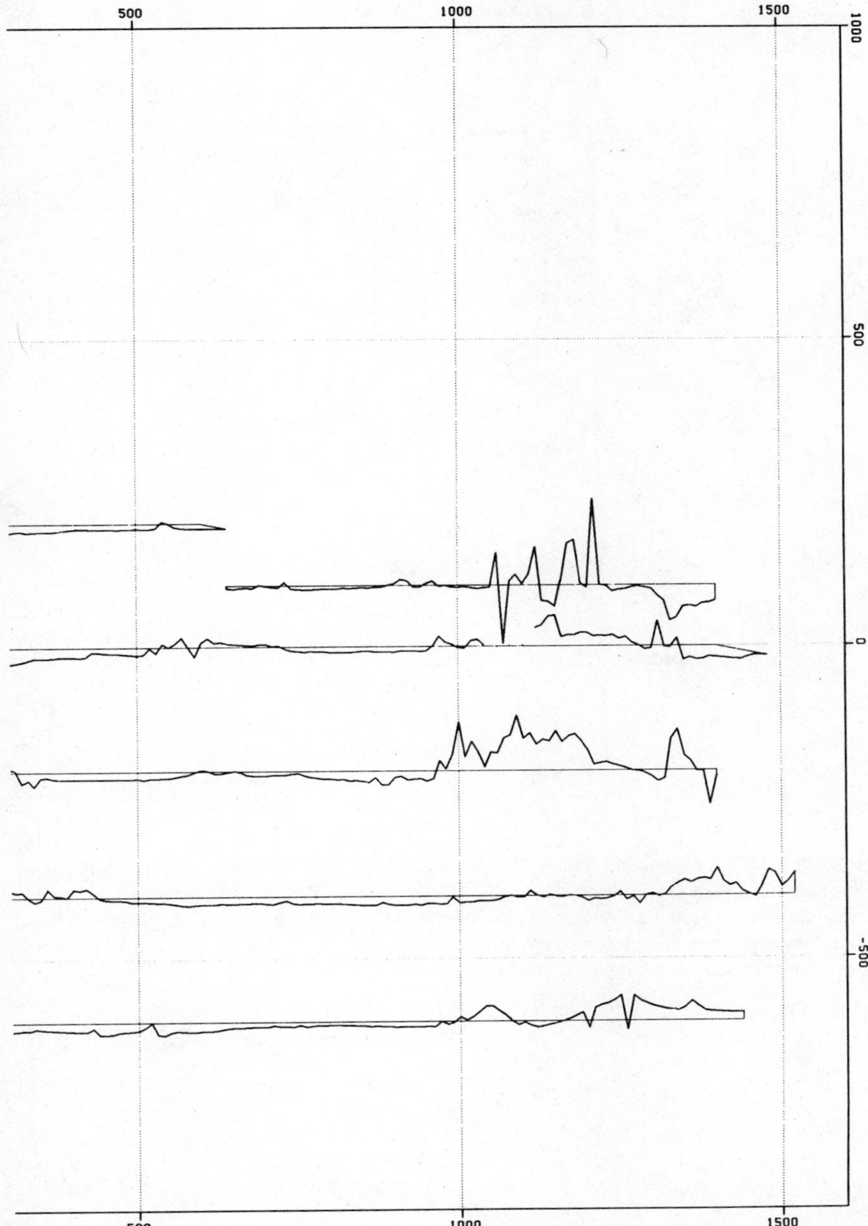
500
1000
1500
1000
500
0
-500
500
1000
1500

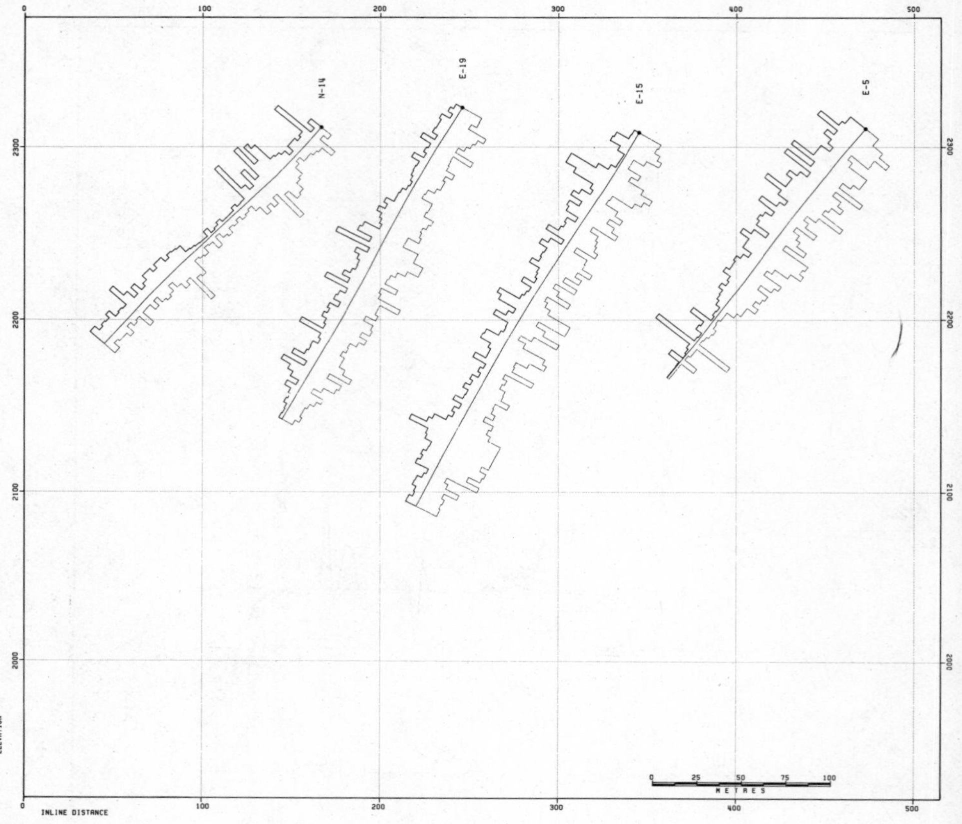

FIGURE 8.12. A cross-section plot. This plot is similar to Fig. 8.11, in that scaled data values are offset from their spatial location. In this case, the survey line is a drill-hole into the earth's crust that has been used to sample an ore body. Note that the data values are plotted as bars, since they represent averages over the indicated interval. In Fig. 8.11., data values are point measurements, and so a simple connecting line is drawn.

data have been measured along lines (e.g., drill-holes into the earth, vertical measurements into the atmosphere), as shown in Figure 8.12.

DETECTION OF ANOMALIES

1. Anomalies Defined as Departures from Regional Structure

Finding a regional structure is often only a preliminary step: the real objective is to find local anomalies (that is, small scale features which do not conform to the regional patterns). If the gross characteristics of the data are well known (and thus predictable), smaller features may be the indication of a new phenomenon or previously unknown structure. Local variations might also be a sign that our knowledge of the process is incomplete, or that the estimate of the regional structure is poor. If there are no anomalies, the phenomenon being investigated is completely predictable, and we can conclude that there is no further need for analyzing the data! This is seldom the case in the real world, of course, which means that this procedure can be applied to locate new resources or discover new phenomena (and indeed that new phenomena remain to be discovered).

Anomalies will often exhibit structure themselves, only on a more local scale than the dominant regional features. By definition, an anomaly is an unusual event. The procedure for locating anomalies, then, is to locate areas where the data characteristics are abnormal. "Normal" can of course take on many meanings, especially in studies involving many variables. Limitations or assumptions inherent in the detection method must be considered in seeking physical explanations for any anomaly.

In examining a single variable, the departure of individual samples from the estimated regional trend is the basic measure of anomalousness. For example, pollution readings from single sites are compared to regional averages to determine their significance. Mineral resources are commonly confined to relatively small geologic features, and may be detected as high concentrations of metals in only a few rock samples from a large survey. Such criteria can equally well apply to one-dimensional data: historical patterns of the price of a particular stock, for example, can be used to define periods of unusual market behavior.

The procedure for displaying anomalous data starts with an estimation of the regional value, which is then subtracted from the original data to produce a "residual" field. As for a smoothing operation, this can be done on the original points, or on a gridded respresentation. If a trend surface is used, this is simply a choice of calculating the polynomial function at the sample locations or the grid points. If the regional is derived by smoothing, an interpolation of gridded values to a sample location within a grid cell is required when the regional is in grid form, and the differences are desired at the original samples.

2. Other Methods for Defining Anomalies

Many other techniques can also be applied to locate anomalous data. Basic statistical displays are often used to set the selection criteria. In studying a single variable, we might decide to plot all points more than two standard deviations from the mean, or to pick thresholds by inspecting the distribution on a histogram or cumulative frequency diagram. When two variables are compared, their ratio can be computed, and extreme values picked, as before. Alternatively, discrete clusters may be observed on a scatter plot, and can be isolated using a polygon selection routine. For the case of three variables, we would use a ternary diagram to look for clustering (an example is shown in Fig.10.4). For larger numbers of variables, we must rely on statistical techniques (e.g., multiple regression or factor analysis), or special plot formats. These topics will be examined in Chapter 10.

Anomalous situations may also be defined in terms of descriptive variables. This is also essentially a problem of data selection. In studying a single variable, each unique value can be assigned a color or symbol, or only samples with particular values of interest can be chosen. Unusual associations of two variables can be shown by selecting those samples which have the desired values for both variables. As shown in Chapter 5, descriptive and numeric variables can also be associated. Selection of samples for plotting them involves testing for specific values of the descriptive variable, and a range of values for the numeric variable. These methods can obviously be extended to more than two variables, although the number of combinations quickly becomes unmanageable unless the variables are restricted to a very limited number of classes. Examples can be found in many types of data analysis. A geologist might search for all copper mines which also contain gold, or which are associated with a specific type of rock. A sociologist may want to find areas where particular combinations of demographic variables occur (for example, high-income districts in the U.S. that voted Democratic in 1980).

In studying large data files, it is often necessary to compute average values, instead of dealing directly with the selected points. This is especially true if the spatial density of samples is highly variable, since apparent clusters of a special category of data may simply reflect more samples in that area. In these cases, maps of percentage values within a unit area are used, which normalize the number of selected points by the number of available points.

Descriptive data are converted to a numeric form by this process, so contour maps can be used to display anomalous areas. Even when plotting selected subsets of data, there may be too many occurrences for any patterns independent of the distribution of all samples on a simple posted map to be seen. A contour map showing relative percentages (e.g., average percentage of copper mines containing gold in each unit area) may show a new pattern. This normalizing process is very familiar in demographic studies, where it is customary to report information in a per-capita form, so that urban and rural areas can be compared.

3. Procedures for Data Display

The display phase is much the same for an estimated anomaly as for the original data. For all types of anomalies, maps can be used to display the spatial relationships (if any). The key is to choose a plot format that makes the anomalous points stand out from the others. This principle is independent of the particular method for defining anomalies.

When using a posted or contoured map format, it may be necessary to modify the basic parameters, if the range of values is greatly altered by the removal of trends. This situation occurs when the regional gradient is large and the magnitude of anomalies is relatively small. The optimum contour interval may be much smaller for the residual map, and a small numeric class size might be needed to plot a symbolic posted map.

A number of additional considerations are also involved. We must decide whether to plot only those samples defined as anomalous, or to show a number of classes with symbols or colors. In the latter case, codes must be assigned to the distinct groups (set by ranges of numeric value, or clusters on a scatter plot, for example). This may be part of the data selection program, or an option in the plotting program. In some cases, it may be desirable to display the data in contour form, or by three-dimensional views, often necessitating a grid interpolation. Hard and fast rules cannot be set since the nature of the data, the spatial distribution of samples, and the individual preference of the analyst must all be considered.

When the density of samples is high it is sometimes useful to plot only the anomalous points in order to avoid excessive clutter. It is important to compare the result to a map of all data, to determine if the anomalies are in undersampled areas, or are adjacent to other samples with normal behavior. This approach is essentially the same as that used in the mineral location maps of Fig. 8.1 and 8.2, where a map of iron occurrences was compared to all known mineral deposits. Any selected data can of course be plotted in this way: the importance of a flexible data selection program (see Chapters 5 and 7) must be noted once again.

When the data do not have a pronounced regional trend, a contour plot of the basic data will often show anomalies, and the process of estimating the trend may be bypassed. The anomalies appear as small closed contours or as areas of unusual complexity. As we saw earlier, such features may also represent noise or data errors, so it is essential to confirm the validity of any anomaly before attempting to find a physical explanation for it.

Some enhancements to a simple contour plot can highlight the abnormal areas. The contours to be drawn may be restricted only to values well outside the normal range, and lines for increasingly larger values drawn progressively thicker (or in different colors). To distinguish positive and negative residuals, one set can be drawn with dashed lines and the others as solid lines. If the plotting system (hardware and software) provides the capability, shading between the contour lines with different colors or line patterns is more effective. An example is shown in Fig. 8.13, where thicker lines are used for the higher values in a contour map of copper content. In this example, most samples have the low values typical of the regional (or "background"), while isolated areas of mineralization show much higher levels. The purpose of the map is to outline these areas, which in this case was achieved by contouring the raw data, since there is no pronounced regional trend. Such procedures create a visual bias, however, and must be used with care to ensure that the resultant map emphasizes the desired features. One must note that a contour map is a selective representation, and be wary of absolute judgments based on a single map.

Where erratic sample distribution and other data-related problems make it difficult to successfully contour data, posted maps can be used. To allow the unusual samples to be quickly identified, the plot format must emphasize these points, so that the eye will be attracted to them. This is most easily done with color (note again that this option is often unavailable). For example, samples near the regional norm may be plotted in blue and then shift to red for values with extreme differences. Intermediate shades can also be used, depending on how many levels must be distinguished. There is often a trade-off between making the extremes noticeable and defining a reasonable number of classes. A continuous color spectrum might also be used. In either event, the range of values to be color-coded must be known so that individual samples can be assigned colors across the range, and not all end up in the same category.

When color cannot be used, a similar procedure is followed, except that the symbol used in plotting sample location must define the anomalous points. This might involve a limited set of different symbols, which must be visually distinct for easy segregation. To highlight large values, symbols with a large amount of blacked-in area are effective, with values close to the norm plotted with more open symbols (e.g., an open circle for values

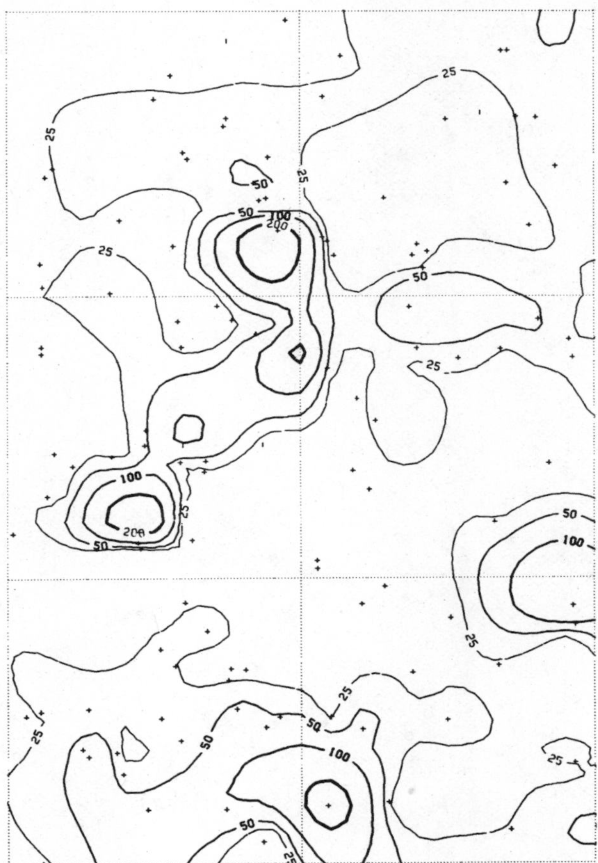

FIGURE 8.13. Contour emphasis to outline anomalous areas. Contour values represent concentrations of copper in stream sediment samples for an area in southwestern British Columbia.

within one standard deviation of the trend, a half-filled circle for one to two standard deviations, and a completely filled circle for greater than two standard deviations). Figure 8.14 shows a posted map of this type, derived from the same set of data contoured in Fig. 8.13.

An alternate, and usually more emphatic form is to plot symbols of varying size, with the size controlled by the data value. As in color coding, a continuous range can be used, or the data might be divided into a limited number of numeric classes, with the extreme values assigned to the largest symbols. The scaling of the plot symbol can be done in a variety of ways with dramatically different effect. The size of a symbol (usually given as the length

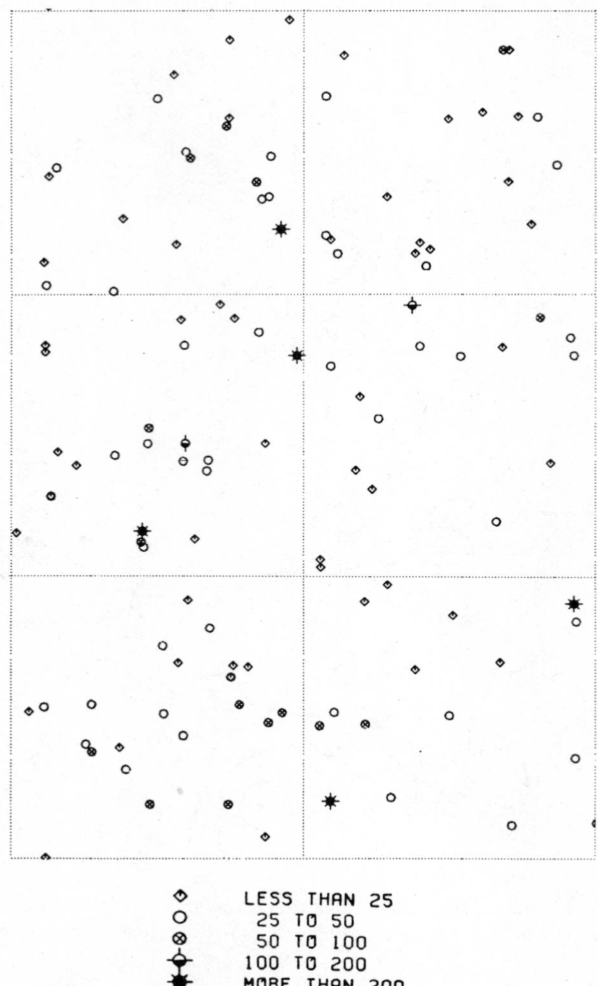

FIGURE 8.14. Symbol coding to show numeric value. The same data as in Fig. 8.13, but plotted in different form.

of a side of an enclosing square) can be made proportional to the numeric value. An alternate method is to make the area of the symbol proportional to the numeric value. For most people, intuitive judgment on relative size is more likely to be based on area than a single linear dimension, as the illustration in Fig. 8.15 shows. The smallest circle has half the diameter of the largest, while the middle-sized one has half the area (hence the ratio of diameters is 0.707). At first glance, the ratio of the sizes appears greater.

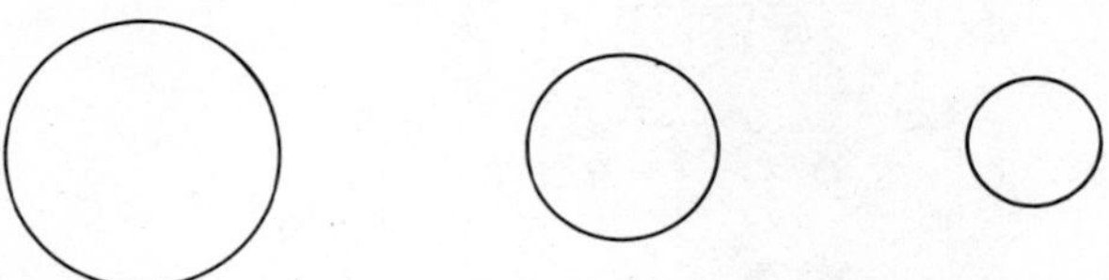

FIGURE 8.15. Perception of relative size. The middle circle has half the area of the large one, while the small one has half the diameter. Which appears to be half as big on first glance?

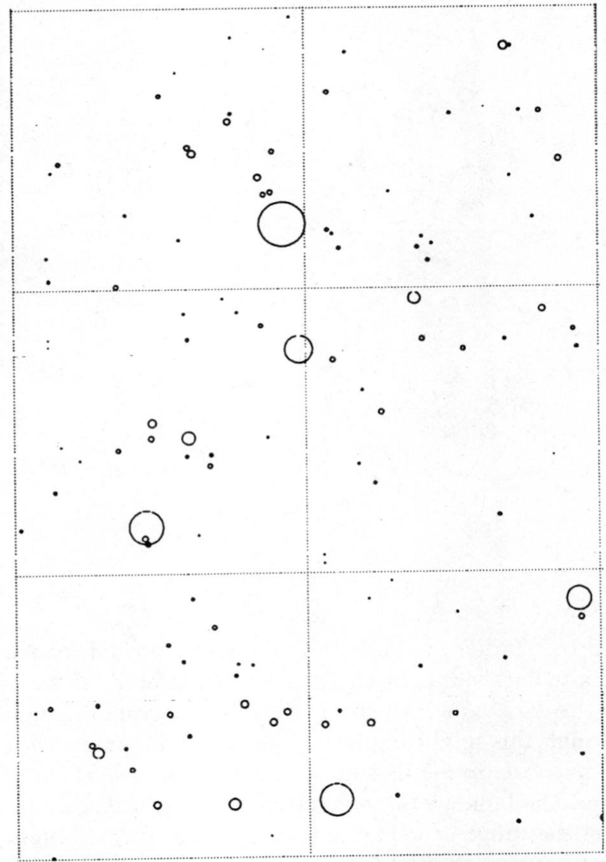

FIGURE 8.16a. Use of symbol size to represent data value. (*a*) A representation of the same data as in 8.13, with the diameter of the circle proportional to the numeric value; (*b*) the same data, but with area proportional to numeric value.

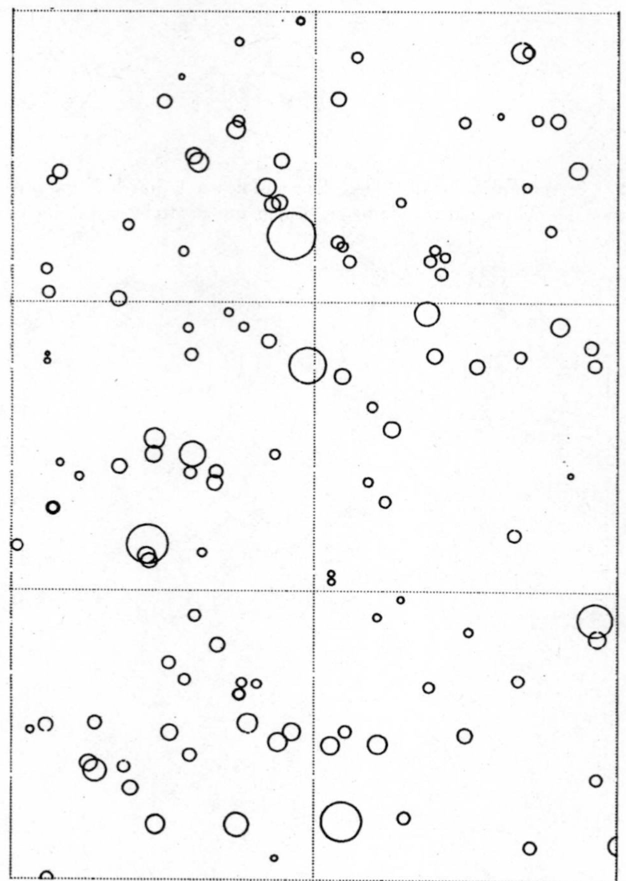

FIGURE 8.16b.

Returning to our earlier example, Fig. 8.16 is a posted map using scaled circles to denote data value. In Fig. 8.16*a*, the diameter of the circle is proportional to the data value, which has the effect of emphasizing the extreme values. Although this might imply a visual bias, the map may be intended for just that purpose. In Fig. 8.16*b*, the area of the circle is proportional to the data value. The largest values are no longer so obvious, although a better impression of the range of values across the map can be obtained.

A combined approach might also be taken, using both size and symbol form to emphasize the extreme classes (or size and color). As with color, the data range may be divided into discrete classes, with size corresponding

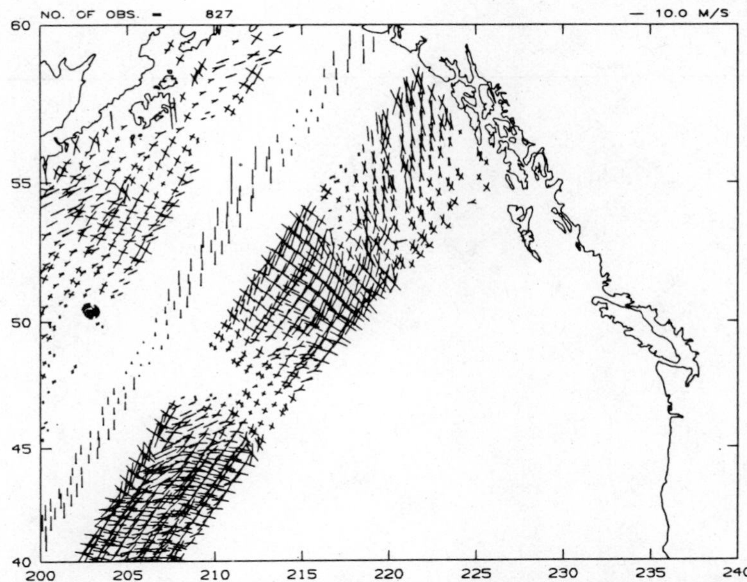

FIGURE 8.17. Scaled symbols for directional data. The direction of the arrow shows the wind direction, while its length is proportional to wind speed. Derived from satellite observations over the north Pacific. (Reproduced from *Computer Graphics World,* December 1983, by permission of the publisher, Pennwell Publishing Co.)

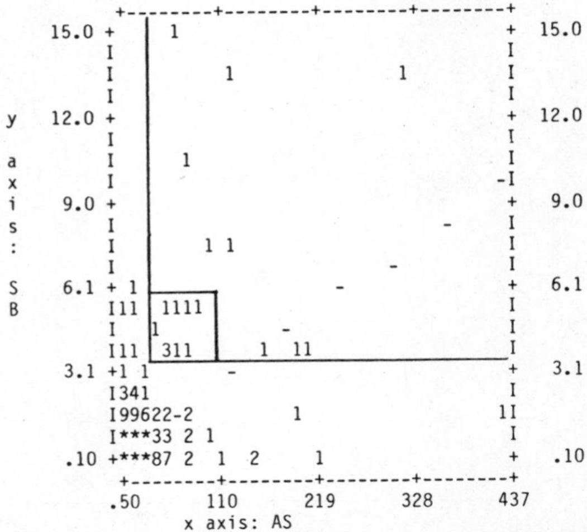

FIGURE 8.18a. Statistical data selection for spatial data. (*a*) A scatter plot comparing concentrations of arsenic and antimony in geologic samples. Two groups of data outside the main clusters are outlined, and selected for plotting in (*b*). (*b*) A map showing locations of all the samples. The points in the small box of (*a*) are marked with solid circles, and those in the larger box with a larger circle enclosing an ×. All other samples are marked with an ×. Note that the selected samples lie within a restricted area, with the exception of three points.

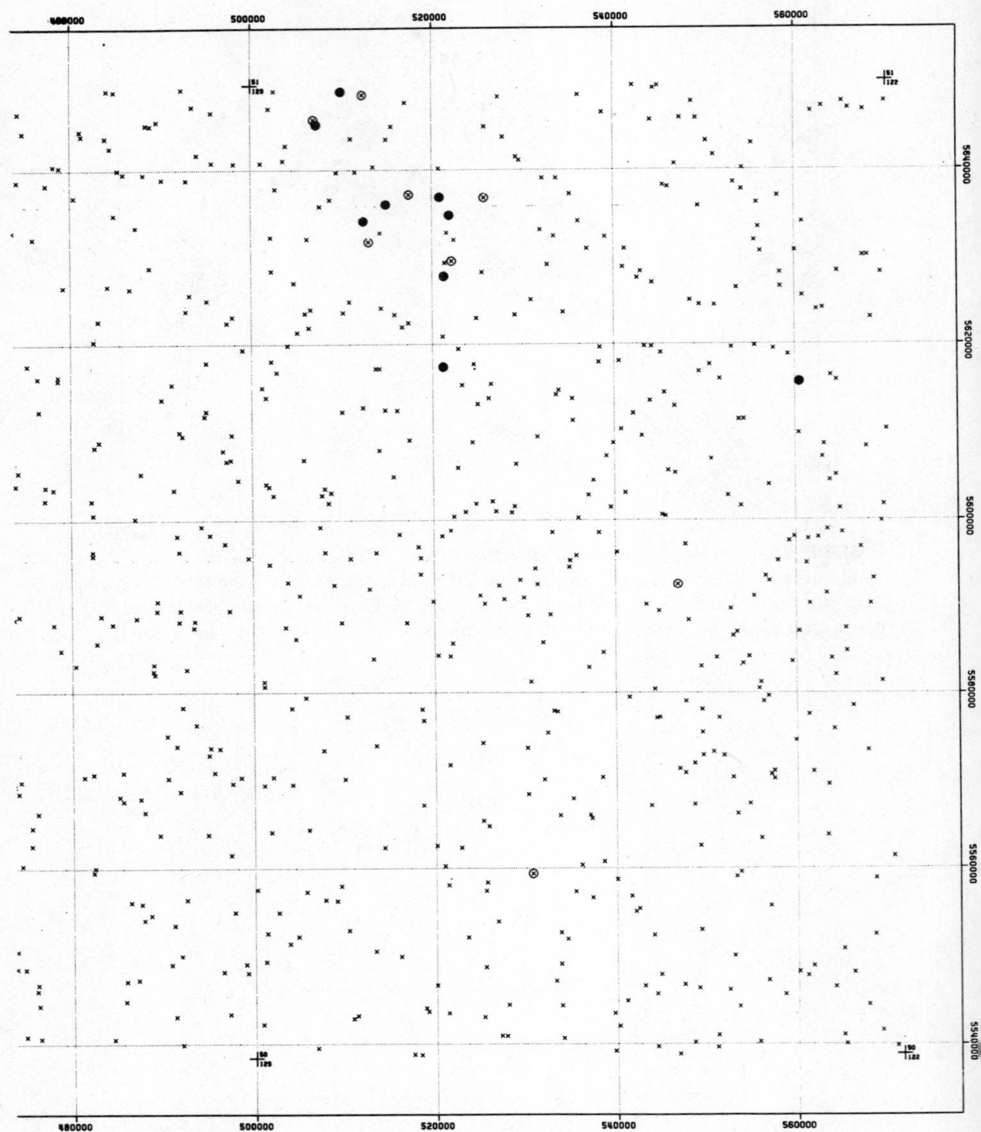

480000
500000
520000
540000
560000
5640000
5620000
5600000
5580000
5560000
5540000

FIGURE 8.18b.

to the average value, or each point can be individually scaled to give a continuous range of sizes.

We have already noted an additional advantage to using color or size coding: the shape of the symbol can then be used to define some other parameter. We might wish to distinguish the sign of the deviation from the trend by plotting positive differences as circles and negative differences as squares, for example. The symbol might also represent some completely independent variable. A geographer studying population trends could plot city populations and growth on the same map, using size for total population, and symbol shape (or color) for the annual percentage increase.

For some types of data, a direction and a magnitude are significant (i.e., the data value is a vector quantity). In this case, both quantities may be displayed simultaneously by using an arrow or a similar shape, and scaling its length according to magnitude. This is illustrated in Fig. 8.17, where wind patterns over the Northern Pacific are shown. This format is equally effective for displaying regional structure, or for searching for local anomalies.

An example of defining an anomaly from basic statistical analysis is shown in Fig. 8.18. The data are from a geologic exploration survey in British Columbia. The concentrations of arsenic and antimony are shown in a scatter plot (Fig. 8.18*a*), and the samples corresponding to the points inside the boxes are plotted on a map (Fig. 8.18*b*) as open or filled circles (all other points are indicated by a +). The main point to be drawn from this example is that the samples associated with the cluster on the scatter plot are also geographically related, which is a key fact to geologists interpreting the results of the survey. Once an anomalous situation has been identified, a location map should be an automatic next step, as it will immediately indicate if a localized source is involved, or whether a phenomenon with erratic spatial distribution had been detected. As we have noted before for other techniques, this procedure can be applied to a wide variety of data, and is not dependent on the particular type shown in the example.

CHAPTER 9

ENHANCED DISPLAY TECHNIQUES

The uses of computer graphics shown in the previous chapter dealt primarily with the value of computer plots to the data analyst. In practical use, the great majority of such plots are considered "working copies," and their aesthetic value is of secondary importance. Inevitably, a need arises to include some computer graphics in final reports, proposals, publications, or presentations. These uses demand a more artistic format, and may place unreasonable demands on a graphics system that was not designed to allow extensive embellishments to its normal output. In this chapter, we consider how standard computer plots can be enhanced, both for easier use by the analyst and for greater impact in presentations. The implications of using a computer for these improvements must also be considered, since additional software and hardware may be required for practical use.

COMPUTER PLOTTING AND DRAFTING

All of the graphical forms considered here were developed manually, and thus do not require the use of a computer. This applies equally to a working copy and a final presentation. Using computer graphics simply means that plots can be produced much more quickly than when drawn by a draftsman, cartographer, or commercial artist. There is one major limitation, however: it is virtually impossible to provide the same level of flexibility in an automated system, which reduces the ability to experiment with different display forms.

The answer to this dilemma lies in computer-aided design (CAD). In effect, CAD provides the best of both worlds with a powerful interactive computer graphics system at the disposal of people skilled in the graphic arts. The objective of these systems is to allow the user to "draw" with the computer, essentially as with pencil and paper. The drawing is displayed on a graphics terminal, and is structured so that individual segments can be easily moved, rotated, scaled, etc. This normally requires a fairly large minicomputer, a number of graphics terminals, digitizers, and plotters, and a vast library of software. Given the infinite variety of graphics displays, it is not surprising that the software is usually separated into packages designed for specific types of drawing. Examples include mechanical design for automobile and aircraft manufacturers, architecture, electronic component design, commercial charts and graphs, and mapping.

Despite the impressive achievements of CAD systems, they are not a panacea for all of the problems in displaying data. First of all, many organizations cannot justify the considerable cost of these systems (which can run anywhere from about $50,000 to millions of dollars, depending on the size of the computer and the number of "workstations" to be supported). A considerable level of training and experience is necessary: as noted above, the operators are normally people skilled in drafting or commercial drawing. This means that the data analyst does not use the system directly, but depends on others (exactly as with a manual drafting department). The productivity of the drafting staff is greatly increased, however, so that delays in getting final drafted plots should be reduced when a CAD system is installed.

When a CAD system is not available, existing plotting software may allow some CAD functions to be added to its normal output displays. There is often a tendency to carry this process too far, and to attempt to add extensive embellishments to a plot, without considering the efficiency of the method. It may be much easier to manually add explanatory text or a legend to a map than to define all of the parameters that a plotting program would need to do this task. This is especially true for "one-shot" jobs, where a special type of plot is needed for a single project, and is not likely to be called for again. It is not uncommon for people to feel that if the computer can take on some of the drafting work, it should be able to do all of it: that is, the computer is expected to create complete drawings to the same standards as an experienced draftsman. In other words, there is a bias against a combined approach of supplementing the computer output by manual methods. When carried to extremes, this feeling can be very counterproductive, since it discourages people from using the computer to do the routine, time-consuming tasks for which it is so well suited.

Over-extension of a plotting program can also consume a great deal of programming and development time. Software development is seldom an easy job, and graphics software is often exceptionally difficult. This is in part due to unavoidable delays in plotting test results (i.e., a printed listing may be obtained almost immediately, while a plot takes an hour or two). The great variety of plot forms is another major factor. A plotted graph requires many more parameters than a printed chart of the same data, for example, since the plot may have colors, dashed lines, variable character sizes, and many other features not possible with a printer. In planning to improve a plotting program, it is important to judge whether the effort involved in adding some new "bells and whistles" will ever be paid back. If the new options will not be heavily used, some of the potenial improvement in productivity is never realized, since the user may have to frequently relearn the new procedures.

IMPROVEMENTS TO A BASIC COMPUTER PLOT

While a data analyst is primarily interested in the characteristics of the data, a computer plot should contain a considerable amount of other information. The objective is to make the task of interpreting the results as simple as possible. As discussed in Chapter 5, this requires that the output contain as much supporting information as is practical, to minimize the need to search for information in other places. Most of the enhancements in this category can be produced nearly automatically, and thus need not be left for manual addition, and do not require the use of a CAD system.

1. Coordinate Reference Points

A major aim of plotting data on a map is to pinpoint the locations of structural features or anomalies. It is essential that a location on the map be immediately relatable to a location on the earth's surface (or within the frame of reference appropriate to the data). A common procedure is to post a number of reference points on the map with the coordinates annotated. These normally include the minimum and maximum X and Y values at the map borders, and points along the axes at a convenient increment.

When the map is relatively large, it is convenient to also post internal reference points, or to draw a grid of lines at regular increments. The coordinate grid is usually drawn in fine or dashed lines, or in a light color, so that it will not divert attention from the data plotted on the map. When locations are to be scaled from the map, the grid provides known coordinates within easy measuring distance of any point. On standard topographic maps, grid lines for the UTM coordinate system are drawn as a background at an increment equivalent to a few inches on the map (every 20,000 meters for a 1:250,000 scale map, for example).

More than one coordinate system may be important in reading a map. The borders of many maps are defined in terms of latitude and longitude, for example, while the locations are measured (and plotted) in an orthogonal projection like UTM. In such cases, two sets of reference lines or points are required, and extra care is needed to make them clearly distinguishable. This can be simply achieved by plotting one system as lines, and the other as discrete points (Fig. 9.1). In some areas, local survey systems are used for land registry, and must be shown if locations are measured in the local system, or if land ownership is a concern. Many parts of the United States and Canada are divided into sections (of one square mile) and townships (of 36 sections), which are clearly marked by survey posts, roadways, fences, or other objects. Such systems then provide reference points on the ground as well as on maps. The problem of clearly identifying the various coordinate

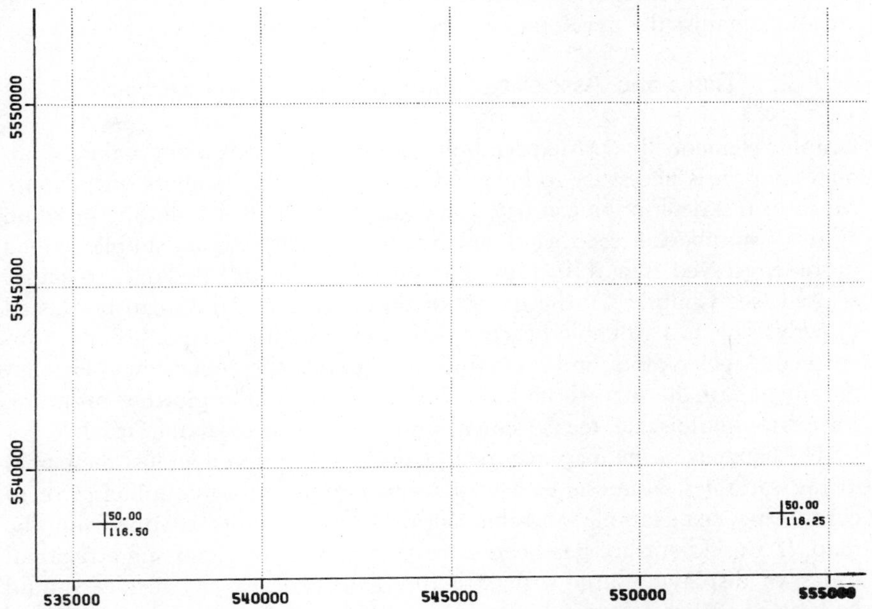

FIGURE 9.1 Plotting coordinate reference points. The fine grid lines mark intervals in the UTM coordinate system, while some latitude-longitude points are simply posted and annotated. This form can be created by a fairly simple plotting program. A more artistic form would require correspondingly more complex software.

systems can obviously become very difficult, especially if the maps must be plotted in black and white.

Sample collection in remote areas may involve a number of local coordinate systems established solely for that survey. The data can be plotted as a series of separate maps, or in composite form, provided that each local system can be converted to a common origin. Once again, it is desirable to show all the coordinate grids on the map for easy calibration to the original designations of the sample locations.

Plotting reference grids is a straightforward procedure, but can become a burden if the result is expected to look like a published map. The intended use of the map must be considered. A simple posting program can display any number of reference points, but will probably not include aesthetic options like an alignment of all the annotations with the grid orientation, or a rotation of latitude-longitude points to allow for curvature of the projected lines. Normal numeric annotations do not include commas, which can make for minor difficulties in reading large numbers (for example a UTM value of 5,600,000 might appear as 5600000). If a large number of maps require these enhancements, it might be worthwhile to add such embellishments to the program, although, as we saw earlier, the long-term benefits must be weighed against the development cost.

2. Titles and Associated Information

Graphic elements like posted symbols and contour lines do not make a complete map: it is necessary to have a description of the contents of the map. Much of this description can be created automatically if the plotting program allows a number of free-form lines of text to be entered and simply echoed in some reserved area of the plot. If an internally documented data structure is used (see Chapter 5), the names of the plotted variables can be posted directly. This is a valuable practice, since it eliminates the possibility of incorrectly labeled plots, and saves time in preparing the map. Other pertinent parameters of the map should also be generated by the plotting program, for example the scale, measurement units, and creation date (Fig. 9.2).

The contents of the map may require more description than just the names of the variables. Numeric transformations may have been applied prior to contouring, for example, and this fact must be known to anyone using the map. If a trend surface has been calculated (either for removing a regional trend, or displaying large scale structure), the order of the surface should be labeled. When locations of a specific subset of data are posted, the selection criteria must be identified. When several subsets are marked by different symbols, a legend is needed to define the various categories. In writing such information directly on a computer plot, we are once again following the general rule of making output as complete as possible. This not only makes the results easier to use, but helps ensure that they will retain their value. An inadequately labeled map is effectively worthless if the supporting information cannot be easily located when the map is retrieved from storage.

The ease of producing such detailed annotation is dependent on the nature of the plotting programs, and how they interact with other components of

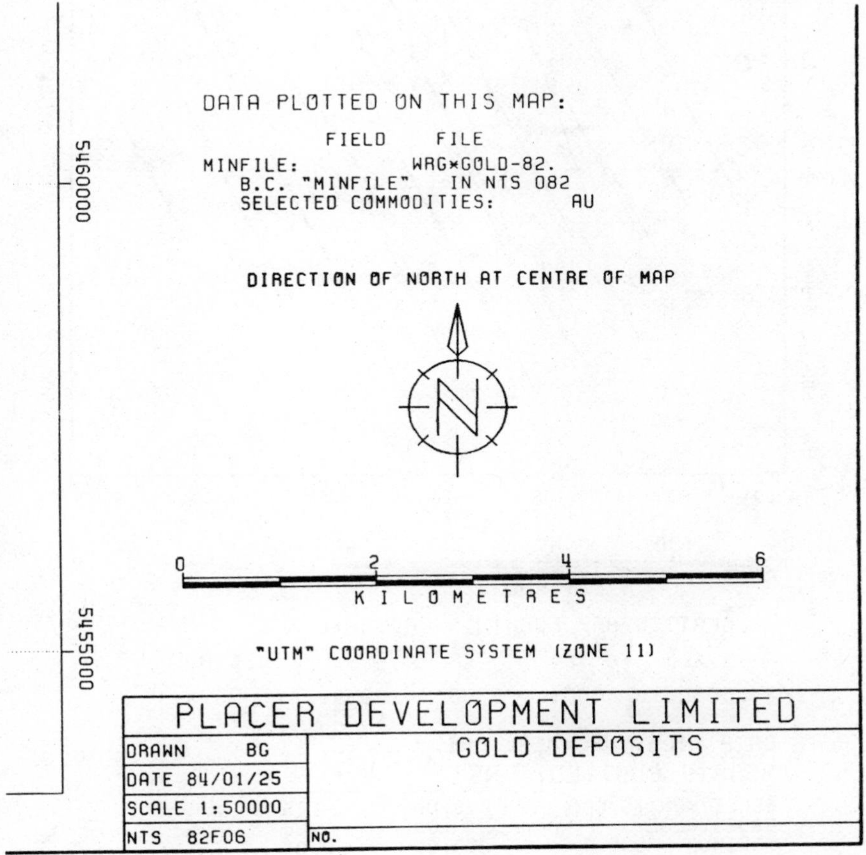

FIGURE 9.2a. Legends for a computer plot. (*a*) A standard legend with identification of important parameters such as scale, and basic information on the data displayed on the map; (*b*) a legend for a more complex display (a cross section), requiring more information, such as the location of the section, parameters to control the plotting of data, etc. This is the legend for the plot shown in Fig. 8.12. With the exception of the main title ("Gold Deposits" or "Test Cross-Section"), these legends are created automatically from the information supplied to produce the basic plot.

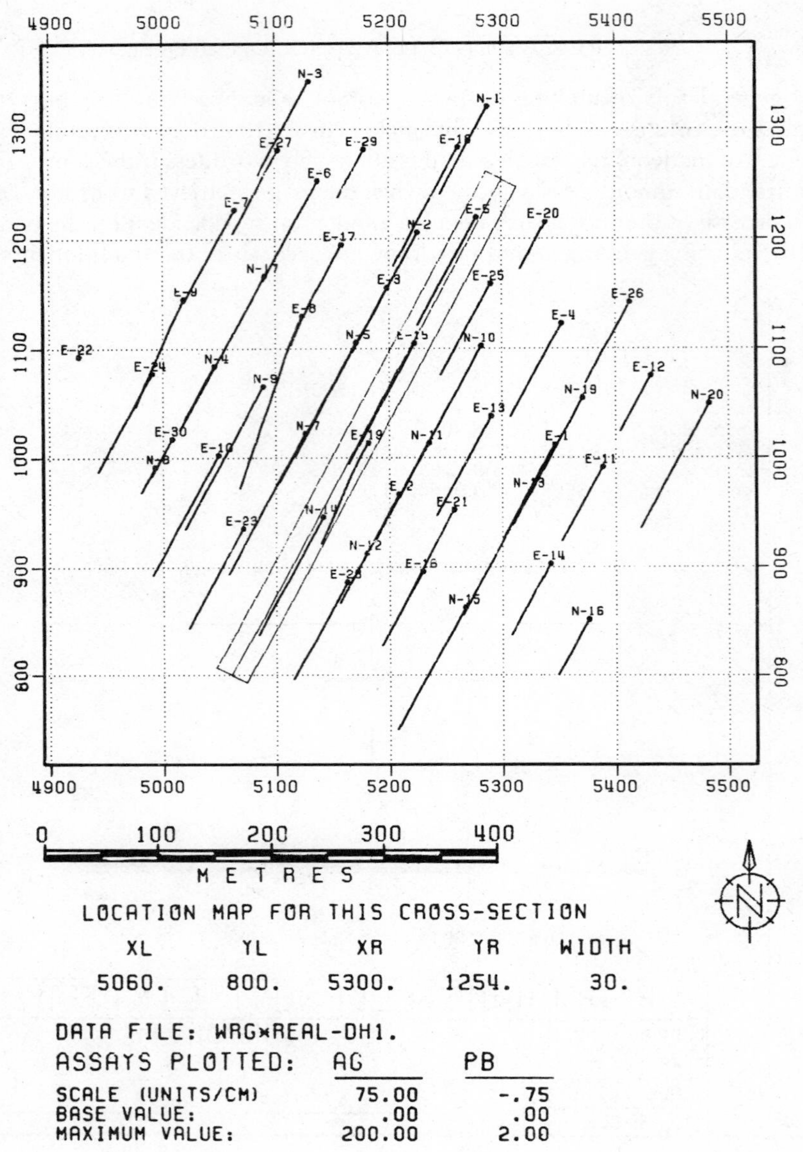

PLACER DEVELOPMENT LIMITED	
DRAWN BG	TEST CROSS-SECTION
DATE 84/01/26	
SCALE 1:1000	
	NO.

FIGURE 9.2b.

a complete data analysis system. It should be possible to automatically display the parameters set in the plotting program without requiring that this information be reentered in the text-labeling phase. Where operations such as smoothing and data selection are run as preliminary steps, this is more difficult, but is still manageable if the other programs involved write the pertinent information into data files used in plotting.

There are limits to the amount of annotation that can be accommodated, of course. First of all, physical size constraints may be involved, which will restrict the space available for extra text. Graphs are often plotted two or three to a page, for example, and maps may be drawn in standard sizes for ease of storage. Secondly, there is a trade-off between the visual impact of the plot, and the amount of text: excessive annotation may serve only to give a cluttered appearance. The use of the plot must also be considered: a working copy might show a complete parameter list, while only the critical values are labeled on the version included in a final report.

If an existing program is to be modified to allow more annotation, the consideration of development effort versus potential benefit arises again. The factors given above are also important: physical constraints and the need to retain a visually effective form may make this task very difficult.

HIGH-LEVEL GRAPHIC ENHANCEMENTS

1. Physical and Cultural Detail

Published maps usually contain many more embellishments than we have discussed in the previous section. Major geographic features (coastlines, rivers, and mountains) are outlined and named. Topography may be shown with contours or color shading. Depending on the intended use of the map, there may also be a great wealth of "cultural" detail, such as cities, towns, political boundaries, parks, airports, and numerous other features. A common road map serves as an excellent example. While not all of this information would be important in analyzing other data, some categories can be very helpful in reading a map. If a computer map combines some cultural detail with the analytical data, it may not be necessary to continually compare it to an existing "base map" for complete geographic orientation.

It is not a trivial matter to have a computer plot such a composite map. Although the basic elements for plotting a base map are the same as for plotting data (posted symbols and continuous lines), a program capable of drawing topographic and cultural detail must be considerably more complex. One basic problem is that the data files involved are massive, and require special access methods for efficient use. Since there may be many types of data, a good index system is needed so that desired features can be easily located for any given map. The variety of types also requires different procedures for selecting the subsets of data which lie within the map boundaries. Line data (such as rivers and coastlines) are stored as arrays of X-Y coordinates, and may require interpolation of intermediate points to terminate properly on the border. Point data may be sorted on the coordinate fields to avoid complete searches through large data files. If areal shading is used, the outline of each area is considered as a polygon. The polygons may overlap (an island within a lake, for example), so it also necessary to define a nesting order in order to set the proper colors for the map.

If the map is to be readable, the various features must be easily distinguished, so the plotting program must have extensive options for variable text size and form, different line weights and patterns, color shading or generation of areal patterns, and so on. In effect, it must provide all of the "tricks of the trade" developed by generations of cartographers. There must also be an efficient procedure for associating the graphic parameters with the corresponding data files, and an ability to quickly view the results to determine if the appearance of the map is acceptable.

Even if the plotting system has these attributes, it may not be possible to draw complete base maps: the necessary data may not be in computer form. Preparing computer files of physical and cultural data is a very time-consuming (and thus expensive) operation, and is practical only for large organizations that make heavy use of maps, and need to redraw maps to show new or revised information frequently. To convert an existing map to computer form, all of the lines must be retraced on a digitizer, point locations marked, and associated text typed. Automatic scanning devices can do much of this work, but are very expensive, and still require a highly skilled operator. Data verification and correction may be equally difficult. Closed features (e.g., lakes or islands) must be checked to ensure that the beginning and ending points match. Similarly, line features that join (political boundaries or road networks) must meet precisely, and not fall short or overshoot slightly. All point locations must be checked for coordinate accuracy, proper symbol codes, and correct associated text.

Many government agencies are now creating maps with computers, or are in the process of converting to automated methods. In addition to preparing files for their own uses, they offer data in computer form for public use at nominal cost. The United States Geological Survey now prepares all of its new topographic maps with computers, and can supply the corresponding "digital terrain models" on magnetic tapes to users. The process of creating such computer files will continue for many years, and should eventually result in widespread use of completely computerized mapping. At present, however, the usual situation is that much of the essential data is not in computer form, and so it is necessary to combine computer maps with existing drawings.

As this brief outline indicates, a complete mapping system is very complex, and requires a number of special characteristics. This is an area where a CAD system is more appropriate than a general purpose computer, since the data structures, operating procedures, and available programs can all be tailored for cartographic applications. A map is visualized as number of separate "overlays" that can be combined in a variety of ways to create different maps. For example, the basic map border and grid might be one segment, with coastlines on a second segment, topographic contours on a third, and other physical and cultural features on other segments. Each segment can be independently displayed and modified, which simplifies the task of entering new types of data. Any combination of segments may be selected; for example, coastlines, major rivers, and lakes might be used as the base for a sample location map.

An overlay procedure can also be used with existing maps. Instead of combining segments from a computer file, several originals are attached together for a composite print. All maps must be at the same scale, of course, and generally must be on a translucent medium (depending on the copying process). Compared to the cost of digitizing a large number of base maps, this process can provide a practical (and affordable) way of combining new and existing data. This is obviously not as flexible a process as a fully computerized procedure, since each hard copy will probably correspond to a number of segments in a CAD file. The maps must be drawn on the scale of the existing copies, and cannot be easily redrawn on any other scale. This may be a considerable inconvenience, but it is not necessarily a prohibitive problem, since it is a common practice to use maps of standard size and scale (as a direct result of the time needed for manual drawing). The quality of the resulting map may be diminished in copying, especially if several originals must be combined.

Despite these problems, it is important to consider complementing computer plots with manual methods as an alternative to expensive computer upgrades. As noted earlier, it is easy to fall into the "computer must do it all" trap, and thus to either avoid using the computer entirely, or to spend more money on improving the system than can ever be recovered in increased productivity.

2. Prevention of Overposting

The problem of overposting—having plotted symbols and text overlap—was outlined in Chapter 7. It is an almost unavoidable situation when plotting data with variable spatial density. As more and more different types of data are included on the map, the problem becomes worse. Overpostings are one of the most visible differences between computer maps and manual maps, and they often create a bias against computer maps, since the cluttered appearance degrades the visual appeal.

A cartographer is free to move textual information to convenient open spaces, since the complete map is visible as each item is drawn. If necessary, letter size and orientation can also be adjusted on an individual point. In principle, a computer program could perform the same task, although in practice this is very difficult, and no completely general algorithms have yet been developed.

The key point is the ability to "see" the complete drawing. Most plotting programs plot different sets of data independently, that is, with no knowledge of other data that will appear on the same map. In plotting a single contour line, labels are usually placed at fixed intervals along the line, and may well overplot on the text associated with a posted point. Posting programs generally plot all annotations at the same angle, or at a fixed orientation to a survey line. Unless a specific test is made on the distance to adjacent points, this can cause overlaps of even points in the same file, let alone independent data which have already been placed on the map.

If a plotting program is to avoid overposting, it must maintain a record of all previously plotted data, so that the "open" areas on the plot are known for each new item. If the standard text position has already been filled, a series of alternate locations are tested until an open space is found. This may well require plotting a tag line to attach the text to the proper location. Ultimately the map may become so dense that some points cannot be labeled: in this case, a listing of such points is created, to be used for later manual insertion of the missing text.

To maintain such a record, the plot area is conceptually divided into many small cells. An internal array in the plotting program can then be used to mark cells containing plotted information. This is not as simple as it sounds, since the cells must be very small to allow for fine detail, which means that the plot array must be very large. The amount of computer "memory" available to any program is limited (to an amount dependent on the particular machine), which often means the cells must be larger than desired. The result is that the program will find some overpostings that are more apparent than real, and encounter the "filled map" situation sooner. Another problem is the algorithm for locating open space, which may be very complex, and so add significantly to the time required to produce the plot. It may involve testing different character sizes and orientations as well as simply testing adjacent cells, to minimize the distance between the annotation and the true location. As with the cell size, there is a trade-off between the ability to correct the overpostings, and the practicality of developing and using the program.

Once again we must look to a CAD system to come to the rescue. The plotting program may perform some overpost checks (perhaps on each segment, and with a relatively coarse grid), but will plot all the data. The CAD operator then displays the map on a terminal, and uses the editing features of the system to select the conflicting annotations and move them as required to eliminate confusion. The first step in this procedure is to check for overpostings within each segment, and make any required corrections. The segments to be combined in the final map are then displayed, to locate overpostings of one segment on another (e.g., the name of a city written on top of a river or some other physical feature). The first stage verifies the basic data, while the second is a custom step that must be repeated for each new map.

3. Using a CAD System with Other Computer Graphics

As we have seen, the thornier problems of plotting complex maps (and other types of displays) are best solved using the sophisticated technology and skilled personnel of a CAD system. In many computer centers, numerous computer plots are created on a central computer system which may not be directly linked to the CAD computer. It is necessary to develop such a link if a CAD system is to effectively supplement other graphics facilities.

This is by no means a straightforward operation, since it usually involves a variety of hardware and software from different sources. To establish efficient communication between computers, it is necessary to develop special software for each machine. The communications program must be aware of the codes and control sequences in both systems, so that it can apply an error-checking algorithm to ensure that the data are not altered in transit. Since the exact form of the program is dependent on the particular computers, each combination of machines obviously needs unique software (although many basic features may be common to a number of systems).

To take full advantage of a CAD system, other plotting programs must be at least partly structured in a similar style. If the plot transferred to the CAD computer cannot be split into a number of segments for different classes of data, much of the editing power is lost. In a CAD system, individual segments are internally structured as well, so that small elements of the plot can be corrected easily. For example, the location symbol and name of a town may be treated as an element, so that the text can be reoriented with a single command. If each letter of the name was generated separately, several commands might be needed to do the same chore.

A plotting program should also account for the "intelligence" of the CAD system, and not reduce the plot file to single vectors. This is often not the case, especially if the program is normally used with a simple plotter. The plot instructions stored in the program's output file will then consist of a large series of vectors, with no internal ordering or identifiers. Each letter of text will be in the form of perhaps eight to ten vectors, and be undistinguishable from a long array of points used to draw a contour line, for example. Once again, such an unstructured form negates much of the power of the CAD system, since it may be very difficult to selectively adjust the positions of conflicting text.

The process of using a CAD system to enhance conventional computer graphics may then require an extensive development effort, both in communications and the existing plotting software. Plotting programs are often acquired commercially, and do not necessarily legally entitle the user to make modifications (or include the "source code" needed to make this possible). As a result, some organizations will have no choice but to use the programs in their current form. Trial projects to judge the potential benefits are always needed, but especially in this situation, since the performance of the CAD system on its own is not an accurate measure of how well it can manipulate externally generated plots.

Communication between a central computer and a CAD system is not a one-way street. It may often be desirable to return edited plot files to the main computer in order to correct data files or create plots on devices not directly linked to the CAD system. In other words, a complete "network" should be established, so that the facilities of both systems can be used interchangeably. A more elaborate communications procedure is obviously required. Magnetic tapes are often used to move plots from a central computer to the CAD system: a more automatic method is needed for the frequent bi-directional transfers of a true network. As always, the volume of work and expected improvement in efficiency are the key factors in deciding whether to install such a complex facility.

PART III

INTRODUCTION TO ADVANCED ANALYSIS METHODS

In addition to the basic techniques for statistical analysis and data display, many special techniques have been developed to handle specific types of data. This section gives a brief review of some of these. Many of the procedures discussed in Parts I and II can be applied to aid in the interpretation of these calculations.

CHAPTER 10. ADVANCED STATISTICAL METHODS

A. Geostatistics

Many problems in determining spatial structure are handled with empirical methods of estimating data values. These problems can be treated more rigorously by employing the principles of geostatistics. The key point is that the variability of a given parameter can be considered as a function of the spatial coordinates by constructing variograms. In estimating average values, or interpolating to create a contour map, the variogram is employed to control the contributions of nearby data to the estimated values. Computer graphics can be a great help, in displaying variograms, plotting estimated surfaces, displaying errors, etc.

B. Multivariate Data Classification

There are a number of powerful statistical methods available to handle cases where several variables are to be considered concurrently. Examples include factor analysis, multiple regression, and discriminant analysis. Proper use demands flexible routines for selecting subsets of data, and efficient means for displaying the results. Special graphical techniques can also be applied to multivariate problems.

CHAPTER 11. PROCEDURES FOR ARRAY-ORIENTED DATA

This chapter is an introduction to some special types of data analysis. Some very powerful computer methods have been developed for data which can be treated as arrays, for example, time series data and spectral data from satellites. Computer graphics are essential in these studies because of the enormous volumes of data involved. In some cases, special "vector" computers are necessary to make the extensive calculations practical.

CHAPTER 12. PHYSICAL MODELS AND DATA INTERPRETATION

The final chapter deals with the interpretation stage which often follows analysis (or perhaps could be considered the final step in analysis). Here, knowledge of physical processes is incorporated in a model of the phenomenon. The aim of interpretation is to find the model that best fits the observations, an aim which may be achieved by comparing the predicted response of the model to the data (the "direct" problem), or computing the model parameters from the data (the "inverse" problem).

To properly illustrate the uses of modeling, a number of examples should be studied. Once again, computer graphics are an essential aid to understanding the results.

CHAPTER 10

ADVANCED STATISTICAL METHODS

The data analysis and display procedures discussed in Parts I and II use only basic statistics, and do not involve complex operations on the data. These procedures are suitable for many types of data, and do not require a background in higher mathematics for proper understanding. In a number of special situations, however, more complex statistical methods are required to gain complete information from a set of data. In this chapter, we briefly examine some of these methods. Mathematical details are omitted, as the main concerns are the general concepts, and the practical problems involved. The References section contains a summary of useful books for those looking for a more thorough introduction.

GEOSTATISTICS

Much of the discussion in Part II dealt with spatial data and the use of maps for investigating spatial relationships. Many of the techniques are empirical, and leave the judgment of the significance of the data largely to the analyst. One of the great advances in the analysis of spatial data over the past two decades is "geostatistics," which provides rigorous statistical procedures for spatial data. In this section, the basic principles of geostatistics are outlined, and some practical aspects of computer implementation are considered.

I. Applications of Geostatistics

Before we discuss the computational procedures of geostatistics, a brief review of its applications will help to explain why these techniques were developed in the first place. In essence, geostatistics is an estimation method for spatial data, similar to the gridding procedures often used for drawing contour maps (see Chapter 7). The main distinction from the usual estimation methods is that a statistical measure of accuracy (or expected error) is produced in addition to the estimated value. The computational algorithm is based on a standard least-squares approach, so the computed value is optimum, in the sense that the total error is minimized.

Geostatistics may then be used whenever data values from randomly located samples must be interpolated to other positions. This often means calculating values on a regular grid as a preliminary to drawing a contour map. In this case, a "confidence" map can also be drawn, by contouring the estimated error at each grid point. In other cases, estimated values at other random locations may be required: for example, rainfall is measured at fixed meteorological stations, but may be estimated for nearby population centers. This type of calculation is also easily achieved by geostatistics.

These examples are cases of "point" estimation: the computed value represents the best guess of the data value at a single location. A common variation is to compute a single value representing the average data value within a predefined area, usually a rectangular or square grid cell. In this situation, the error estimates provided by geostatistics may be of great importance, especially if the implied range of values is large. Using the error estimates, decisions can be based on standard statistical methods, rather than on subjective judgments that rely on past experience.

To illustrate this point, consider the problem of deciding whether a mineral deposit can be profitably mined. There are many factors in this decision, of course, but the fundamental question is "how much ore is there?". This simple question seldom has a simple answer, since the answer must be based on a very tiny fraction of the ore-body (perhaps a few hundred kilograms of rock samples drilled from various places in a volume of rock weighing hundreds of millions of tonnes). To evaluate the risk, it is necessary to estimate the possible upper and lower bounds on the average "grade" of the ore. As we might expect, this range might be very large, leaving a large uncertainty in as to whether the amount of ore actually present is greater than the economic "cutoff" value. As a result, the best possible estimation technique must be applied.

Such problems in mining were a large factor in the original development of geostatistics, and are still the most common area of application. The technique is not restricted to geological problems, of course, and can be used in a variety of other fields. In forest ecology, for example, the average density of certain species of plants or animals can be calculated from actual counts taken in small sub-areas. Meteorological data analysis involves many types of measurements at point locations, while a computer program for prediction requires averaged values in a three-dimensional grid. Geostatistics have also been applied in oceanography (e.g., for accurate estimation of sea-floor topography), oil production (e.g., to estimate reserves in an oil field), and a number of other fields.

2. Regionalized Variables and the Variogram

A basic assumption in drawing a contour map, or indeed in any procedure involving interpolation, is that the variable in question is continuous. In other words, it is assumed that readings taken close to each other will tend to have similar values, and that in the limit (when the points are essentially coincident), the values are the same. As in grid interpolation, this means that the closest samples are given a dominant role in estimation, and very distant samples are not even considered.

Variables that behave in this fashion are called "regionalized variables," to denote the tendency for similar behavior to persist over a spatial region. The basic principles and terminology of the study of regionalized variables were developed by Georges Matheron and his associates in France during the 1960s. Matheron is also responsible for the term "geostatistics," and for establishing the first formal research organization in the field (at Fountainbleu in 1968).

The essence of the theory of regionalized variables is that the statistical variations between samples are related to the distance separating them. The mathematical formulation does not invoke completely new procedures, but simply allows classical measures like standard deviation to be expressed as functions of the separation.

A number of quantitative measures can be used to express the variations between samples. All begin by simply computing the difference in data values between two samples, and saving this new variable along with the associated separation distance. Statistical values like mean difference or the variance of differences are calculated for groups of samples with the same separation. The result is a series of points describing the variation as a function of the distance.

a. The Variogram

The primary tool for examining the spatial characteristics of data is the "variogram," shown in Fig. 10.1. This is a standard two-dimensional graph, where the horizontal axis represents the distance between pairs of samples, and the vertical axis the variance of the difference in data values for all samples having a particular separation distance. The expected tendency for

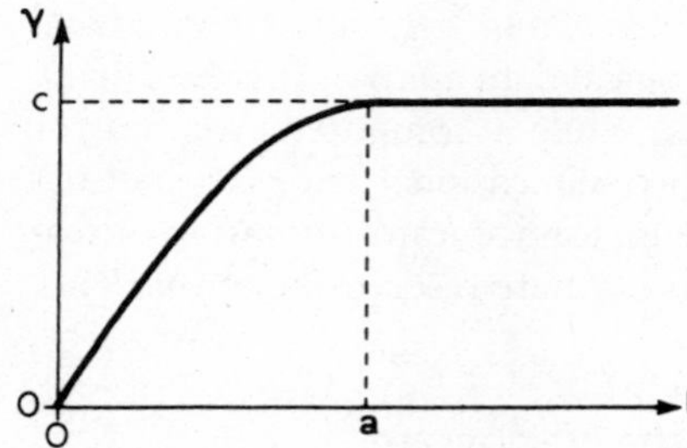

FIGURE 10.1. The variogram. The horizontal axis represents the distance between pairs of samples, and the vertical axis is the variance for each group of samples with the same separation distance. (Reproduced from *Practical Geostatistics,* by Isobel Clark, copyright Applied Science Publishers, 1979, by permission of Elsevier Applied Science Publishers Ltd.)

adjacent samples to have similar values then appears as a curve which is near zero on the left, and increases to the right (as the separation distance gets larger). Note that the curve may not terminate at zero if the samples have random variations in addition to a smoothly varying spatial pattern. This is called the "nugget" effect, after the erratic distribution of nuggets of gold, which cannot be predicted from adjacent samples.

For mathematical convenience, the graph usually shows half the variance on the Y axis (the factor of two simplifies many equations in the estimation process). To be precise, the display should be called a "semivariogram," although the term variogram is often applied. The form of the graph does not change, of course, but it is important to know whether a true variogram or semivariogram was used when applying the variogram parameters. For simplicity, the term "variogram" is used thoughout this chapter.

Other statistical measures besides the variance can be plotted in the same fashion. The choice of the particular function used to measure variability is somewhat arbitrary, depending on the preference of the analyst, past experience, and other subjective factors. Strictly speaking, the term "variogram" should not be applied to measures other than the variance, although the term is often used in other contexts. Geostatistical estimation employs the parameters of the variogram, so each different statistic requires its own algorithm for computing the estimated values.

One fairly common alternate to the standard variogram is the "relative variogram," where the variance is divided by the square of the mean value of the differences. This is often used where there are large regional trends that may result in both the mean and the variance having larger values in certain regions (called the "proportional effect"). Consider for example a set of topographic data from an area including both plains and mountains. The relative variogram is an analog to the coefficient of variation (standard deviation divided by the mean), sometimes used for skewed distributions.

b. Experimental and Model Variograms

Like any statistical measure, a variogram is only an estimate of the true characteristics of the data. The graph derived from the data is thus called an "experimental" variogram, to distinguish it from a theoretical model. As we will see later, certain types of models, with a few basic parameters, are used in estimations, rather than the experimental variogram itself. The most common type of model is shown in Fig. 10.1. Here the variance at zero distance may be zero, or the data may exhibit a nugget effect. The variance increases up to a distance called the "range" (marked "a" in the graph) after which it is constant. This is considered as a range of influence (i.e., the maximum distance between samples for which data values are likely to be influenced by other samples). The "sill" (marked "c") is the level of variance beyond the range. Within the range, the variance is related to distance by a cubic function (which is why this is called the "spherical" model). Alternately, an exponential function can be used (the "exponential" model). Other formulae have also been used on occasion, some without a sill, but a discussion of their relative merits is beyond the scope of this introduction.

Computing the points on an experimental variogram is not a difficult task, although it can be very time consuming. The basic procedure is to locate all pairs of samples that have the same separation distance, and then to calculate the variance of the associated data values. In practice, a small range of distances is considered acceptable, so that enough pairs can be selected for the calculation to be statistically significant. This procedure is repeated many times to generate a series of values for a complete range of distances. It is obviously not practical to do this manually, and even with a computer it is important to have an efficient sorting and selection algorithm to quickly find all pairs of samples for each group.

Fitting a model to the experimental variogram is a prerequisite for estimation. In practice, there is a considerable degree of subjectivity to this operation, and the previous experience of the analyst is often brought into play. A model curve is plotted over the experimental points, either manually or with a computer plotting routine, for visual inspection (Fig. 10.2). In principle, this could be defined as a least-squares procedure, although the degree of scatter is often large, and it may be necessary to "weight" the points according to the number of sample pairs associated with them. A number of different models can be tried, to see the effect of changing the basic parameters. Different types of models (e.g., spherical and exponential) might also be tested.

In addition to calculating the experimental points, the computer is also of great value in plotting the results in graphical form. The principles of earlier chapters should be considered in this application as well. To interpret a variogram properly, it is important to know the number of pairs of samples involved, a value which can be shown as a second curve on the graph. Other statistical parameters might also be displayed: for example, confidence limits on the estimated variances. Interactive computer graphics can also be very useful in model fitting, if a program is designed to overplot a number of

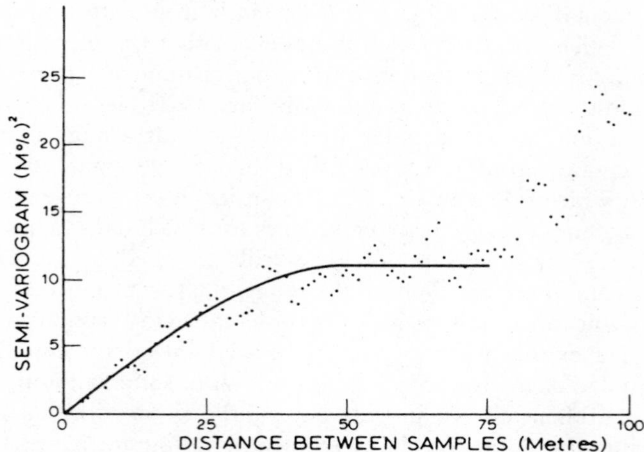

FIGURE 10.2. Fitting a model to an experimental variogram. (Reproduced from *Practical Geostatistics,* by Isobel Clark, copyright Appplied Science Publishers, 1979, by permission of Elsevier Applied Science Publishers Ltd.)

model curves on the experimental points for immediate evaluation by the analyst.

c. Anistropic Data

If the spatial behavior of data is not isotropic (i.e., if there are significant directional trends) it will be necessary to construct a number of variograms in different directions. In selecting the sample pairs, the alignment of the samples must be tested to see if it lies in the allowed direction. For example, all pairs which line up within 30 degrees of a north–south line might be retained for one variogram. To check for all possible trends, a complete range of variograms would be plotted, each representing an angular range of perhaps 30 or 45 degrees.

In some situations, variograms are computed for different sub-areas of the total region which are suspected of showing different characteristics. For example, counts of insect population might be analyzed separately in areas of forest and grassland. The samples must then be isolated into geographic regions by testing their locations against the appropriate boundaries.

When the coordinate system is three-dimensional, the number of variograms that might be required can quickly become unmanageable, since a complete test involves subdividing the volume of a sphere, not just the area of a circle. This type of analysis is often necessary in mining, oil production, atmospheric modeling, and other areas. Instead of a complete three-dimensional analysis, the region is sometimes divided into a number of layers which can be treated in two dimensions. Alternately, a selected number of variograms may be used to test for anistropy if preferred orientations can be established. A mineral deposit may be confined to veins of known extent, in which case the analysis can be restricted to samples within the veins.

3. Estimation Using a Variogram Model (Kriging)

Computing a series of variograms and deriving a model from them is not usually an end in itself, of course. The objective of such studies is to determine the characteristics of the data in a statistically optimum fashion (i.e., to obtain the best estimates possible with the available samples).

a. Global Averages

One common application is to estimate the average value of the variable in question throughout the sampled area. A simple calculation of the mean may be very inaccurate because of spatial trends, erratic distribution of samples, and other such complications of the real world. The variogram model may be combined with the observed frequency distribution of the data to make an optimum estimation.

Global averages are used as a measure of the cumulative sum of the variable, so it is necessary to adjust the data to account for differences in areal distribution. Each sample can be considered to represent a certain area (or volume); the desired sum is a product of data value and area (or volume). For example, population densities measured in local regions are multiplied by the total area to estimate the total number of individuals in the area. To remove the effects of variations in region size, the data are "declustered." This process is usually a matter of averaging within blocks of uniform size, or weighting data values according to local sample density prior to computing a histogram.

The variogram model is used to compute an "estimation variance" for the global average. The estimation variance is a function of the geometry of the blocks, the variogram parameters, and the spatial distribution of samples. As a result, it is possible to test the gain in accuracy that might be obtained by varying any of these without actually repeating the complete calculations. For example, new sampling patterns can be evaluated to determine which will give the greatest improvement in accuracy. Similarly, the effect of using a number of smaller blocks instead of one large one can be measured.

b. Kriging

To examine detailed characteristics of the data, we must go beyond gross measures, and estimate many local values. In practice, this usually involves computing values on a regular grid, which can then be used for other calculations or graphic display. As noted in Chapter 7, there are many ways of computing grid values from the original data: the advantage of using a geostatistical approach is that the computed values will be optimum, in the sense that the error in estimation will be minimized. The acronym BLUE (Best Linear Unbiased Estimation) is sometimes used to characterize this method.

Grid estimation using variograms is called "kriging," after D.G. Krige, a South African mining geologist who first developed the technique in the 1950s. As in most empirical gridding algorithms, the first step is to select a number of samples in the vicinity of the grid point. The range of the variogram model can be used to set a maximum selection distance, and thus reduce the amount of time involved in this step. The actual calculation of the grid value is a weighted average of the individual data values; again the technique resembles conventional methods. The difference lies in the method used to set the weights: instead of a simple function of distance, the weights are chosen to minimize the estimation variance for the grid point.

Estimation variance can be expressed as a function of the variogram model, the weights for each sample, and the geometry of the samples relative to the grid location. Considering the weights as unknowns, a series of equations can be defined following standard methods for least-squares minimization. The weights are then obtained by solving the set of equations by matrix manipulation. The form of the equation may vary, depending on whether the grid values represent "point" estimates, or averages for the complete cell. The kriging calculations are the same in either event.

It is obvious that the amount of calculation required in kriging is much greater than for conventional algorithms, since a matrix equation must be defined and solved for every grid point. The size of the matrix depends on the number of samples used in estimation, which is another reason for selecting only a limited set of samples. There is a tradeoff of computer time against the reliability of the estimate, of course, as sufficient points must be retained to keep the estimation error within acceptable limits. With the ever-increasing power of computer hardware, and efficient routines for data selection and matrix manipulation, these are not insurmountable problems, but are nevertheless an important consideration when a large number of grid values are involved.

In addition to providing optimum estimated values, the kriging approach can apply an error estimate for each point (by simply taking the square root of the estimation variance). The estimated errors may be very important in using the grid values. For example, in producing a bathymetric map for navigation purposes, it is essential to know the possible error in water depths, so that ships can safely choose proper channels. In this case, the contours can be drawn to show the possible minimum depth, rather than the probable depth, by subtracting two or three standard deviations from the estimated value.

The accuracy of the kriged values can also be estimated by calculating values directly at the sample locations, for comparison to actual data values. The procedure is the same as before, except that instead of computing values at an array of grid points, the known sample locations are used. The known data value for each point is excluded in kriging that point. The difference between the kriged and original value is then treated as a direct measurement of the estimation error. This approach is especially useful when the variogram shows a large nugget effect, as it can quickly detect samples with large differences from adjacent values.

4. Applications of Computer Graphics

Like most other statistical computer methods, geostatistics can produce a vast amount of output, which cannot easily be assimilated by the analyst. This is an ideal situation for computer graphics, and not surprisingly, graphic displays are an integral part of most geostatistics programs.

As noted earlier, many variograms may be required to adequately define the spatial behavior of the data. A program for plotting variograms should be able to display many of them together for easy visual examination. It might also provide an overplot of a variogram model, or an "average" variogram (constructed from all samples) to emphasize differences from the norm. The usual rule of having complete annotation must be considered as well. In this case, the nature of the different variograms must be noted (e.g., taken in specific directions, or limited to a particular type of sample). The graph should also show the number of contributing points, and basic statistical parameters, which are often useful in judging the significance of individual variograms which are "noisier" than the rest.

When fitting a model to a variogram, an interactive graphics approach is desirable. This would be a separate program from the variogram calculation, which would simply read the experimental variogram from a data file, rather than computing it directly. The model parameters would be entered at a terminal, and the model curve plotted over the experimental points. The analyst would adjust the parameters until an acceptable fit was achieved.

In the estimation phase, a general-purpose contouring and map posting program can be used to display the results. Since an error estimate is available for each grid point, an error map can be produced to supplement the basic contour map (Fig. 10.3). This might be in the form of another contour map, a second set of contour lines overplotted on the first (in different colors or line patterns), a symbolic posting at the grid point, or any of the other procedures used for examining two spatial variables (see Chapter 8).

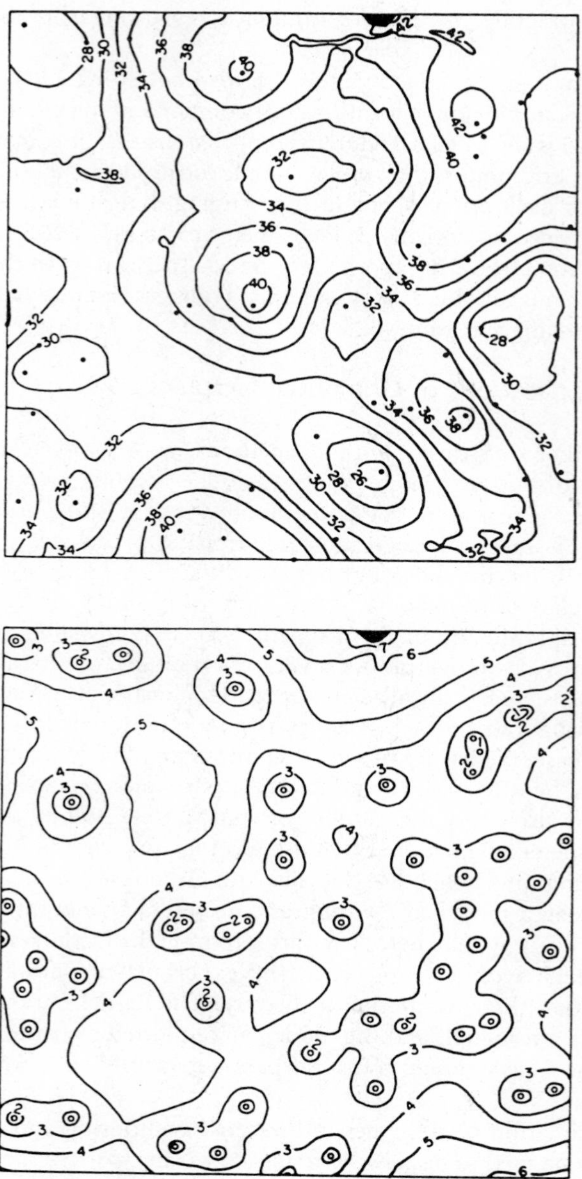

FIGURE 10.3. Display of kriging error estimates. The top map represents the kriged data values, while the bottom map is the estimated error (used as a "confidence" map). (Reproduced from *Practical Geostatistics,* by Isobel Clark, copyright Applied Science Publishers, 1979, by permission of Elsevier Applied Science Publishers Ltd.)

MULTIVARIATE DATA ANALYSIS

As we saw in Chapter 4, correlation matrices and scatter plots can be used to study data with many variables. They do not provide a direct measure of the relationships between a number of variables, however. When this type of analysis is required, more advanced statistical methods must be employed. Such procedures will not be considered in great detail in this book, as the applications tend to be specialized, and a good knowledge of the mathematical procedures is necessary for proper use. The book by P.M. Mather in the References is an excellent survey of the field, containing the essential theory, practical examples, and valuable suggestions (and programs) for implementation on a computer. A brief outline of the more common methods follows.

1. Multiple Regression

In many cases, analysis attempts to predict the value of a particular variable from the other available data. "Multiple regression" is an extension of the procedure for fitting a straight line to two variables. In this case, the equation of the line includes coefficients for a number of variables:

$$z1_n = a + bz_1 + cz_2 + dz_3 + \cdots \qquad 10.1$$

where a, b, c, are the coefficients, and $z_1, z_2, \ldots, z_n$ are the variables. The estimated value for z_n is $z1_n$. The solution is obtained as before, by requiring the sum of squares $(z_n\text{-}z1_n)**2$ to be a minimum, when all samples are considered.

A number of different strategies can be employed in selecting variables to use in the equation. Note that z_n is simply chosen as the variable to be predicted. The other z values might be defined as all available numeric fields, but in many cases this will yield an unwieldy (and possibly uninterpretable) result. The analyst may specify the choice arbitrarily, or use statistical methods to select the other variables which have a significant influence on z_n. The procedure known as "stepwise" regression attempts to do this automatically. It may proceed "forward" by first using only one independent variable (that which has the highest correlation coefficient), or "backward" by initially using all variables. After the solution, the differences of z_n from $z1_n$ are used to select additional variables to include in the equation (or to reject from the solution in the backward case). The process continues until a statistical significance test indicates that all pertinent variables are included in the regression equation.

2. Principal Components and Factor Analysis

Any problem involving N different variables may be considered as an N-dimensional problem, where each variable is a coordinate in an N-dimensional space. Since the variables may be related, it may be possible to define the data in terms of an M-dimensional space, where M is less than N. A set of independent (orthogonal) coordinate axes may be determined by computing the "principal components" of the data. These orthogonal variables are linear combinations of the original variables, obtained by eigenvalue analysis of the correlation matrix. There are N eigenvalues, so, to reduce the number of axes, a significance test is applied. For example, we might wish to have 95 percent of the variance explained by the principal components. By proceeding through the eigenvalues in inverse size order, we can quickly find how many of the values are required to give the desired level of significance.

Eigenvalue analysis involves the solution of matrix equations, so appropriate computer programs must be available to implement these techniques. Matrix methods are used in many other areas, so this is usually not a problem in a computer center accustomed to scientific data analysis. Mather's book contains a number of *FORTRAN* programs for the basic matrix manipulations, as well as for the analytical procedures.

Factor analysis has a similar aim: to reduce the number of variables needed to adequately describe the relationships between them. The computational procedure involves eigenvalue analysis as well, and produces a set of "factors" which are functions of the variables. For each sample, factor "scores" are then calculated, to show the relative contribution of each factor to the observed data for that sample.

There are two different methods of application. In R-mode analysis, the factors represent combinations of the variables, derived from the correlation matrix. In Q-mode analysis, the approach is to look for groups of samples that are related: this requires the roles of observed values and samples to be reversed, with the samples treated as "variables," and different data fields treated as observations. In this case, a "similarity matrix" is used in the eigenvalue analysis. Note that this is often more difficult to implement, simply because of the size of the matrices. If we have a set of data containing 200 samples with 10 variables, the R-mode solution involves inverting a 10 by 10 correlation matrix. The Q-mode solution requires the inverse of a 200 by 200 similarity matrix, which demands that much more computer memory be available for the matrix solution.

3. Classification Methods

Q-mode factor analysis can be considered as one of a number of methods for classifying multivariate data. The aim is to subdivide the available samples into a relatively small number of groups, based on the statistical behavior of the different variables. In effect, this is the multivariate equivalent of the problem of identifying multiple populations in the analysis of one or two variables. These techniques are employed when there are no additional variables that can be used for a separation. There is no guarantee of success, however, and the statistical parameters of the particular method must be examined to evaluate the significance of the result.

A variety of "cluster analysis" methods have been proposed for this type of problem. The key element of the process is the measure of similarity between samples. A number of algorithms have been developed for specific applications. Once again, matrix solutions are required, along with significance tests to limit the number of groups.

"Discriminant analysis" carries the process one step further. Clustering techniques are used to find groups of samples, whose common characteristics are not predefined. With discriminant analysis, we define groups of samples believed to have common properties, and compute a discriminant function for each group, based on the statistical behavior of the variables. These functions can then be used to assign additional samples to one of the groups. This type of approach is employed in pattern recognition problems like identifying land-cover on satellite images, by comparing unknown areas to selected regions known from surface study.

MULTIVARIATE DATA DISPLAY

Graphical displays are very useful in multivariate analysis, as well, since the many permutations of the variables can quickly lead to an overwhelming volume of statistical calculations. The simple two-dimensional scatter plot is a common example, although many other techniques have been developed for special types of data.

1. Direct Displays of Two or Three Variables

The simplest multivariate problem is the study of two variables, as we saw in Chapter 4. Graphical displays of two variables usually take the form of a X-Y scatter plot (often termed a profile plot for single-valued data). Additional variables can be represented on the plot as well, by using coded symbols at the plotted points. A number of examples were shown in Chapters 4 and 8, and need not be discussed further here.

To examine three variables, a "ternary diagram" can be used. This is often used in chemistry and metallurgy to show ratios of the elements in a three-component system. A sample containing 100 percent of one component is plotted at the vertex representing that variable, while samples with a mix

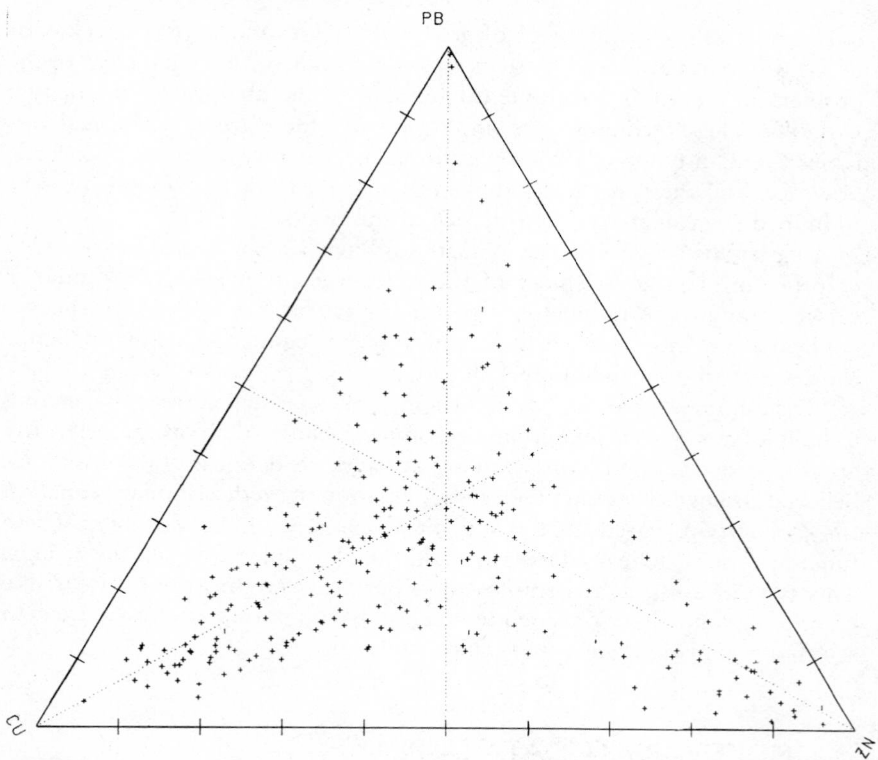

FIGURE 10.4. A ternary diagram. This plot represents the ratios of copper, lead, and zinc in a group of rock samples. Like a scatter plot, the objective is to find distinct clusters of points on the plot.

of components will plot inside the triangle, at a position determined by the percentages of each one.

Ternary diagrams can also be used to show relative abundances of trace components, where the complete system has more than three components. In this case, the values of the plotted variables for each sample are scaled (to have a sum of one) prior to plotting. This may require more than a simple addition of data values, if the ranges (and units) of each variable are fundamentally different. An example is shown in Fig. 10.4.

Like the scatter plot, the ternary diagram is used to determine if the samples can be separated into groups. Distinct clusters are isolated from the other data for independent analysis. This might involve searching for differences in the other variables, or testing for spatial correlations by plotting maps showing the locations of samples in each group.

2. Symbolic Coding

When displaying more than three variables, direct scaling of the values onto a two-dimensional graph is no longer possible. Special coding schemes or more complex projections are required, and generally must be tailored to the specific type of data. Because so many special graphical procedures have been developed, only a few examples are discussed here in the interests of brevity.

As was seen in Chapter 8, one or more additional variables can be represented on virtually any plot, by using color, size, or symbol shape as a code. Combinations are also possible, of course, although in designing any graphical display one must be careful to maintain readability (which usually means striving for simplicity). An effective format usually requires considerable experimentation, and thus a flexible and easy-to-use program, to allow different forms to be tried quickly. This involves efficient data selection in addition to the actual plotting, once again calling for a structured data management system (as outlined in Chapter 5).

Symbolic coding can be applied to any type of plot where discrete points are plotted or where specific data values are assigned to various sub-areas. This includes many of the examples from Chapter 8: scatter plots, ternary diagrams, demographic maps, and profile plots.

3. Use of Special Figures

The composite effect of many different variables can be graphically presented by using the values of each variable as the parameters of a figure of distinct shape. When the majority of variables have similar values, the shapes are also similar. The figures are plotted for all samples, and then grouped by visual inspection. This approach can be applied to non-numeric data as well, since the parameters of the figure can be defined according to any classification scheme desired.

A form widely used in the social sciences is the "Chernoff face," developed by Herman Chernoff of MIT in the early 1970s (Fig. 10.5). The parameters of the face (e.g., the size of ears and nose, the spacing of eyes, the curvature of mouth) are determined by the values of perhaps 15 to 20 variables, for a number of different samples. In the example, the samples are countries in Africa, while the variables are various indicators of Soviet foreign policy towards those countries (such as amount of economic and military aid, and the number of Soviet technicians in the country). Face diagrams have also been used to analyze such data as economic and social characteristics of cities, diagnoses of psychiatric patients, exploration success of major oil companies, and morphological features of lunar craters.

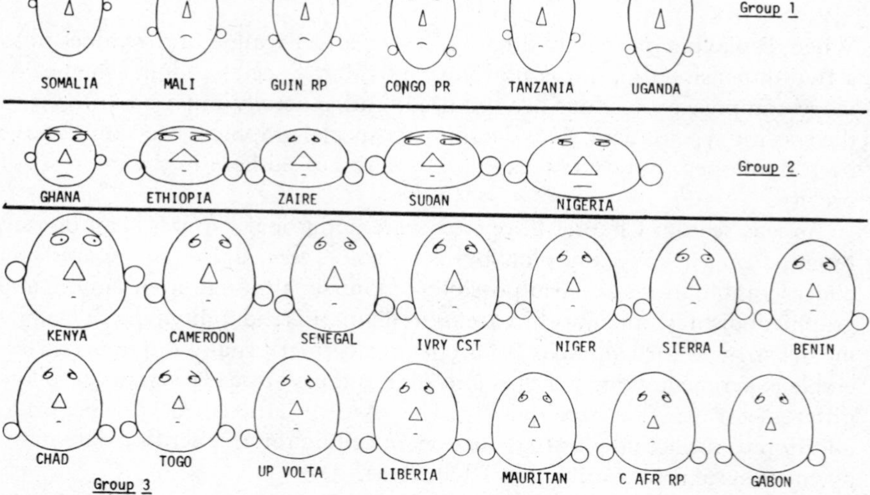

FIGURE 10.5. A set of Chernoff "faces." The parameters of the face were set according to various measures of Soviet foreign policy toward countries in Africa. (Reproduced from "Application of Graphical Multivariate Techniques in Policy Sciences," by P.C.C. Wang and G.E. Lake, in *Graphical Representation of Multivariate Data,* copyright 1978, Academic Press, New York, by permission of the publisher).

A potential problem with "faces" is visual bias: a pleasant looking face will probably get more attention than an angry one. This opens the door to tuning the parameters to provide a display favorable to the argument being presented by the author. For this reason, more abstract figures (like those described below) are preferred by many analysts.

The same basic method can be applied with figures of different shape: for example, "trees," linear profiles, and polygons. In a "circular profile," the vertices of a polygon are set according to the values of the selected variables (Fig. 10.6). A similar form is a "star" diagram, where the lengths of arms of the star are the parameters. Star diagrams are used to characterize different types of petroleum, since oil from the same source will have very similar ratios of constituent hydrocarbons. When plotted on a map, similar shapes may show the migration of oil from the source region to a reservoir.

Any of these shapes can be plotted on a map to test for spatial correlation, of course. A natural extension of Fig. 10.5 would be to show the "faces" on a map of Africa, to quickly see whether the visually determined classification has a geographic basis.

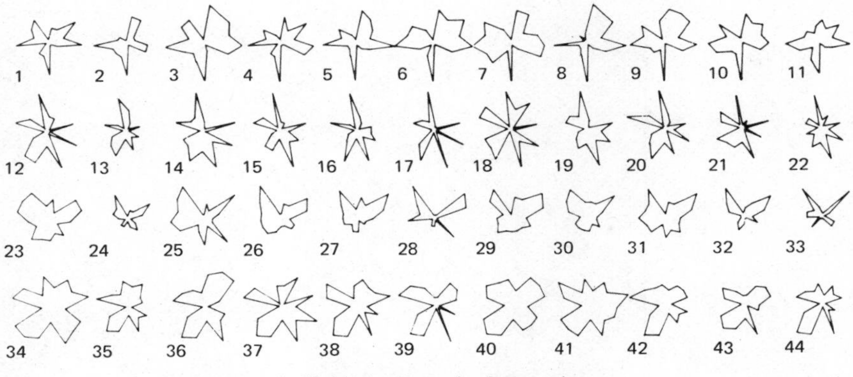

FIGURE 10.6. "Circular profiles" for data classification. An abstract multivariate figure is pictured. It is used here to display characteristic symptoms of psychiatric patients. (Reproduced from "A Comparison of Graphical Representations of Multidimensional Psychiatric Diagnostic Data", by J.E. Mezzich and D.R.L. Worthington, in *Graphical Representation of Multivariate Data,* copyright 1978 Academic Press, New York, by permission of the publisher)

4. Displays That Support Multivariate Classification

Computer graphics can also be used to advantage in studying the results of statistical techniques like multiple regression and factor analysis. As always, the key to success is to have an easy-to-use plotting program that allows different symbols to be assigned to discrete groups of samples.

Multiple regression is in effect a predictive tool, and can be used to define large-scale structure in the data. Following the methods presented in Chapter 8, anomalous samples can be identified by taking the difference of the observed and predicted values for a given variable. Different groups then are determined by setting numeric ranges, such as 0 to 1 standard deviations from the mean, and so on. There are many other possibilities, such as picking points that are anomalous in predicting two or more variables.

Similar procedures can be applied in factor analysis by using the factor scores for each sample. Once again, a variety of criteria can be applied to define distinct groups. In addition to plotting maps to test for spatial separation, scatter plots of pairs of factor scores are often used to locate clusters of samples (Fig. 10.7). Other clustering methods for reducing dimensionality might also be displayed in this form.

With direct classification techniques, the need is simply to assign a symbol

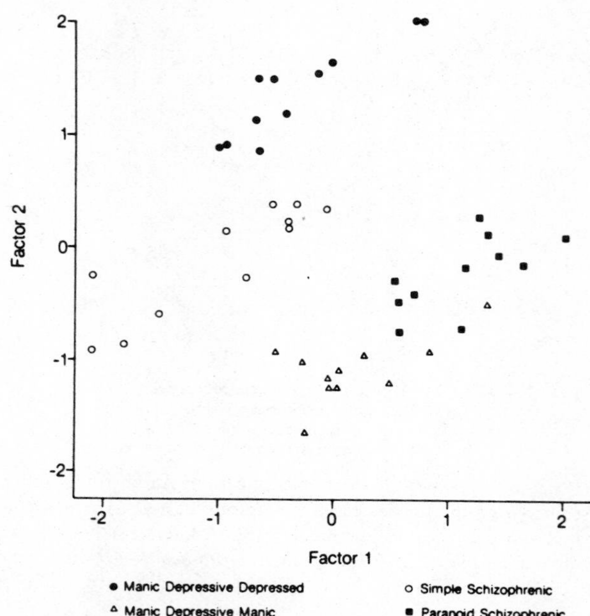

FIGURE 10.7. Use of scatter plots in factor analysis. The same data as in Fig. 10.6 are shown, with the results of factor analysis used to group the patients. (Reproduced from "A Comparison of Graphical Representations of Multidimensional Psychiatric Diagnostic Data", by J.E. Mezzich and D.R.L. Worthington, in *Graphical Representation of Multivariate Data,* copyright 1978 Academic Press, New York, by permission of the publisher)

to each sample according to its classification. If the samples represent spatial averages, the map might show a shading pattern or color throughout the region. The result is much like demographic maps which are based on discrete political boundaries.

To use these kinds of plots, the multivariate analysis programs should be able to add new information to the original database. This allows normal plotting programs to use derived data directly, without requiring special procedures to be developed (e.g., adding limited plotting functions to each program). As outlined in Chapter 8, a general-purpose mapping program would have options to set symbol codes, sizes, or colors according to the values of any field in the database.

CHAPTER 11

PROCEDURES FOR ARRAY-ORIENTED DATA

We have so far made few assumptions about the organization of the data being analyzed: in effect, all variables have been considered to be randomly distributed. In many situations, observations are made in a prescribed pattern so that the coordinates of each point will have a uniform distribution. In such cases, special analytical techniques can be developed to take advantage of this regularity, providing more powerful insights into the nature of the data, and dramatic improvements in computational efficiency. The dependent variables can be considered as elements of an array in the computer, and the coordinates as a simple function of position in the array, which need not be explicitly treated during the analysis.

In this chapter, two common categories of array-type data analysis are reviewed. First are "time-series," by which we mean any observations made at fixed intervals of time. Examples are countless, including daily stock prices, hourly weather information, annual economic indicators, and so on. There is only a single coordinate, so the computational methods involve one-dimensional arrays.

As we have already seen, spatial data analysis often involves interpolation of randomly positioned samples onto a uniform two-dimensional grid. Data collected by automatic scanning devices (like the LANDSAT satellites and other remote-sensing instruments) are often in the form of a two-dimensional array, or are routinely converted to such a form as part of the data collection process.

Since these topics are complex, mathematical details will once again be omitted. More specialized texts are noted in the References section for anyone wishing to pursue the subjects further.

TIME-SERIES ANALYSIS

In almost all human endeavors there is an interest in observing phenomena which change over a period of time. To record such data, the usual method is to make a series of observations at fixed intervals of time (hence the name "time series"). In analysis, the objective may be to gain an understanding of past events by determining the structure of the data, or to predict the future by extrapolating from past behavior. Some examples of time series are shown in Fig. 11.1. This line graph format is perhaps the most common type of display, although many other variations are possible, as we shall see later.

1. Recording Time Series

Acquiring data at regular time intervals is not always a simple process. The variable may be directly related to the time interval by definition: variables like the total precipitation in a day or the number of houses built in a month are of this kind. In these cases, each data value is unambiguously associated with a particular point in time. The variable may also be continuously changing, so the observations must be considered as "samples" of instantaneous values, or averages over the time interval. Depending on the method for taking meaurements, the data may also represent an intermediate case if the recording device averages instantaneous values over a period shorter than the nominal time interval. When instantaneous readings are taken, care must be taken that the interval is short enough to observe all significant fluctuations. If this is not the case, "aliasing" occurs, and high-frequency oscillations appear as spurious lower frequencies. A common example is the apparent backward spinning of a stagecoach wheel in cowboy movies, which is due to continuous motion being recorded as a series of still pictures (typically at 24 frames per second). The effect of "digitizing" or "sampling" a continuous variable is illustrated in Fig. 11.2.

FIGURE 11.1. Examples of time-series. (*a*) Annual count of sunspots from 1749 to 1924; (*b*) price of IBM stock from May 1961 to November 1962.

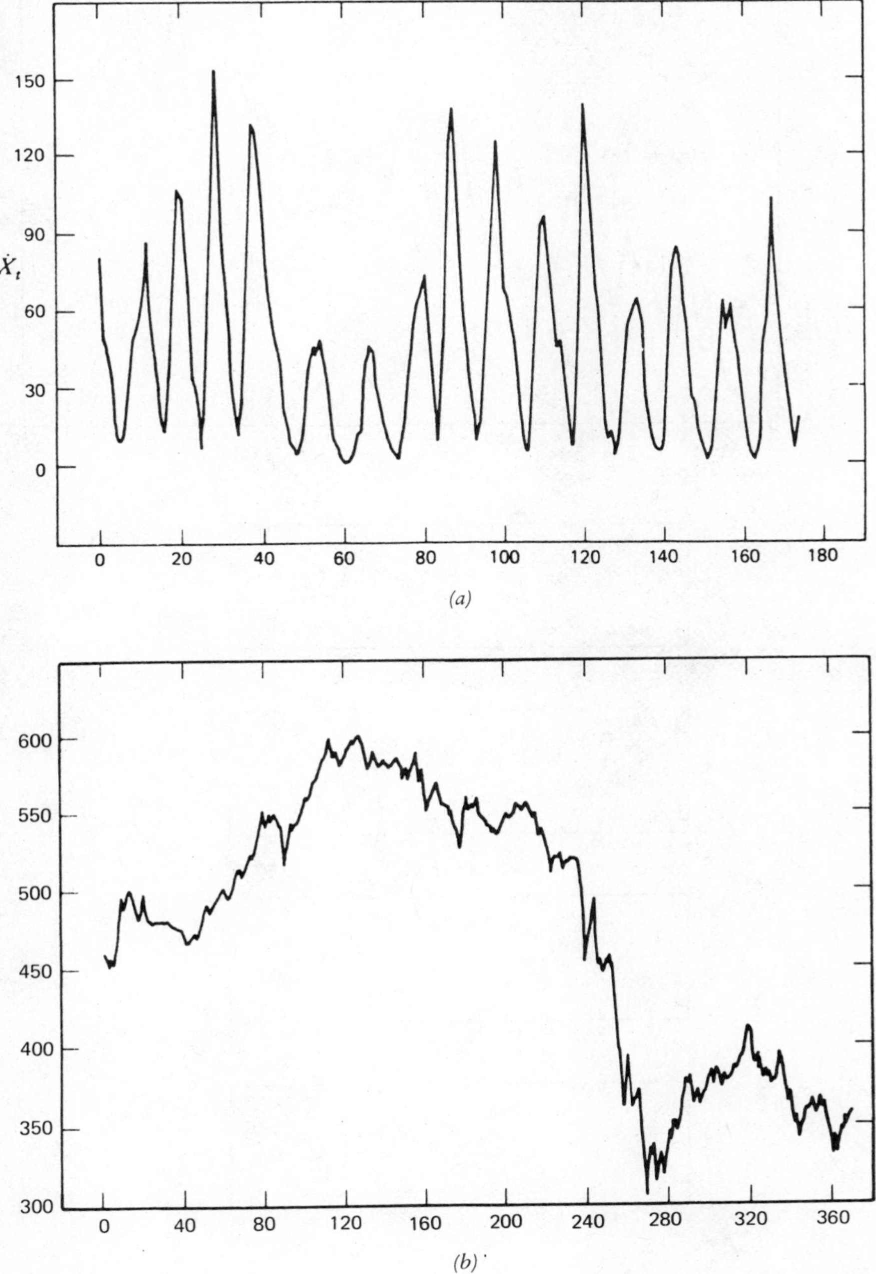
150
120
90
$\dot{X}_t$
60
30
0
0 20 40 60 80 100 120 140 160 180
600
550
500
450
400
350
300
0 40 80 120 160 200 240 280 320 360

(a)

(b)

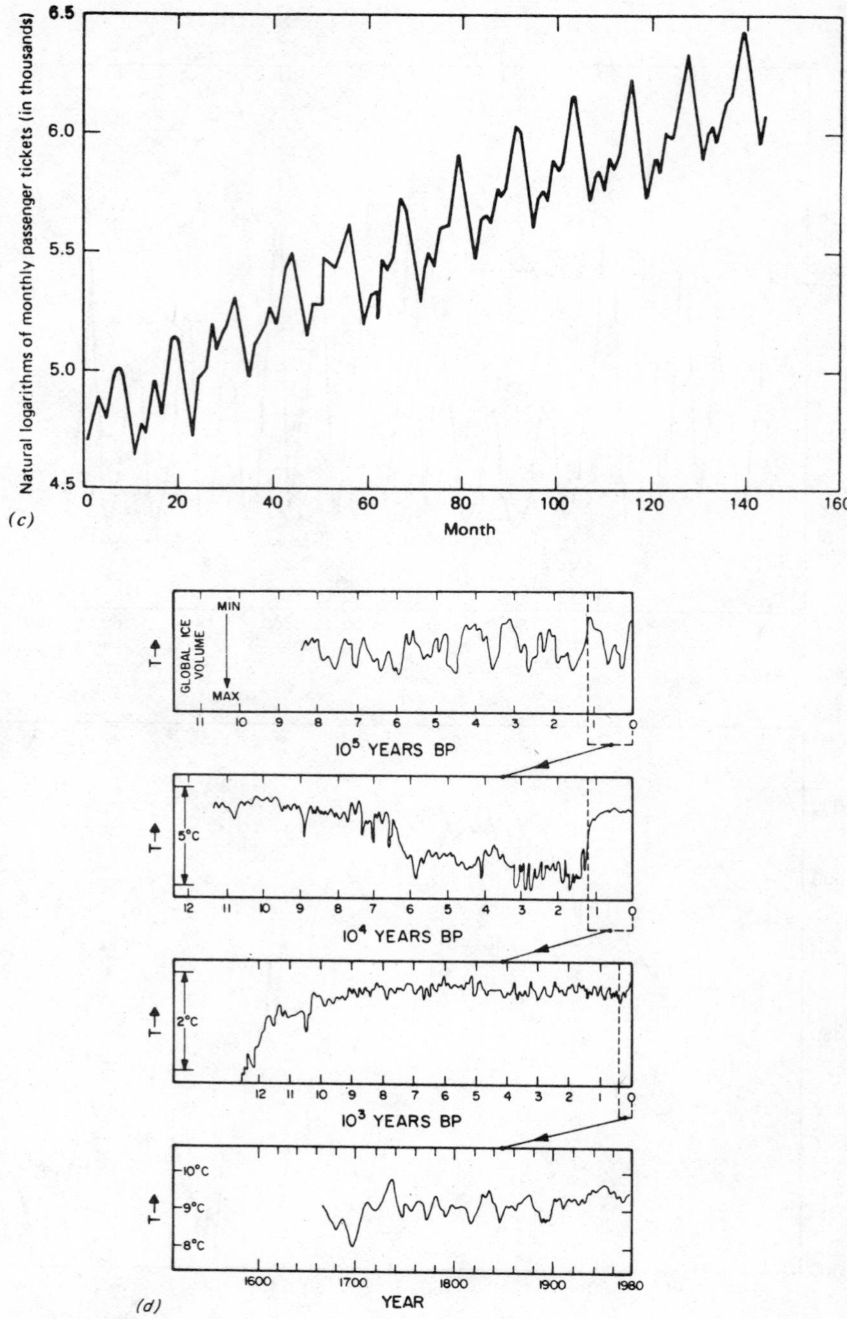

FIGURE 11.1. *(Continued).* (*c*) Airline ticket sales from January 1949 to December 1960 (note the logarithmic scale). (Figures 11.1*a*–11.1*c* reproduced from *Time Series and Systems Analysis with Applications,* by S.M. Pandit and S.M. Wu, copyright 1983 John Wiley & Sons, New York, by permission of the publisher). (*d*) Climatic trends over the past 1 million years. Each curve was derived from a different type of measurement. Note the use of expanding scales to show more detailed information for the recent past. (Figure 11.1*d* reproduced from "Climatic Systems Analysis", by B. Saltzman, in *Theory of Climate* B. Saltzman ed., copyright 1983, Academic Press, New York by permission of the publisher).

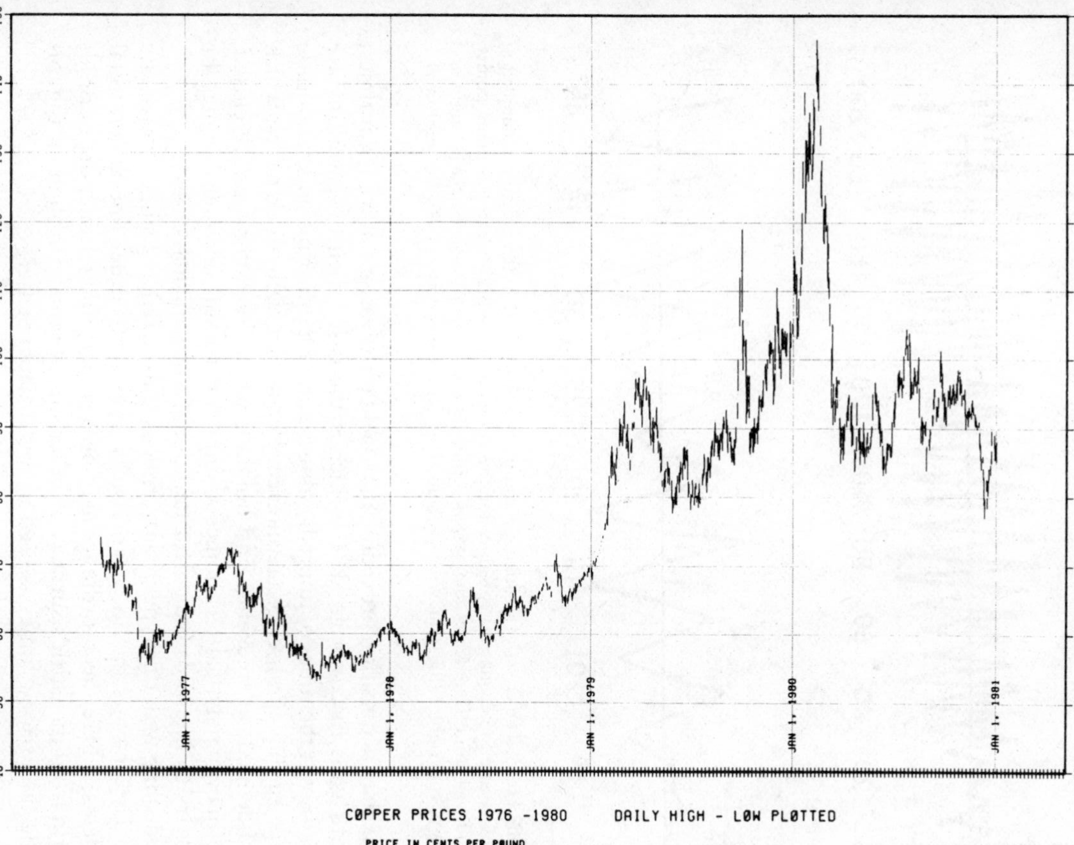

FIGURE 11.1. *(Continued).* (*e*) The price of copper from 1980 to 1982. The daily high and low price are shown as a vertical bar, instead of in the connected line form of Figs. 11.1*a*–11.1*d*.

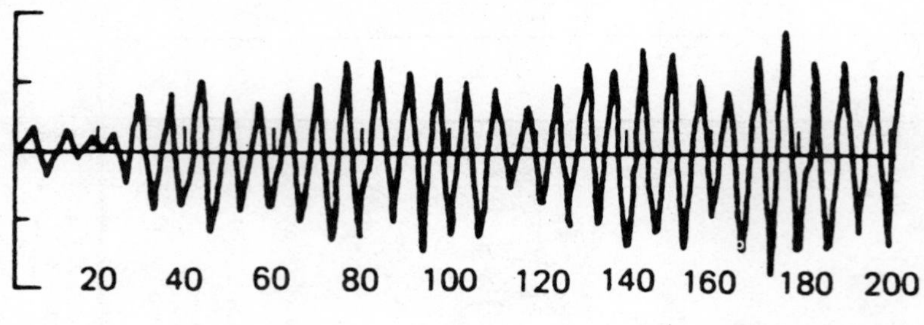

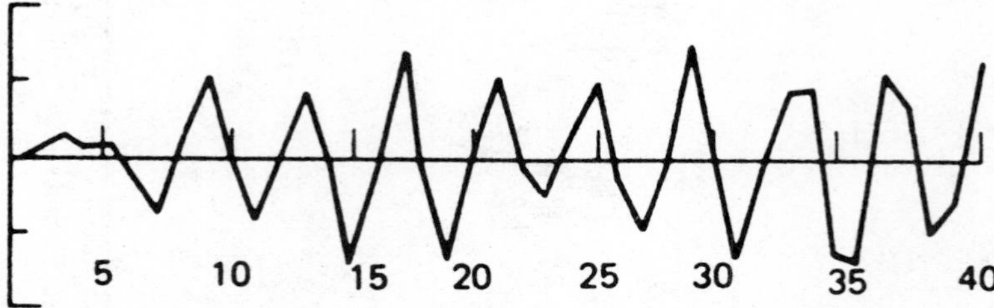

FIGURE 11.2. The effect of digitizing a continuous series. The bottom figure is sampled at too slow a rate to adequately reproduce the top curve, which has four times as many points. (Reproduced from *Time Series and Systems Analysis with Applications,* by S.M. Pandit and S.M. Wu, copyright 1983 John Wiley & Sons, New York, by permission of the publisher).

The data acquisition procedure may yield observations at irregular times, or with gaps in coverage. The former is the case when observations are taken only at the times of unpredictable events (e.g., the time and magnitude of large earthquakes). Gaps are inherent in data like daily stock prices, which are undefined on weekends and holidays when the exchanges are closed. Since many analytical techniques assume a constant increment, it may be necessary to interpolate data for additional times in such cases.

In dealing with this type of data, time is considered as a single coordinate field. The analysis methods can also be applied to other one-dimensional problems, where the coordinate may be distance along a line, depth or elevation from the earth's surface, or other spatial units. Throughout the following discussion, "time" is used in this broader sense.

2. Structural Analysis of Time Series

In general, the determination of data structure can be considered as the first objective of analysis. In dealing with time series, the presence of structure means that the data behavior at a particular point in time will be at least partially predicted by its values at other times.

The first step is usually to see if the data have any trend, that is, whether there is a tendency for the values to increase or decrease with time. Consider the earth's population, which has increased throughout man's history with occasional short-term setbacks due to major epidemics, and variations in the growth rate due to economic and cultural factors (see also the examples in Fig. 11.1). As we saw in Chapter 4, we can treat this kind of situation as a two-variable problem, and define the relationship of population to time mathematically. A straight line, a higher order polynomial, or some other function (an exponential curve, perhaps), can be "fit" to the data by least-squares methods.

Whether or not there is a long-term trend, we might expect observations taken a short time apart to have similar values. This is the case whenever the phenomenon is essentially continuous in nature, that is, if the variable in question cannot take sudden jumps, but must change gradually. The time interval of the data may be of importance here, for if the time scale of fluctuations is much shorter than the observation period, the data may appear to be changing erratically, since the details of the transition from point to point cannot be seen. Alternately, if the measurement process is an average over the interval, short-term fluctuations can be smoothed out. As noted earlier, these problems are inherent in the process of recording a time series, and must be adequately handled at that time to prevent aliasing.

3. Prediction (Extrapolation)

To predict future values, an "auto-regressive" model of the time series is developed. In essence, this quantifies the basic principle of similarity of adjacent values, by estimating the next value in the series as a function of a limited number of the most recent values. Normally a linear regression equation is used:

$$x(t) = a + b*x(t-1) + c*x(t-2) + \cdots \qquad 11.1$$

where $x(t)$ is the value of the series at time t. The coefficients $(a,b,c, \ldots)$ are computed by standard least-squares methods, and the quality of the prediction is measured by comparing predicted values to observed values. This formulation can be considered as a weighted average of a portion of the data, or a "moving average." The acronym ARMA (autoregressive moving average) is often used in time-series literature to describe this model. The number of samples required for adequate prediction is obviously very data dependent. Similarly, the maximum attainable accuracy and the distance of reliable extrapolation are controlled by the complexity of the data, the relative magnitude of random components, and other factors. A number of statistical techniques are available to aid in defining these parameters, although the analyst must generally apply considerable knowledge and experience to produce useful results.

Applications of time-series predictions are widespread, and in some fields are perhaps the most important aspect of data analysis. In economics, for example, there is great interest in defining expected patterns in interest rates, unemployment, inflation, and many other parameters. Stock market analysts all dream of being able to reliably anticipate price fluctuations, although if anyone has achieved complete success, they are keeping the method to themselves. In control systems for industrial processes, machine performance is monitored to detect trends toward unacceptable results, so that problems can be corrected before actual failure. If manufactured parts must be within certain size limits, sample measurements are studied to detect a possible drift away from the desired values. This is done instead of simple checking to see if parts are within the allowed tolerance. Climatologists study long-term records of temperature, precipitation, and other data to determine whether fundamental changes in climate are underway (e.g., whether a new ice age is starting, or whether the earth will become much warmer due to the "greenhouse effect").

4. Frequency Analysis

In addition to trends and short-term continuity, time series often have strong cyclical components. Daily maximum temperatures are strongly influenced by the seasons, for example, as well as by short-term fluctuations imposed by changing weather conditions, and long-term trends which reflect shifts in climate. There may be a great many periodic components, many of which cannot be easily detected in the data because of the obscuring effect of adding them all together.

Each cyclic component can be defined in terms of its "period," which is the length of time required to complete one cycle. An alternate and mathematically equivalent form is to define its "frequency," which is the number of cycles completed in a given time. These quantities are simply the reciprocals of each other:

$$P = 1 / F \qquad \text{and} \qquad F = 1 / P \tag{11.2}$$

where P is the period, and F the frequency. For example, a wheel spinning at 1000 revolutions per minute has a period of 0.06 seconds (1/1000 * 60). This behavior can be represented graphically in the form of a sine or cosine function, for which any two points separated by a distance P on the time axis have the same value.

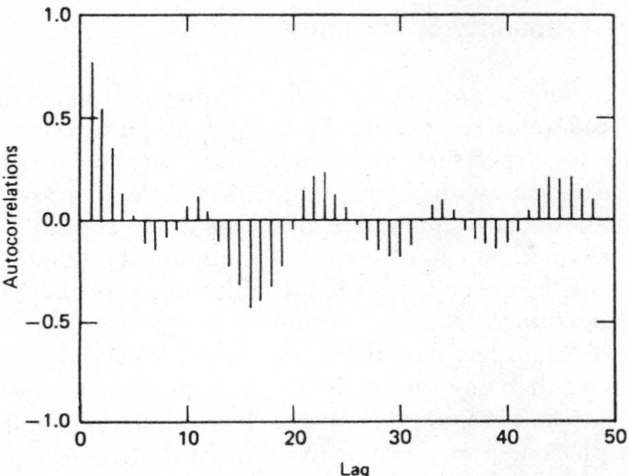

FIGURE 11.3. An autocorrelation function. (Reproduced from *Time Series and Systems Analysis with Applications,* by S.M. Pandit and S.M. Wu, copyright 1983 John Wiley & Sons, New York, by permission of the publisher).

With sampled data (but not with a continuous function) there is an upper limit to the frequency that can be represented. This is called the Nyquist frequency, which is $1/(2*t)$ where t is the time interval between samples. An alternate description of this limit is the "sampling theorem," which states that at least two samples must be taken within one period to accurately define the frequency. If the data contain components with periods shorter than twice the sampling interval, aliasing results.

The aim of frequency analysis is to find the periods and relative amplitudes (strengths) of these components. In some instances, the period may already be known, as with yearly and other cycles determined by astronomical events. The amplitude of the particular frequency will probably still be unknown, however.

To test whether a given time series has a cyclic nature, we can calculate its "auto-correlation":

$$A(T) = \text{Avg}\ (x(t) * (x(t-T))) \qquad 11.3$$

where "Avg" denotes the average value for all t, $x(t)$ is a sample point of the series, and T represents a time "lag" between two sample points. To compute each value in $A(T)$, at least N squared multiplications are required, where N is the number of points in the series. If the data contain a component of period $T1$, the function $A(T)$ should have a local maxima at $T = T1$. This simply reflects the fact that sample values at any time t will be similar to those at $(t \pm nT1)$ (see Fig. 11.3).

5. The Frequency Spectrum

The relative strength of each component is expressed by its "amplitude," which is the peak value reached during each cycle. To compare the amplitudes, a frequency "spectrum" is plotted, as shown in Fig. 11.4. This is much like a histogram, with the amplitude taking the place of the sample count, and the frequency represented along the other axis.

The essential operation is of course to compute the amplitudes corresponding to each frequency. This is normally done by taking a Fourier transform of the autocorrelation to produce the "power spectrum" of the data. This procedure is based on the work of the 19th century French physicist, who showed than any time series can be represented by a summation of a series of sine and cosine functions, each with a unique amplitude and "phase." The phase is a measure of the shift of the curves from the time origin (i.e., the peak of a cosine function need not occur at zero when a phase shift is allowed). The "time domain" and "frequency domain" representations of the data can be used equivalently in analysis, since the transformation between them is unique.

The standard mathematical definition of a Fourier transform involves an integral over the complete time axis (i.e., for all possible times). As we are normally dealing with a sampled series, the integral is replaced by a summation over all the samples. In practice, the time range is limited, and it

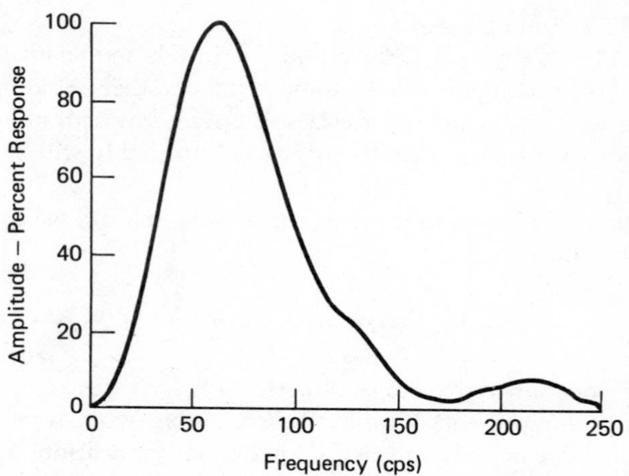

FIGURE 11.4. A power frequency spectrum. (Reproduced from "The Design of High-Resolution Digital Filters", by S. Treitel and E.A. Robinson, in *IEEE Transactions on Geoscience Electronics*, vol GE-4, no. 1, 1966, by permission of the IEEE).

must be assumed that the data have the same statistical properties throughout time (this is termed "stationarity"). This avoids the need to sum over the entire time axis (which is infinite). With the further assumption that the time period of observations is in fact a fundamental period of the data, the Fast Fourier Transform (FFT) was developed in the 1960s, to greatly reduce computing time. This may appear to be a strong assumption, but, provided the length of the time series is long relative to the periods of interest, it does not profoundly affect the results. When dealing with short time series, however, the FFT can introduce serious errors, and more sophisticated techniques must be used. In situations where very low frequencies are not present (or have been removed in the process of recording data), the autorrelation function will tend toward zero at longer periods, and can safely be assumed to remain at zero outside the available range. The FFT is itself a series, defined in terms of regular intervals of frequency instead of time. It is thus also treated as an array in a computer, so that efficient procedures for array manipulation can also be applied.

In many cases, computing the spectrum of the data is a major result in itself, since identification of unknown components in the data is a basic objective. For example, it has often been suggested that the 11-year sunspot cycle has an influence on weather. To test this hypothesis on a set of meteorological data (average monthly precipitation or temperature, perhaps), the frequency spectrum is calculated, and examined for significant peaks in the region corresponding to an 11-year period.

We often need to go a step further, and remove the dominant frequencies to make smaller amplitude features more visible. This requires that the data be "filtered," to selectively remove components within a specified band of frequencies. The operation can be performed on the original data by convolution with a filter operator, or on the Fourier transform of the data by applying different weights to the frequency components. In either event, it is necessary to have a transition zone between accepted and rejected frequencies. This is an inevitable consequence of working with a series of finite length, and must be considered in designing a filtering algorithm.

6. Other Procedures

Another common goal in analyzing time series is to test for the occurrence of isolated "events," or unexpected departures from normal behavior. This can be described as detecting a "signal" in the presence of "noise." This is of major importance in such fields as radio astronomy, radar, and digital data transmission. For example, in transmitting data between computers, the receiving device must translate a series of electric pulses into bits, and be able to reject any random noise fluctuations that are received simultaneously. The classic application of statistical "communication theory," developed during the Second World War, is the analysis of radar signals to distinguish real "targets" from false echoes.

A basic concept in signal detection is that any time series can be considered as a combination of a "deterministic" and "random" components. A "decomposition" of the observed series can then isolate the random part, which is expected to include the unknown signal. This concept is related to the principle that the information content of the series is related to its uncertainty, that is, that if the series is completely deterministic (predictable), then it contains no new information. The actual mathematical methods involved are much more complex than this simplistic overview: the interested reader should consult the References for details.

7. Multiple Time Series

It is often important to examine the relationships of several variables, each recorded as a function of time. Provided that the measurements are taken at the same times, any two variables can be compared using the standard methods presented in Chapter 4 (i.e., scatter plots and correlation coefficients). This procedure ignores the time dependence, however, which is often of major importance when cyclic components are present. In the sunspots and weather example, there may be a delay between significant changes in solar activity and consequent weather variations. The first step in such cases is to compute a "cross correlation" function for the two series (instead of the simple correlation coefficient):

$$R(T) = \mathrm{Avg}(x(t) * y(t-T)) \tag{11.4}$$

Like the analogous autocorrelation, this function can be used to compute a "cross-power spectrum," in order to graphically illustrate the frequency content of the components common to both series.

One common use of cross correlation is to determine an unknown time shift between similar series. The assumption is that a single strong peak will appear in the cross correlation, corresponding to a difference in the time origins or to an inherent delay in the physical process. For example, it is often suggested that the stock market is an early indicator of trends in the general economy. This theory might be tested by comparing the Dow Jones average to the growth rate of the gross national product. The amplitude of the peak in the cross correlation is a measure of how strong the association is, while its position on the time axis gives the delay.

The same procedure is followed to adjust two different time series to a common origin, with redefining the time axis of one series as a final step.

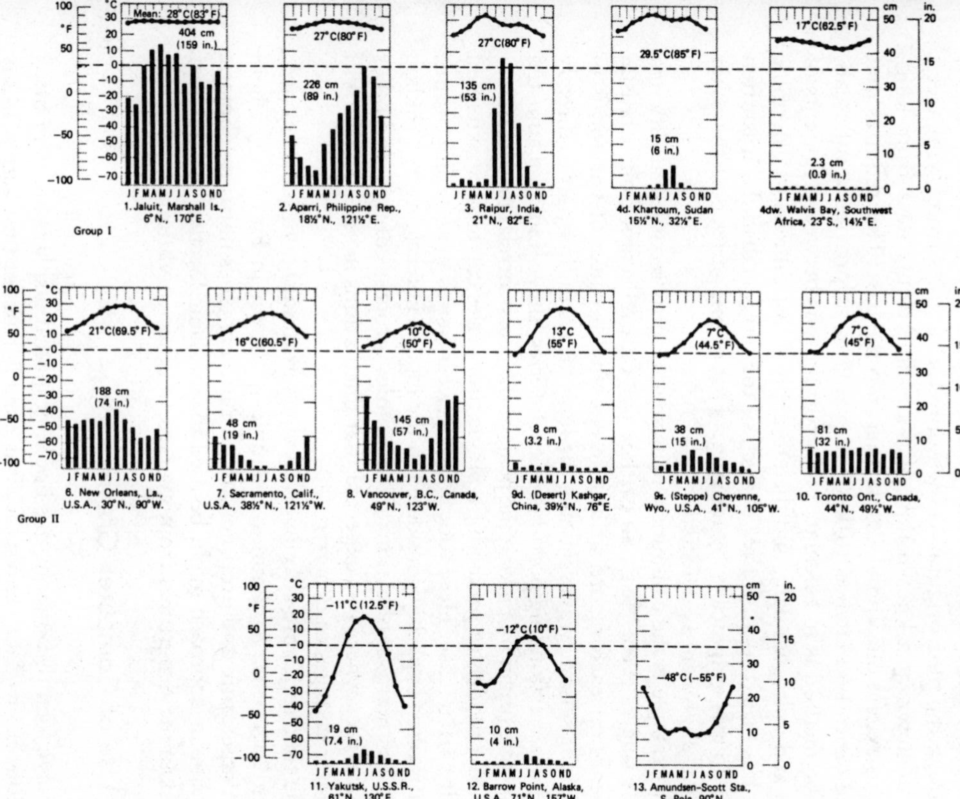

FIGURE 11.5. A comparison of the same time-series variable at different locations. These "climographs" provide a compact display of average weather patterns at different locations around the world. (Reproduced from *Modern Physical Geography*, 2nd ed. by A.N. Strahler and A.H. Strahler, copyright 1983 John Wiley & Sons, by permission of the publisher).

This is required in situations where it is difficult (if not impossible) to synchronize the measurement times. In studying past variations of climate, "dendrochronology" (the dating of tree rings) is a powerful tool, especially in arid regions such as the southwestern United States where wood is preserved for many centuries. Here the variable is the width of each annual ring. Although the time origin is known only for samples from living trees, or those cut down at a known time, it is possible to use data from long-dead trees to extend our knowledge farther into the past. This requires that part of the series be matched to known examples to provide a time calibration. The method is to calculate cross correlations between segments of the known and unknown data, and then to apply statistical tests to determine if a match has been found. If the "shape" of the series is distinct, it is often possible to do this graphically by moving a plot of one series past the other until a visual alignment is detected.

Another example is the calibration of seismic records recorded at different locations. A single "event" (e.g., an earthquake, or a reflection from a crustal layer) appears on each record at a different time because of variations in the speed of the seismic waves passing through the earth. In order to directly compare the corresponding portions of each series, they should be adjusted to the same time origin by picking the peak of the cross-correlation function.

The ARMA model for predicting a single time series can also be extended to the multivariate case. Here too, a lag between series may be important, and in fact is often explicitly considered in the model. Forecasting by "leading indicators" has many applications in economics, process control, and other fields in situations where it is expected that fluctuations in one variable will trigger similar changes in others.

Multiple time series are also involved when examining the same variable at different locations. A common example is shown in Fig. 11.5, where charts of temperature and precipitation for different cities illustrate climatic groups. A similar approach might be used for the same location but different years, to examine departures from average weather conditions.

8. Use of Computer Graphics

As we have seen throughout this book, graphical displays are very often a tremendous aid to data analysis. This is equally true for time series. Many types of computer plots can be used to study time series, although the most common form by far is a simple two-dimensional graph, with time on the horizontal axis and the data values shown as a continuous line (by connecting the discrete points). For multiple time series, several variables can be displayed on the same plot, by using different symbols, colors, or patterns to distinguish the lines. Some examples are shown in Figure 11.6.

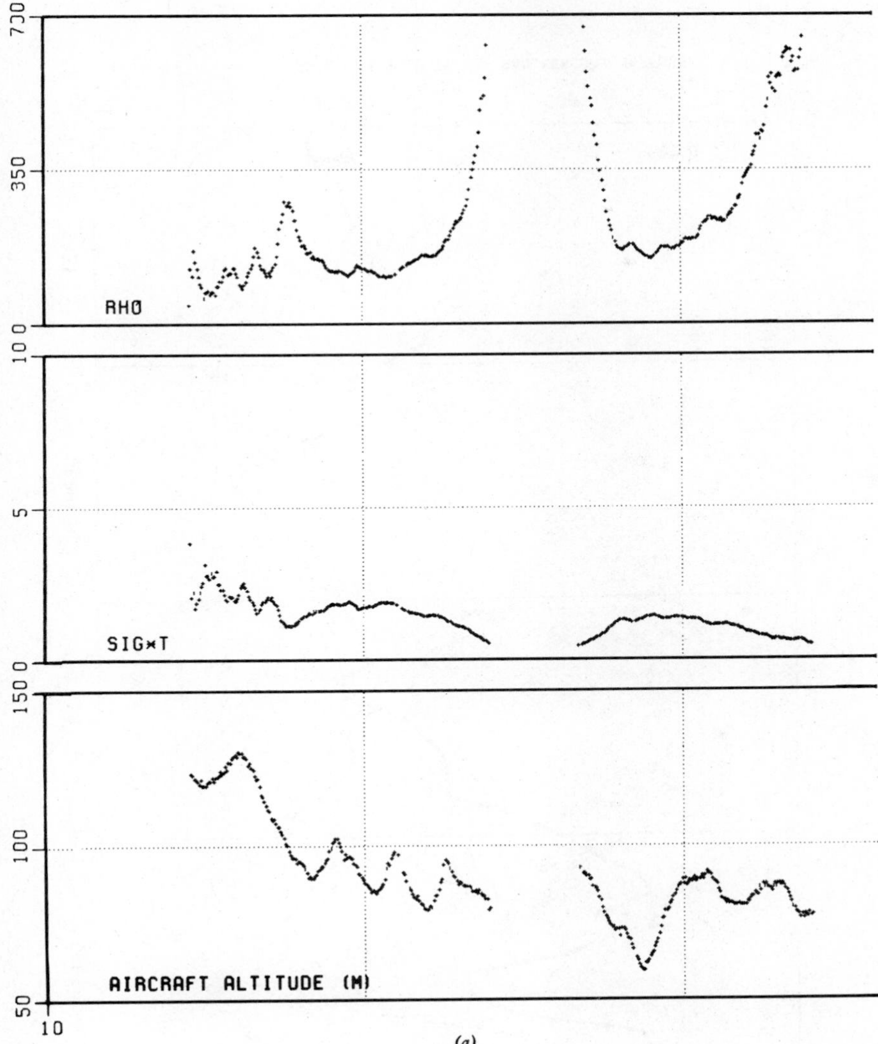

(a)

FIGURE 11.6. Display of multiple time series. (*a*) A stack of individual time-series plots. In this example, "time" also represents distance along a flight line in an airborne geophysical survey; (*b*) plot of each series with different line patterns. Note that silver is plotted on a different vertical axis; (*c*) The use of multiple bars. This format is suitable for short series, and is often used in reporting annual financial data and other business graphics. (*d*) A plot of cumulative traces. This assumes that each series is part of a larger total, so the distance between the lines represents the particular data value. In this example, the world's stock of copper is subdivided by major sources.

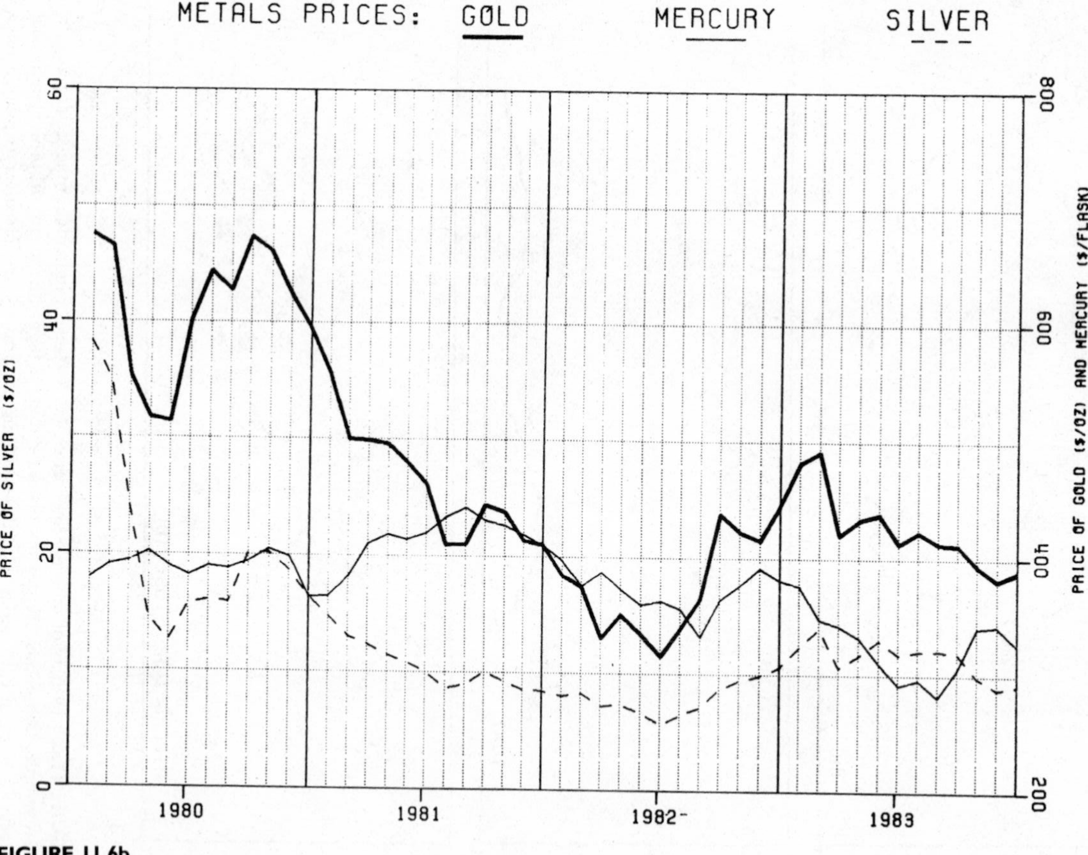
METALS PRICES: GOLD MERCURY SILVER
PRICE OF SILVER ($/OZ)
60
40
20
0
PRICE OF GOLD ($/OZ) AND MERCURY ($/FLASK)
800
600
400
200
1980
1981
1982
1983

FIGURE 11.6b.

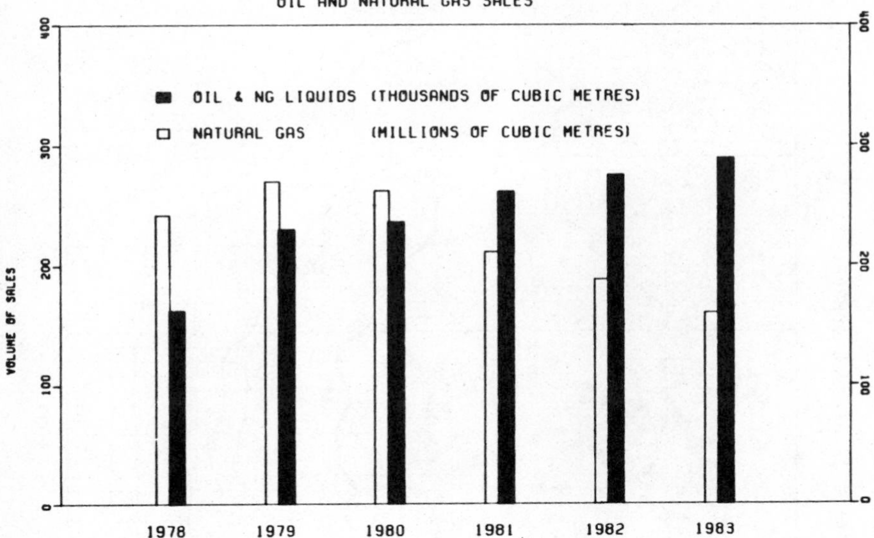

FIGURE 11.6c.

In many cases, simple plots can provide a great deal of information without involving complex statistics or more abstract approaches like Fourier transforms. Any sudden changes are clearly visible, and can be highlighted by overplotting a trend line or plotting residuals from a trend. In the examination of multiple series, a composite plot can allow immediate visual correlation of similar features.

In addition to the basic data, plots of frequency spectra, correlations, and other derived quantities are often employed in analysis. To allow such a variety of outputs to be used effectively, a computer system must include the features outlined in Chapters 5 and 8. It must be able to select a variety of data from a database, and to add the results of calculations to the database. In plotting, flexibility in combining different displays, adjusting scales, and highlighting lines is essential. Ideally, the system should allow immediate display on a graphic terminal, and interactive revision of plotting parameters before final copies are produced.

IMAGE PROCESSING

A natural extension of the one-dimensional methods of time-series analysis is to consider data that are defined on a regular grid in two dimensions. As discussed in Part II, gridded data are often required in spatial analysis and

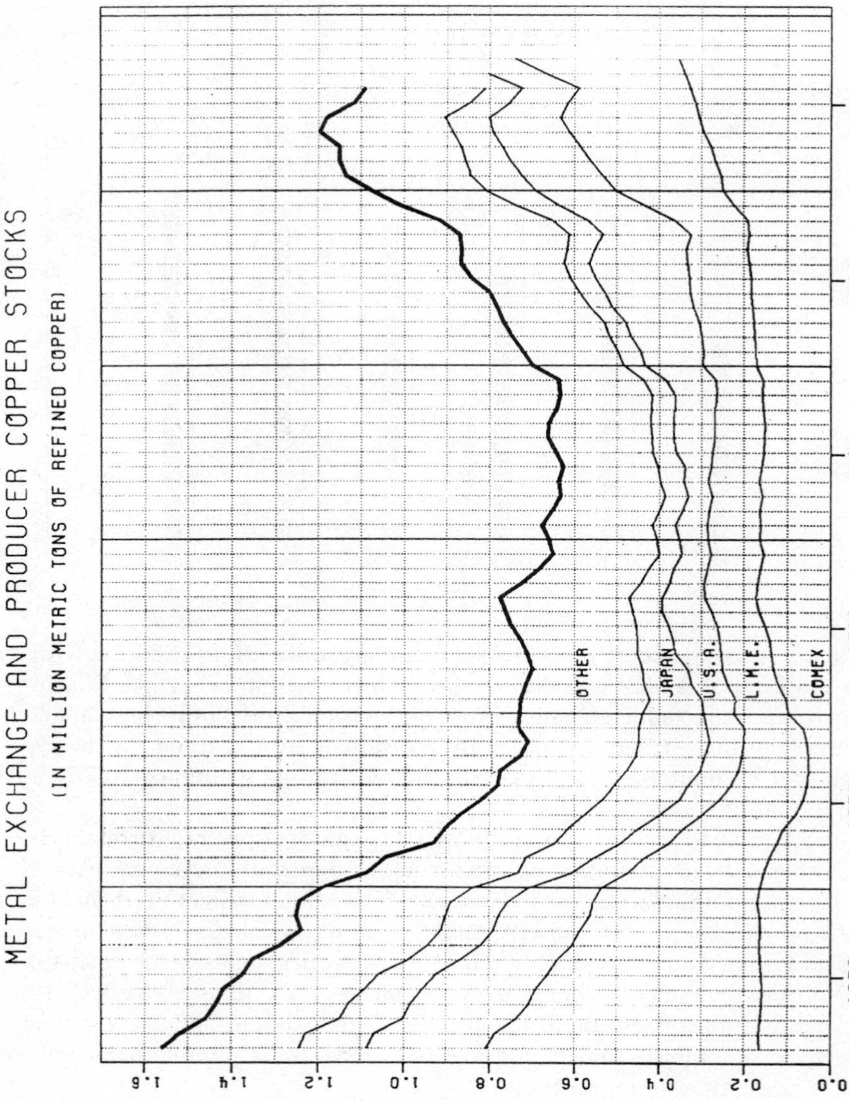

METAL EXCHANGE AND PRODUCER COPPER STOCKS
(IN MILLION METRIC TONS OF REFINED COPPER)
OTHER
JAPAN
U.S.A.
L.M.E.
COMEX
1978
1979
1980
1981
1982
1983
0.0
0.2
0.4
0.6
0.8
1.0
1.2
1.4
1.6
REFINED COPPER (MILLIONS OF METRIC TONS)

for many forms of graphical display. By extending the techniques of time-series analysis to two dimensions, it is possible to perform spectral analysis, filtering, extrapolation, and similar operations on spatial data.

One major area of two-dimensional analysis is "image processing," which is a general term for computer manipulation of data which are normally presented visually (photographs, for example). As handled in the computer, an "image" consists of many small cells arranged on a two-dimensional grid. Each cell is called a "pixel," or picture element. As a simple analogy, consider a newspaper photograph, which consists of a matrix of black and white dots (as with the "raster" approach to computer graphics). When the image is large, or has high resolution (i.e., a small cell size), there can be an astronomical number of data, requiring large computers and special computational methods for practical use.

The examples in this section involve data which are essentially recorded in a gridded form. The procedures can be applied to randomly located data by first interpolating values onto a regular grid. As noted in Chapter 7, this can be a difficult problem, and may well add considerably to the amount of computer time needed to prepare the basic data for analysis. Like the one-dimensional case, aliasing is a potential problem if the observations are point values not taken at a sufficiently fine spacing. Here too, aliasing must be treated in the gridding or recording procedure to avoid later problems.

1. Remote Sensing from Satellites

The advent of satellite technology has brought profound changes in many scientific fields. In the earth sciences, satellites provide an unparalleled viewpoint for observing large scale features and monitoring dynamic surface phenomena like weather systems and seasonal changes in vegetation. Data from satellites are now routinely used in meteorology, agriculture, forestry, geology, and a variety of other disciplines.

Although such information is usually presented visually, a satellite survey cannot simply use conventional cameras because of the logistical problems of retrieving photographic film. As a result, the observations are encoded into digital form for radio transmission to a surface station, and require a computer for preparing a visual presentation. Although this means that sophisticated hardware and software are needed for simply displaying data, there is a major added benefit in having the data in computer form: many complex mathematical operations can then be applied to the data, and a great deal more information derived than from a photograph.

All satellite observations can be considered as a form of "remote sensing," in that information is obtained at a distance from the source and without direct contact. In the earth sciences, a major source of remote-sensing data is the LANDSAT series of satellites which started with LANDSAT 1 in 1972. They are in near-polar orbits at an altitude of about 920 kilometers. Each satellite completely covers the earth's surface in 18 days, so that a new image of any particular area is obtained every 18 days. As more satellites are launched, the effective period between images will be reduced.

The data recorded by LANDSAT satellites consist of four values of reflected energy from the earth's surface, each corresponding to a different frequency "band" in the visible and infrared regions of the electromagnetic spectrum. (The latest in the series, LANDSAT 4, records seven bands). The infrared bands are included with the visible, since they are more sensitive to certain surface conditions (e.g., type of vegetation). Each set of readings defines one pixel, which represents a square block on the ground about 80 meters square (30 meters square for LANDSAT 4). Data are collected as a series of images, each measuring about 185 by 170 km on the surface. An individual image thus contains millions of data points which are usually treated as a single entity.

Other types of satellite data are recorded and handled in a similar manner. Resolution, area of coverage, and time between observations may vary, of course, depending on the intended use of the data. As a general rule, all types involve vast numbers of pixels and specialized computer systems for practical use. The GOES system for weather observations takes an image of the entire Western Hemisphere every 30 minutes, with a resolution of about four miles. The data are collected in 1821 scans from pole to pole, each with eight channels (so the image contains over 14,000 lines). As with LANDSAT, multiple sensors are used, which further multiplies the amount of data to be transmitted and processed.

2. Basic Computer Manipulation of Satellite Images

Satellite images are normally studied in map form, which means that the raw data must be corrected to show a proper projection onto a two-dimensional surface. As recorded, the pixels represent areas of somewhat different size because of the effect of the earth's curvature and distortion in the imaging system. The correction involves a calibration to known points on the surface, and interpolation of new values on a regular grid in terms of the chosen map projection (the UTM system is normally used for LANDSAT). Gridding problems are not as serious as in some of the applications discussed in Chapter 7, since the coverage is essentially complete, and the interpolation does not demand extrapolation or extensive infill in uncontrolled areas. This process of "geometric correction" is done routinely for each new recorded image, and the results are then considered to be the basic data in further processing.

Given the enormous volume of data, the next problem is simply to effectively display an image. It can be presented in a variety of ways. Individual bands are plotted in shades of gray, according to the energy level for each pixel. Composites of different bands are usually shown as "false-color" images, by adapting a color-coding scheme for each band and employing colors that mix distinctly. "False" here means that the colors do not necessarily correspond to visible light: vegetation, for example, is most often shown in various shades of red. A standard color pattern has been established by the United States Geological Survey for basic display, although for specialized uses custom coding schemes are often used. These might involve the use of ratios of bands or other derived measures in addition to different color assignments. Some of these "image enhancement" methods are designed to employ the statistics of all data in the image, and thus can be invoked automatically. For example, contrast "stretching" is often used to ensure that a wide range of colors (or grey levels) are used. Color is not set by the absolute data values, but rather a fixed number of classes are assigned to the observed range of the data. This avoids situations where most of the pixels have similar shades when the range is limited (perhaps because of instrument problems, or simply as a result of similar characteristics of all areas within the image). More sophisticated methods can be used to make corrections for the movement of the source, which otherwise can blur the image and reduce resolution.

Color, then, is used extensively in plotting remote sensing data. There are a great variety of effective forms that cannot easily be illustrated with a limited set of examples. For this reason, no sample images are shown here. The books on remote sensing in the References provide many illustrations.

3. Computer Analysis of Images

Computer algorithms are often used to subdivide images into distinct regions on the basis of the characteristics of the data. This is essentially a multivariate classification problem, where the variables are the data values (or derived quantities like ratios) in a number of adjacent pixels (perhaps a three-by-three block). The statistical parameters of each set of variables are then used to define unique classes. In "unsupervised classification," a computer program assigns each block to one of an arbitrary number of classes (as in cluster analysis). In "supervised classification," the characteristics of particular areas of interest are first determined in known regions of the image. The computer then finds all blocks similar to each of the "training" areas. This is the same principle used in discriminant analysis, where different subsets of a large group of samples are used to define discriminant functions for classifying the other data.

Many uses for these classification procedures have been developed, and special computer systems are available for these applications. To take an inventory of the types of trees in a large forest, the approach might be to do an unsupervised classification and then to determine which particular species are present in the major areas. Alternately, areas known to contain species of particular interest might be defined and a supervised classification run to find other such regions. The inventory by type would then be a simple matter of computing total areas for each class. The results would be plotted in map form, as well, by drawing polygons around each region or shading with patterns or color.

Other examples include crop inventory in agricultural regions, detection of diseased areas, monitoring water pollution, and many other problems related to land use. There is no single procedure that works for all of these situations, since the different items being studied do not reflect electromagnetic energy in the same way. In other words, each has a distinct spectral pattern and requires data-specific analysis methods. Within each scientific discipline, many case histories have now have published, and successful techniques documented, so that an analyst new to this type of work can take advantage of the experiences of others.

Another common use of satellite images is to search for linear features corresponding to regional geologic trends. The existence of such "lineaments" is important in resource exploration, siting of major engineering projects (e.g., dams and pipelines), evaluation of earthquake hazards, and other fields where geology is a controlling influence. In many cases, lineaments can be easily detected on the original image. Special algorithms are sometimes used to search for such features automatically, and can be used in conjunction with image enhancement techniques when there are no apparent alignments. The selections of the computer are then plotted over the image for evaluation by the analyst.

SPECIAL SYSTEMS FOR HANDLING LARGE ARRAYS

Many time series are quite short, and do not place a great burden on the computer even when doing extensive calculations like correlations and Fourier transforms. Similarly, two-dimensional gridded data are often of manageable size for conventional computer processing. Many effective methods can be run on a personal computer, provided the size of data sets is kept within reasonable limits. In some fields, however, the volumes of data are enormous, and the entire resources of even a large computer may be required to achieve reasonable speed. For this reason, specialized hardware and software has been developed to take advantage of the array format and to provide much greater calculation speed for this type of data.

1. Examples of Large-Volume Data Sets

To illustrate the volume of data that may be involved, consider a typical seismic survey for oil exploration. The basic procedure is to transmit acoustic waves down into the earth's crust from the surface and then to monitor the vibrations at the surface for a period of time so that any waves that have returned after reflection from structural features in the crust can be detected. Each "shot" (be it a dynamite explosion or some other means of generating waves) is recorded at perhaps 96 different locations, for a period of four to six seconds, with readings taken every one or two milliseconds. A single record thus consists of 96 different time series, each containing 4000 to 6000 samples. To survey a complete prospect area, a number of shots are taken along multiple lines to form a grid throughout the area. A survey of moderate size might have 20 lines of 100 shots each, so that the total number of samples taken is around 800,000,000. These figures might easily be an order of magnitude larger for offshore exploration, since it is much easier to record a large number of shots from a continuously moving ship than on land.

As we saw earlier, similar numbers may be involved in processing data from satellites. A single LANDSAT 4 image contains about 35 million pixels (30 meter spacing, for a 185 by 170 km area), and seven different variables for each pixel.

The processing applied to these data can be extensive, often requiring hundreds or thousands of calculations for each sample. Before a seismic survey can be interpreted, extensive preparation is required, involving many correlations, filtering operations, frequency transforms, summations, and similar operations. In the case of satellite images, calibrations to proper mapping coordinates are necessary, along with a variety of scaling operations to produce a basic image. Detailed analysis may entail a number of complex multivariate techniques, which again means many computations for each pixel.

2. Scalar and Vector Processors

Although software may define data as arrays and allow easy programming of operations to "loop" through an array, conventional computer hardware does not distinguish an array from a set of unrelated variables. In order to perform calculations on an array, each member must be retrieved from memory, operated on as required, and stored back in memory independently. This is called a "scalar" operation, as distinct from a "vector" operation, following the mathematical terms, a scalar quantity being a single number, and a vector an ordered set of N numbers denoting position in an N-dimensional space.

This is not a fundamental limitation of computer hardware, however: it is possible to design hardware that operates much more efficiently when handling arrays. The key is to perform some tasks simultaneously: several elements of an array, for example, could be multiplied by a scaling factor at the same time. This is called "parallel processing," by analogy to parallel circuits having multiple paths for electric current.

Another method for increasing speed is to "pipeline" operations, that is, to break a task into a number of sequential steps that require only that the previous step be finished (and not the complete task). For example, the next element of an array can be loaded from memory while calculations are proceeding on the current element. New data can then enter the pipeline before previous data have left.

All modern computers make some use of these techniques, although they are not heavily exploited in most scalar operations. Hardware intended specifically for vector operations can be designed to have most operations on arrays organized in a pipeline, so that one complete result can be produced for each machine "cycle," even though many individual operations are involved. By contrast, a scalar operation can take many cycles to do the same job, as only one instruction is completed in each cycle. Similarly, large arrays can be routinely segmented into several pieces, each processed through a separate pipeline.

3. Array Processors

One method for implementing these procedures is to attach an "array processor" to a large scalar computer. An array processor is essentially a computer in its own right, although it is completely controlled by the other machine, and is generally capable of performing only a limited number of tasks. When extensive array manipulations are needed, data are passed from the main computer to the array processor, and returned when the desired operation is completed. This external transfer is essentially invisible to the applications program, which simply loads an array, calls an array function (perhaps a correlation or Fourier transform), and waits for the results. Note that this configuration allows some parallel processing capability, if the program can be structured to do other tasks during the waiting period.

4. Supercomputers

In some fields it is worthwhile to have a complete computer system to use just for vector operations, rather than just a peripheral device like an array processor. Such vector machines are often called "supercomputers," since they are orders of magnitude faster than even the largest scalar machines. They are also very expensive, and are still quite rare, with less than 100 in existence. Right now there are only two companies building these computers: Cray Research and Control Data Corporation.

As an independent system, a vector computer must be able to perform tasks such as data I/O, program scheduling, and other "system" functions, just like a scalar computer. The tremendous speed can create problems, since it becomes quite difficult to get data in and out of the CPU fast enough to take full advantage of its power. A large scalar machine is usually employed as a "front-end processor" to a supercomputer, to take over such tasks as control of I/O devices, loading of data arrays, etc. This is the reverse of an array processor configuration, since the scalar computer is controlled by the vector machine.

As we shall see in the next chapter, the primary use of supercomputers is in complex modeling problems like reservoir simulation for oil field production, atmospheric modeling for weather prediction, and aerodynamic simulation. These models may have millions of individual cells, and normally involve iterative solutions of complex equations, so that the number of calculations done in a single job may be many times greater even than the largest of the array manipulations referred to earlier (e.g., correlating thousands of time-series). In some cases, jobs run on a supercomputer would take weeks on a large conventional computer. Even so, there are problems demanding even more power than supercomputers can supply, and as with all other aspects of computer technology, impressive advances are expected in this area in the next decade.

CHAPTER 12

PHYSICAL MODELS AND DATA INTERPRETATION

The ultimate aim of data analysis is to gain an improved understanding of some phenomenon. The methods we have examined to this point all contribute to this goal, but do not directly provide information on the significance of the data with respect to the phenomenon. The final stage of analysis, then, is to "interpret" data, that is, to define the relationships of data to physical processes.

Although interpretations can be developed intuitively or by analogy to past experience, the scientific approach requires a model for phenomena. The "model" is a mathematical description of the relationships between the different variables associated with the phenomenon. Two types of variables can be distinguished. "Parameters" can be set independently in any particular model. "Predicted variables" are functionally dependent on parameters and must be computed from them. The modeling process is in essence to calculate theoretical data (i.e., predicted variables) from parameters, and to compare them to real values. If the observed data show a good "fit" to these estimates, we consider the model to be an adequate representation of the real world. If not, the model must be revised, to consider additional variables or modify the equations defining the relationships.

A modeling study, like other types of computer processing, can be viewed as a three-stage system, with input, computation, and output. Input here is a set of specific values for the model parameters. The computations involve the mathematical formulae which describe the functional relationships. The normal output is the theoretical values to be compared to real data. In many cases, the roles of input and output may be wholly or partially reversed, depending on which variables are defined as independent, and which are being estimated.

In this chapter, the procedures involved in interpretation and modeling are examined. General principles for effective computer application are considered, by relating this process to the methods discussed in earlier chapters. It is more difficult to generalize here, since each particular problem requires its own special model. The discussion necessarily concentrates on specific examples in different fields. This is in distinct contrast to the rest of the book, where methods for data analysis and display are applicable to many situations, and the nature of the examples is secondary to the techniques.

THE NATURE OF MATHEMATICAL MODELS

In a broad sense, any mathematical equation relating different variables can be considered a model. The function may be (by definition) an exact measure, for example $Y = 2*X$, where Y is always a derived quantity. More commonly, though, we use functions as approximations or summaries of statistical relationships, as when we fit a regression line to two variables.

Many such simple uses of models have been employed in earlier chapters, often without being explicitly defined as such. As we have just noted, a regression line is a two-parameter model that describes a linear dependence of one variable on another. Statistical inferences with the normal distribution are an implicit use of a theoretical model, since they entail the assumption that the data have a true normal distribution. In spatial analysis, gridded representations are often used as models for continuous variables like topography. The procedures in Chapter 8 for estimating structure and locating anomalies all employ mathematical models: weighted averages of adjacent points, polynomial fits, and Fourier transforms are some examples.

1. Physical Models

Often the term "modeling" is used in a more restrictive sense, to mean only those cases where a large set of equations are used to describe a complex process involving many variables. For example, economic models are used to predict future trends in inflation, unemployment, productivity, etc. A model must be able to define relationships between these items, and parameters such as population growth rates, technological change, depletion of resources, and so on. In this sense, a model attempts to describe the physical relationship of the variables, and is not just a mathematical abstraction that provides a reasonable fit to the data.

With spatial data, a physical model must allow for spatial variations as well as interrelationships among a number of parameters. This is normally achieved by subdividing the region into a number of cells, each of which can have different data values. Mathematical equations define any physical contraints on spatial variation, as well as the functional dependencies of the variables. For example, the earth's atmosphere is considered as a set of three-dimensional blocks in weather prediction. Parameters such as temperature, humidity, pressure, and air flow are specified for each block. The physical laws governing these variables are incorporated into the model using the theories of fluid dynamics. From a series of recent observations, new model parameters are then calculated to produce the basic information for predictions.

2. Empirical and Theoretical Models

As we have just noted, the physical laws relevant to the phenomena under study must be formulated into the model. This implies that the cause-and-effect relationships operating among the model parameters and the observed data are known. This is often not the case, of course, since all of the potentially important variables may not even be identified, let alone quantified in mathematical terms. In economic and sociological studies, for example, many different aspects of human behavior and the physical world are interrelated in complex forms which frequently defy precise analysis.

In the absence of a rigorous theory, models can be developed empirically. This means that the governing equations are defined on the basis of providing an acceptable fit to the observations, and do not necessarily correspond to a known physical process. Derivation of the equations is largely a trial-and-error process, based on intuition, experience with similar problems, and other subjective criteria.

Empirical models are used in many situations, often by necessity. In fields like economics where it is impossible to perform rigidly controlled experiments, cause-and-effect can never be unambiguously defined. There is always the possibility that some unknown factor is influencing all of the data, and thus biasing the interpretation. Empirical relationships can be used to test correlations between different variables, and judged for statistical "goodness-of-fit." It is always desirable to have a plausible explanation for such apparent relationships, but it may not be possible to express them in exact mathematical terms. It is well known that a change in the U.S. economy, for example a rise in interest rates, is generally reflected in other countries after a period of time. The delay time, and magnitude of the change, cannot be predicted except in terms of past averages, since there are so many modifying factors which cannot be determined ahead of time.

An empirical model may be just the first step in studying a new phenomenon. The next phase is to develop a theoretical model in which the equations have a precise physical significance. Early attempts to calculate the orbits of the planets relied on empirical formulae which were eventually replaced by the physical theories of Kepler and Newton. A model of the solar system can now be used to compute the orbits of spacecraft to a high degree of accuracy, given parameters such as starting velocity, rocket burning time, etc. In atmospheric modeling, the laws of thermodynamics and fluid motion can be defined mathematically so that the result of a change in any parameter can be computed.

Such calculations can also be used to test the relative importance of parameters. A series of calculations are performed with all parameters but one fixed. Changes in the computed variables are recorded as a function of the value of the chosen parameter. The process is repeated for all of the parameters in the model, to find those which have the greatest effect. The end result may be that the modeling problem can be greatly simplified by reducing the number of parameters used in the calculations. This is more than a linear savings in computer time, since there are *N* squared relationships among *N* variables.

THE MODELING PROCESS

Once a mathematical model has been defined, it must be tested to determine how accurately it describes the real world. It many cases, this can be done directly, by considering various observed data as unknowns, and calculating their values from the other data. Like the process of testing for significance, the operation can be repeated for all variables, to give a relative ranking of the model's success in predicting each one.

If the accuracy of the results is deemed insufficient, it may be necessary to revise the model. The errors may also result from imprecise data, of course. The effect of data errors can be evaluated by the type of significance test used to determine important parameters. Calculations are run using the observed data and for possible extreme values due to errors (some assumptions about the range of errors are obviously required). There may also be fundamental limitations in the model itself, requiring either changes to take account of additional parameters, or more rigorous definition of built-in assumptions. The range of problems to which the model applies may become more restricted. If this is the case, it is desirable to have a modeling program test the data for suitability, whenever possible, so that warnings can be issued that some basic criteria are not met.

In many modeling studies, the objective is to derive optimum values for the model parameters. The data are assumed to be correct, and the model to provide a complete description of the problem. The difficulties described in the previous paragraph can then be ignored in modeling, although one must always be prepared to reconsider them if the need arises. This is a process of fitting theoretical estimates to actual data: something we have already seen in other situations (as when fitting a regression line or polynomial surface to estimate gross trends).

Although the model parameters and observed data can all be considered as variables, there is often a fundamental difference which affects how they are used. By definition, observed data can be measured directly, and thus a true value is available to compare to the model's calculations. The parameters of the model may not be directly measurable: they can only be estimated. The accuracy of the parameter values must therefore be inferred statistically from the quality of the fit to the observed data. Some observed values may also be parameters, in that they influence the values of other variables. In an analysis of the stock market, prices and averages are known precisely, while delay times and multiplying factors can be defined as parameters in order to quantify the relationship between them. When the model equations are empirically derived, the unknown parameters may include numerical coefficients. Some of the observed data are used as input to the model, while others are reserved for comparison to the predicted values. Different combinations of input and output might be tested as well.

In general, then, we require a method to calculate unobservable parameters from observed data. There are two different strategies for doing this: "direct" and "inverse" modeling. These terms can be misleading, as there are implications of forward and reverse motion, when in fact the direction is purely a matter of convention.

1. The "Direct" Problem

The direct (or "forward") problem in modeling is to predict data values from the model parameters. There is an implicit assumption of cause and effect in this procedure: the data are viewed as observational variables controlled by the model. In other words, the data change in response to changes in the model, and cannot be modified directly. For example, a simple weather model might calculate the temperature as a function of the time of year, time of day, and degree of cloud cover. These variables are important controls on temperature, but are not controlled by it.

To use a direct modeling approach, the mathematical equations relating the chosen parameters and observed variables must be known. The model must also provide a unique solution, that is, any particular set of parameters must correspond to only one value for each predicted variable. If this is not the case it is impossible to make comparisons to the real observations.

In practical use, the first step is to define some reasonable initial values for the parameters and then to run through the calculations to produce a set of predicted values. By comparing these to the real data, an experienced analyst can make adjustments to the parameters, to reduce the differences after recalculation. Multiple iterations continue until a satisfactory fit is obtained.

Adjustment of parameters after each step can be performed automatically, if a set of rules has been included in the modeling program. A combined interactive approach is also possible, where the computer sets new parameters, but allows the analyst to override its choices. As we saw in Chapter 5, the program can also be used in a "batch" mode, simply performing the model calculations and displaying the results. The analyst may then choose another set of parameters after examining the output from the last run. The relative merits of these different approaches are very dependent on the nature of the problem, the experience of the analyst, the amount of computation required, and other factors.

2. The "Inverse" Problem

In some cases it is possible to follow the reverse strategy and to calculate the model parameters from the data. Given the objective of obtaining the best set of parameters, it might seem more logical to call this a direct approach, since it aims at a direct calculation of the parameters instead of employing the iterative trial-and-error method of the previous section. The name "inverse" reflects the view that the natural flow is from parameters to data, and not the reverse.

In general, solving an inverse problem is much more difficult than the corresponding direct problem. Well-behaved mathematical functions are not necessarily so well behaved when they are reversed, and may not even have a closed solution. Errors may always be present in the data, and can lead to wildly unrealistic results by moving the data outside the stability limits of the model. The possibility of multiple solutions (see the next section) may impose restrictions on the type of model which may be used.

The equations for an inverse calculation may be nonlinear, which means that an iterative solution will probably be required. While this does not require the analyst to supply additional information, it may demand a considerable amount of computer time. There is also the possibility than a satisfactory result will not be obtained, which means that the program must have checks to allow it to stop after a specified number of iterations or when successive steps produce no significant improvement.

3. The Problem of Non-Uniqueness

A major problem in inversion is "non-uniqueness": many different models may fit the observed data equally well. Intuitively this is to be expected when the model has more parameters than predicted variables. Furthermore, the physical process itself may preclude uniqueness. In gravitational theory, for example, many configurations of different bodies can produce the same gravitational field. As a result, there is no general solution to the "multibody problem," so that simplifying assumptions are necessary in computing satellite orbits and in interpreting gravity surveys in mineral exploration.

Regardless of the approach, non-uniqueness poses a serious problem in any modeling study, since it implies that there may be many solutions to the problem. Although the objective of a study may be to derive a single model, it is important to also be aware of other models that might also be acceptable. There may be a very large number of these, so rather than try to find them all, we should attempt to set limits on the parameters which will define the range of all possible models. The basic philosophy is analogous to the setting of confidence limits in statistics, where estimated extremes for a mean value are used to judge risk in decision making.

The range of solutions is often defined by a "Monte Carlo" modeling method. The model parameters are all considered as independent random variables so that a potentially infinite number of models can be generated. For each one, the direct calculations are performed, and the results tested against the available data to decide if the model is accepted. The operation is repeated until a reasonable number of models are obtained, or the amount of computer time exceeds a pre-set limit. As the name suggests, there is a random chance of any given model being accepted. The range of possible models is defined according to the statistics of the sets of selected parameters.

While this brute-force approach may seem absurdly inefficient, it is frequently the only practical method. Depending on the mathematics involved, it may be possible to set parameter limits with an inverse method. This has been done with considerable success in a variety of problems in geophysics, remote sensing, and other fields. As we noted before, the inverse problem is often insoluble, however, so that some type of direct modeling will be required. The advantage of the Monte-Carlo method is that it is unbiased.

An analyst could define a series of models to perform the same test, but might well restrict the parameters to preconceived notions of what will be acceptable.

Although a true random model could have any value for each parameter, practical considerations usually dictate that each parameter vary within set bounds. For example, if density is a parameter in a geologic model, it might be limited to values between 0 and 10, to avoid pointless testing of models with completely unrealistic densities. Setting such limits may reintroduce a bias, so they must have a wide tolerance to allow a thorough test. To judge whether the limits are too narrow, the parameter values for all accepted models are examined to see if any have come close to the limits. In other words, we expect the range of accepted values to be much smaller than the limits applied for generation of the random models.

Increased speed can also be gained with other shortcuts. Instead of performing the complete prediction of all observed variables, we can compute one at a time, so that the operation can stop as soon as any test fails. The tests could be ranked in order of significance so that the most critical variables are checked first. It may be possible to perform a simplified calculation as a first-level test, so that a more complex operation is used only when truly necessary. For example, in testing whether a point is inside a multisided polygon, a program can first compare its coordinates to the extremes of the polygon vertices (i.e., decide whether the point is within the rectangle which encloses the polygon). There are many other possibilities, many of which are specific to particular problems, and thus cannot be easily summarized.

PREDICTIVE MODELING

Mathematical models are extensively used in prediction problems. Once again, the basic principle is that some unmeasurable variables are derived from the observed data. The difference is that the observations are taken over a period of time and the model is used to estimate values for the same variables at times outside the observed range. As we noted in Chapter 11, "time" can be viewed more generally as any coordinate, to include spatial data in one, two, or more dimensions.

An immediate problem arises: with predictive modeling it is no longer possible to compare the output of the model to real data. As a result, a modeling study confined to the available data is a prerequisite to a predictive study. In other words, the model must first be used to compute values for observed times and then adjusted as necessary to produce acceptable results. This requires not only that the interrelationships of the variables be defined, but also that the changes over time be quantifiable. We must be able to produce realistic values for the model parameters, before we can use them to compute the extrapolated values.

This procedure can be viewed in an alternate light: all of the observed data can be considered as parameters of the model, and future values treated as dependent variables to be predicted. There are additional constraints to be considered, since the variables are usually expected to be continuous, and the time dependence must follow the physical laws incorporated in the model. The test of the model is then to see how well it can predict data for part of the observation period from the remaining times (for example, how well an economic model can estimate the Dow Jones average for the current month from data for the previous year).

The effect of time dependence is to add another dimension to the model, which demands a great increase in computer resources. Spatial problems normally treated as an array of cells will require much larger arrays. Atmospheric models in weather prediction require several parameters to be defined at each point of a three-dimensional grid. Each grid point is also defined at a number of times which normally correspond to a fixed interval. While not all of these may be simultaneously required in computer memory, a number of adjacent points will generally be treated together, as required by the constraints of continuity in time and space.

Predictive modeling, then, is normally a problem requiring large computer systems, unless there are a limited number of variables and data to be considered. In this case, the problem is more in the nature of short multiple time series than complex time-varying physical models, and it may be possible to run a modeling study on a small computer.

EXAMPLES OF MODELING

As noted at the outset of this chapter, generalizations about modeling and interpretation cannot be taken too far. The methods that are most successful in particular fields tend to be largely dependent on the specific details of the problem. To illustrate the use of modeling techniques, a variety of examples are presented here.

1. Geophysical Exploration with Gravity

Exploration for oil and minerals has the basic goal of defining the geologic structures in the earth's crust. A variety of different techniques can be used, and in most cases more than one type of data is acquired. The interpretation process involves developing a geologic model consistent with all the available data. Each set of data can be interpreted separately, although the results of the other types will be used as constraints in modeling. Gravity surveys are often used as a preliminary stage of exploration, or as an adjunct to other methods which yield more information. The gravitational attraction is measured at various locations on the surface, perhaps along a line or at locations chosen to cover a two-dimensional area.

Although the readings of a gravity meter are dominated by the attraction of the earth as a whole, there are subtle fluctuations due to density changes in the earth's crust. The objective of a gravity survey is to determine these density variations by examining the components of the gravity readings that are due to near-surface sources. Prior to interpretation, a considerable amount of data processing is required to separate the desired portion of the observed "field." This is by no means a trivial operation, although for the purposes of this example we will assume it has been done. The problem is then to find the geologic model which provides the best fit of the computed gravity to the data. Conceptually this is a fairly simple modeling problem, involving only one type of computed data and a limited number of parameters.

There are several ways of defining a geologic model suitable for computing a gravity field. Since the key parameter is density, one obvious approach is to divide the crust into a number of cells, specifying the density of each. This does not necessarily correspond to a simple structural picture, however, so a more common alternative is to consider that the gravity field is due to a number of separate sources, each with a constant density. The model parameters now are the geometric factors which define each source (e.g., shape, size, depth of burial), and its density. The source bodies can be collections of simple shapes (e.g., spheres or prisms), or have a complex configuration defined by vertices of polygons at various depths.

A gravity modeling program can proceed by a direct or inverse approach, since mathematics for both procedures can be derived using potential field theory. Since there are a relatively limited number of parameters, and generally not an excessive number of observations, results are obtained quickly, and the process can be performed interactively. This means that the analyst can examine the results of a model calculation (as displayed on a terminal), and immediately revise the parameters for another run, if desired. A single display is usually adequate to show all of the results (this is not the case in the more complicated problems to be discussed later). If the problem is two-dimensional, the display may be of the form shown in Fig. 12.1, where the model represents a cross section and the computed and theoretical gravity fields are plotted as profiles above it.

In a three-dimensional model, the gravity field is computed at various locations on a two-dimensional surface (e.g., a regular grid for contouring, or at the points where the observations were taken). The theoretical data

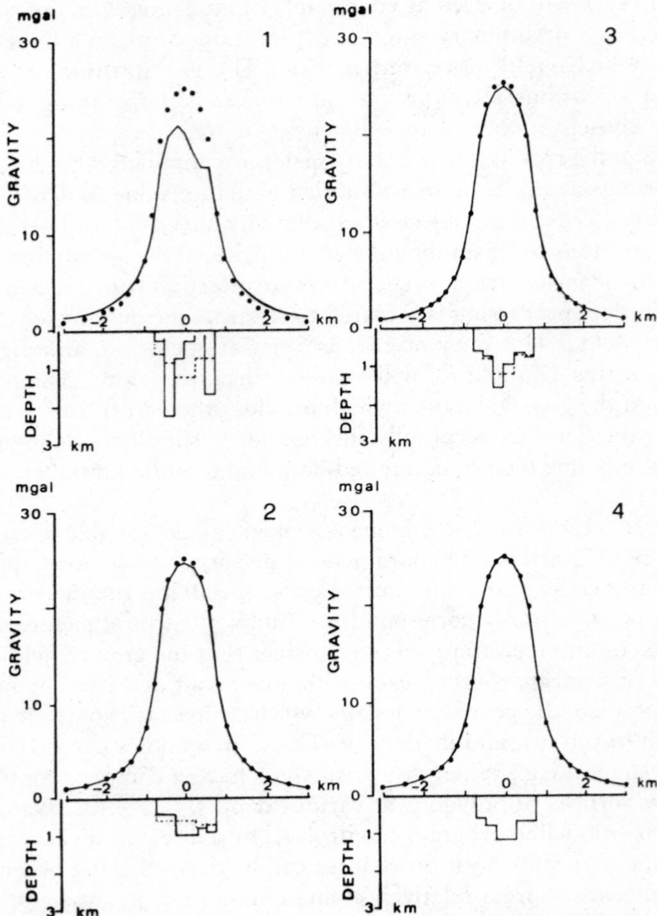

FIGURE 12.1 Results of modeling a gravity profile. The model is shown in simple block form at the bottom of each diagram. The observed data are shown as points, while the value computed from the model is plotted as a line. Successive steps of an automatic iterative process are shown, with the final model represented by a dotted line on the preliminary trials. (Reproduced from "Some Aspects of the Interpretation of Gravity Data for the Study of Regional and Local Structures", by A. Rapolla, in *The Solution of the Inverse Problem in Geophysical Interpretation,* copyright Plenum Press, New York 1981, by permission of the publisher).

can be plotted on a map, for comparison to the real data. Difference maps can also be used, to show areas where the discrepancies are greatest.

Since gravity fields are non-unique, it is necessary to apply constraints in the modeling process to derive a unique solution. This generally means that the form of the model is subject to such limitations as a fixed number of source objects, or sources confined to a small range of depths in the crust. In addition, any information available from other sources is incorporated whenever possible. For example, the density at the surface may be known from geologic sampling, to provide fixed values for at least part of the model.

Figure 12.1 is an example of the simplest kind of gravity problem. The source of the gravity field is a single body, represented as a collection of blocks. The computed field and real gravity data are plotted as profiles above the surface. In practical use, this type of plot might be drawn on a graphics terminal, and the configuration of the body changed by entering new parameters from the keyboard, or by drawing the new outline directly on the screen with an input device like a digitizing tablet. In a three-dimensional problem, the procedure is conceptually the same, but considerably more difficult to perform interactively, since it is difficult to plot a three-dimensional object on a flat surface, and computation time is necessarily much longer.

2. Economic Forecasting

In recent years, many organizations have attempted to use computer models to predict the future course of the world economy. The most widely publicized study to date is the 1972 report of the Club of Rome, "The Limits to Growth," which projected economic trends into the 21st Century and showed that expectations of continued growth were unrealistic at the least, and at the worst an invitation to disaster. Such results were obtained only by a consideration of the interaction of different variables, since they are a result of the conflicting demands of population growth and depleting resources.

This study and others like it are based on the techniques of multiple time-series analysis. Using a number of recorded economic parameters and a numerical model of the relationships between them, future values can be predicted. This is more complex than simply extrapolating observed patterns, since the possibility of fundamental changes in some parameters cannot be discounted. For example, projections of energy supply depend on potential new oil discoveries, development of new technologies, and other factors which cannot easily be estimated.

The method for handling these contingencies is to do the prediction for a number of different models in order to produce results that are dependent on the particular scenario. There may be a great many possibilities to test, and no absolute method for judging the results, so the significance of any single model is largely left to the judgment of the analyst. It is fairly common in such studies to see conflicting reports based on apparently similar models, since the authors may have different opinions on the most likely course of events.

Economic models are by nature empirical, since the variations due to such diverse elements as changing weather and human decisions cannot be rigidly defined. This can also contribute to great differences in reported results, even when the same basic equations are used, since each analyst may derive different values for the numeric "constants" in the model.

The results of economic prediction are usually presented in multiple-time-series plots extending into the future. A single graph can represent only a few of the many variables included in the model, so it is clear that extensive use of computer graphics would be required to examine all of the results. To compare results of different scenarios, output from separate models must be saved, and combined in plotting. This is another situation where the data handling routines that support the basic program must be flexible and efficient so that the analyst will have complete freedom in evaluating the computer output.

3. Reservoir Simulation

"Simulation" is a term describing the use of computers to model time-dependent processes. The aim of a simulation study is often to test whether a large project will perform up to expectations, before a large amount of money is spent on its development. The project might be an economic feasability study for business expansion; an engineering plan for a large project like a dam, a pipeline, or a new industrial process; or an automobile or aircraft design; and many others. Simulation is also used extensively as a training aid in areas like aviation and spaceflight, where it is desirable to train an operator without risking potentially fatal and expensive accidents.

Our example for simulation is a very complex modeling problem, combining some aspects of the three-dimensional gravity model with the prediction of the economic model. Reservoir simulation is a procedure for studying the production of oil from an oil field and for designing optimum methods to extract the greatest possible amounts of oil (and natural gas). A large field may produce oil worth hundreds of millions of dollars over a period of a few decades, so the decisions based on computer prediction are very important to the future of the organizations that own the oil.

It is never possible to extract all of the oil in the ground, and in fact recovery rates of 25 to 30 percent are all that can reasonably be expected in many areas. An improvement of even one percent can be very significant, considering the total volume (and value) of oil in place. To increase the total recovery, a variety of secondary (and tertiary) methods can be used. These generally involve drilling additional wells to pump in water, steam, and other fluids to maintain pressure and/or improve the flowing characteristics. Reservoir simulation is used to choose the best locations for additional drilling, and to minimize the number of wells required.

The "reservoir" is the portion of the earth's crust that contains both the oil and the wells. The model consists of a number of blocks for which such parameters as porosity, permeability, pressure, temperature, and oil content are specified. The positions of all of the wells are defined, along with the pumping or injection rates. The size of the blocks can vary throughout the reservoir, to allow more resolution in the densely drilled areas without requiring an excessive number of blocks in the outer areas, where there may be only a few injection wells.

The model equations apply various laws of fluid flow, conservation of matter, and so on, to estimate new parameters for each block at increments of time throughout the expected lifetime of the field. The physical constraints imposed by the well locations, maximum practical pumping rates, and so on, must also be followed. The objective of the study is to maximize the total production from the field. This requires that various pumping rates, different patterns for additional drilling, and other operational factors be evaluated. Since these imply different operating costs, the rule of maximum production really means maximum earnings (which may not necessarily coincide).

To plan the development of an oil field, simulations must be run for each proposed scheme. The results are then compared to determine the effect of adding new wells, using different pumping rates, and so on. Since there are so many variables, and each simulation requires a great deal of computer time, careful selection of the models to be used is essential. This is obviously not a problem for a novice, but rather for expert engineers experienced in reservoir simulations.

The amount of computation required demands the use of very large computers. Reservoir simulation is in fact one of the major areas where supercomputers are used, although scalar machines with array processors can also be employed (see the previous chapter for a discussion of these systems).

In addition to the heavy computing, reservoir modeling poses another major problem: the sheer volume of output makes it difficult to interpret the results. The model may contain thousands of blocks, and may be defined at intervals of one year over a period of 30 years. For each block, and each time, all the dynamic parameters (flow rates in various directions, oil/gas/water content, pressure, etc.) must be defined. For any one variable, this is essentially a four-dimensional problem, which means it cannot easily be shown in a single display.

As we might expect from previous discussions, reservoir modeling is a prime candidate for computer graphics. To show the depletion of oil from a given level, a series of maps can be plotted, each corresponding to a given time and showing the type of fluid in each block (e.g., oil in red, gas in white, and water in blue). If the appropriate equipment is available, these might even be presented in "movie" form, by creating a plot for each time and displaying them rapidly in sequence. Even with such techniques, a great deal of graphic output is necessary to allow the behavior of each variable to be examined. There are other variations: plotting cross-sections through the model to show the variation of each parameter with depth, and using three-dimensional views to depict the region of influence of each well, for instance.

4. Atmospheric Modeling

Numerical weather prediction is similar in many ways to reservoir simulation. The basic structure of the model is once again a large number of blocks spanning a three-dimensional region (here the lower atmosphere). For each block, temperature, humidity, pressure, velocity, and other parameters are defined. The variations of parameters in time and space must obey physical laws of continuity, fluid dynamics, and thermodynamics. Boundary conditions are also important, since the configuration of land and water, ocean currents, mountain ranges, and other geographic factors are a major influence on the atmosphere.

Since weather phenomena may have a great range of scales, the computational problem is even more complex than in the previous example. Strong weather systems range from tornadoes a few tens of meters across to hurricanes measuring several hundred kilometers, to the jet stream, which is essentially global. Significant changes can occur in a matter of hours or take several months or years. With present technology, it is impossible to use a single model to encompass these extremes. Phenomena of different scales are studied independently, employing block sizes appropriate to the scale. Although some events are thereby excluded from the model, it may be necessary to consider their effect as a statistical average. For example, in global circulation studies individual thunderstorms will not be explicitly defined, but the average number of storms can be used as a contributing factor in calculating net transfer of energy and moisture.

Like any other prediction, the results of atmospheric modeling can not be verified directly, but must be checked against actual events. For short-term weather forecasts, this means fairly immediate answers. For long-term

FIGURE 12.2. A display of the results of atmospheric modeling. These two plots show the pressure distributions obtained from two different models of global circulation. (Reproduced from "Parameterization of Travelling Weather Systems," by G.J. Shutts, in *Theory of Climate*, ed. B. Saltzman, copyright 1983, Academic Press, New York, by permission of the publisher).

climatic shifts, the prediction ranges far into the future, and thus can only be tested by using the historical record to make hypothetical predictions about actual events in the recent past. These predictions, of course, are then compared to what actually happened.

Atmospheric modeling also demands the most powerful computers, and is probably even more likely than reservoir simulation to be run on a supercomputer. The calculations are equally complex, and must be performed much more frequently. After an initial study, the model for an oil field might be recomputed every year so that new information can be incorporated. Because of rapid changes in weather patterns, new predictions must be run on a daily basis, if not even more frequently. Large scale forecasts (e.g., for an entire country) might be revised every month.

Computer graphics are again essential for an understanding of the results. Many different types are used, including maps of different variables, profile displays along latitude or longitude lines, vertical profiles to show variations with elevation, and time series displays. An example is shown in Fig. 12.2, in which contour maps of atmospheric pressure are used to compare results from two different models of global circulation.

5. Modeling of Dynamic Structures

One of the fundamental questions in any science is how natural objects evolved into their presently observed forms. In chemistry, the structure of complex molecules must be related to a progressive addition of atoms to simpler forms. In biology, the evolution of life from the components of the earth's early atmosphere and crust is not clearly known. Geophysicists and astronomers seek to explain how the earth and solar system developed from an amorphous cloud of interstellar gas and dust. In cosmology, the key question is how the universe expanded into its observed form after the "Big Bang."

To answer such a question, it is necessary to have a model that describes the initial situation, and then to apply known physical laws (or the best available theories) over the requisite period of time to produce a result that can be compared to the present. The normal principles of modeling apply: if the comparison is judged to be inadequate, the initial model or governing equations must be adjusted for another trial. Unlike many other problems, the modeling process is built entirely on assumed quantities, that is, no observed data are included in the initial model (simply because it is impossible to make observations in the past). The results, then, are very dependent on the assumptions made by the analyst, and are frequently discounted.

In some cases, if it is practical to duplicate the assumed initial conditions, dynamic structures can be modeled in a laboratory. In a classic experiment performed in the 1950s, Stanley Miller showed that simple organic compounds could be produced in the atmospheric environment thought to exist in the earth's early history. (He placed the appropriate mixture of gases in a sealed container and applied elevated levels of ultraviolet light and synthetic lightning discharges.) It is impossible to perform such an experiment for large scale phenomena, of course. It is difficult to visualize the Big Bang, when the entire universe was essentially concentrated at a point, let alone try to duplicate it! Once a mathematical theory has been developed, it becomes possible to replace a physical experiment with a computer model.

To illustrate this application, we examine the cosmological problem in somewhat more detail. As briefly noted earlier, the simple picture of the origin of the universe is that all matter was concentrated at a single point, perhaps 20 billion years ago. Since such a discontinuity cannot be maintained, there was an immense explosion (the "Big Bang"), and all matter rapidly expanded in all directions. In recent years, a great deal of research has contributed to a detailed understanding of such an event. All of the laws of physics are important, especially in the early stages when only fundamental particles could exist. Later, the nuclear forces become less significant, and gravity becomes the dominant force.

This picture would suggest that the average density of the universe is constant, since there would be no preferential direction for the initial expansion. Astronomical observations show, however, that there are definite large-scale structures in the universe. To determine whether this represents a flaw in the theory, or whether it is a situation where intuition is misleading, computer models have been developed to simulate the development of the universe after the Big Bang. The initial model presents a uniform distribution of rapidly expanding matter. Other initial conditions (e.g., the presence of small "density waves") are defined in accordance with the predictions of particle physics for the very early evolution of the universe. Applying the laws of gravitational attraction over many intervals of time, later distributions of matter can be calculated. The results show that there is a clear tendency for large-scale structures to develop. The model does not yield the actual structures, of course, but this result shows that the existence of structure does not pose a conflict with current theory.

CONCLUSION

As we noted at the outset, a successful modeling study often is the ultimate goal in analyzing any set of data. The end of a project, though, seldom leads to a complete end of a study. Many different circumstances can arise that necessitate a further examination of the problem.

New data may be acquired, demanding at the very least a check for consistency with previous data. This might involve more samples of the same type, or new types of measurements. In the latter case, it may be necessary to expand the model to account for additional variables. Observation methods are continually being improved, so it is often advantageous to record new data to see if higher resolution allows more detailed interpretations to be derived.

The physical theory behind the model is not necessarily unchanging, either. In many cases, of course, new data point out inadequacies in the theory, and stimulate research toward a more complete model. Einstein's theory of relativity was stimulated by observations made in the late 19th century which failed to find variations in the speed of light coming from stars moving in different directions. Advances in science can also work in the opposite direction: new theories may require new observational techniques before they can be adequately tested. The concepts of black holes and neutron stars were derived strictly from considerations of the effects of the gravitational collapse of large bodies. These concepts were developed decades before astronomical observations became sufficiently advanced to detect these objects.

Given a high probability that parts of any set of data will have to be reevaluated in the future, care should be taken in organizing a computer study to enable it to be quickly reactivated. As we saw in Chapter 5, such flexibility is largely dependent on the operating practices of the analyst, regardless of the hardware or software. Two main points should be emphasized: first, all computer files associated with a project should be logically named, and be as descriptive as possible of their contents. Second, data files, special techniques, problems, and results should be documented as thoroughly as possible. This will allow experience from an earlier study to be relearned quickly, and not have to be redeveloped from scratch.

As a final note, the analyst should always be willing to try new approaches. Perhaps the greatest single advantage of using a computer is that the machine takes over the routine, repetitive tasks, leaving the analyst more time to investigate special problems, study new types of data, try different interpretations, and so on. Following the principles of this book, it should be possible to make this a practical reality, not just an ideal goal.

APPENDIX A.

CHARACTERISTICS OF EFFECTIVE ANALYSIS SYSTEMS: A SUMMARY

Computer systems may be quite easy or extremely difficult to use, depending on the level of the software and the degree of logical organization in the operating procedures. These topics are discussed in detail in Chapter 5, and noted in many other parts of the book. This appendix is a brief review of the key points to consider in designing and using a computerized data analysis system.

1. Use a consistent structure, with
—standard parameter names and meanings
—similar sequence of operations

2. Provide help to the user, but allow shortcuts like
—"menu" method for describing parameters,
—complete parameter checking before starting computations, and
—detailed tutorials that can be bypassed by expert users

3. Don't try to be all-encompassing:
—design a system as a number of component programs, rather than

as one massive program which does everything
—limit the options in each program to those which are important

4. Strive for independence from specific devices or data structures:
—put data in a self-documenting database
—send graphical displays to a variety of plotters or terminals

5. Make output easy to interpret:
—use compact forms, especially with graphics
—annotate as completely as possible such items as file and variable names, key parameters, creation date, etc

6. Take advantage of utility programs for
—sorting
—general purpose data selection
—listings and file summaries

7. Develop complete documentation with
—fully descriptive names for files
—"index" files describing available databases
—internal comments in programs and run-streams
—concise "cook-books" to describe operations requiring a number of independent steps
—"master" copies of important parameter lists, etc

8. Stress flexibility
—programs should allow different analytical methods to be applied with equal ease
—the analyst must be willing to experiment, and not just stay with "tried and true" techniques

APPENDIX B.

AN EXAMPLE COMPUTER SYSTEM FOR DATA ANALYSIS AND DISPLAY

To illustrate how the principles of this book can be applied, a brief outline of an existing system is given here. Some of the features discussed in the main text are not available in this system because of the inevitable budget and manpower constraints faced by any organization.

Placer Development Ltd. is a major Canadian mining company. Placer uses computers in all facets of its operations. The system of interest here was developed for the analysis of data in the exploration and evaluation of new mining prospects. It is also applied to a variety of other problems, including price trend analysis (by the marketing department), financial data reporting (accounting), and computer performance monitoring.

1. Data Structure

The key to effective use of a computer in data analysis is an organized and easy-to-use method for storing and locating data. Placer's Data Analysis and Display System employs a fairly simple database structure. All data files have a short "header" in the first few records, containing the format description, variable names, and a short description of the file contents. Data fields are classified in three groups: character identifiers, coordinates, and numeric analytical data. The files are stored in character format, and can be accessed (and revised, if necessary) by system utility programs like text editors.

The analysis programs read sequentially through data files, so simple read-write commands are sufficient for all input/output operations. In most cases, the procedure is to read a single record, perform the desired calculations, and then write an output record (if required). With this approach it is generally necessary to read every record in a file, so in practical use the system is not applied to large files. The limit is perhaps 5000 records, although the programs can handle more. Larger files are more structured, to allow immediate retrieval of subsets of data without a complete search through the file. This requires special programs which are not considered part of the data analysis system. Some programs have limitations on the number of records they can handle, since they retain all data in memory for recursive operations. These restrictions are necessary to allow use of available utility programs for data revisions, and to keep the programs relatively simple and easy to write.

2. Data Management Programs

Data files can be created by normal system programs, independently of the data analysis system. For example, tabular data on prices can be entered by conventional methods, and the appropriate header records added to the file by means of the text editor. In many cases, data files with the header are created automatically by programs which load particular types of data. This approach is used at Placer's laboratory: all geochemical measurements are stored in a single segmented file, and any data retrieved from this file is in the form described above.

Various utility programs are used to manipulate the data:

SMERGE: Merge two or more files into one, either as a simple concatenation or by matching on specified identifier fields; this program is also used as a general-purpose sort program.

COORD: Coordinate transformations such as latitude-longitude to UTM and general translation and rotation.

LISTDF: List data files, and produce summary statistical information (to verify contents of a file, and as a first step in analysis).

SELECT: Is used for general-purpose data selection: subsets of a data file are created by tests on specified fields:

(a) Match character fields to list of values.

(b) Test numeric fields against minimum-maximum limits.

(c) Combine (a) with (b).

(d) Test if any two numeric fields define a point within an arbitrary polygon.

3. Data Analysis: Statistics

A variety of basic statistical measures can be computed using an interactive program called STATS. It can produce histograms or cumulative frequency diagrams for any numeric field, scatter plots (with least squares lines or curves) for any two fields, or a correlation matrix for up to 20 fields. The results of each operation are first displayed on a terminal screen (in standard printed characters), at which point the user may decide to alter parameters (e.g., limiting the range of values to include in the histogram, or applying a logarithmic transformation). If the results seem acceptable they are saved in a file and printed when the session is finished. Since all results are simply printed, any terminal or printer can be used, even ones at remote locations connected to the main computer only by a telephone line

In multivariate problems, STATS and SELECT are often used iteratively. SELECT prepares subfiles of a database, according to specific criteria defined by the analyst. STATS is then used to study the statistical characteristics of each group. This procedure allows possible relationships between numeric and non-numeric data to be tested. It is also used to isolate clusters of data observed on scatter plots. The STATS results may indicate a need for additional subdivision, in which case SELECT is run again, followed by another pass through STATS.

More complex statistical procedures are available, but generally in programs that are not fully interactive. They are still linked to the same database structure, but require prior knowledge of parameter conventions, etc. As the majority of users of the system are not familiar with the mathematical details, the programs tend to be used only by people who have studied the techniques thoroughly. Such people also tend to be experienced computer users, so there is less incentive to expend the effort to develop self-tutoring programs. This policy also reduces the danger of having inexperienced people attempting to use advanced methods which they do not completely understand.

4. Data Analysis: Graphical Display

Extensive use is made of computer mapping to investigate spatial characteristics of various types of data. Placer uses a general purpose mapping program called CPS1 (licensed from Radian Corporation, of Austin, Texas). This is a batch-oriented system, and is very much an "expert" type of program, having a great number of options to consider in setting such parameters as scales, contour levels, gridding techniques, and the like. While making the program difficult to learn, the wide range of options provides great flexibility in preparing computer graphics tailored to different applications.

To allow novice computer users to run CPS1 directly, an interactive "front-end" program is used to prepare a "run-stream" for CPS1. This program (called MAPS) uses menus to prompt the user for all necessary information, and provides as many reasonable default values as possible. It is linked to the data structure, so selection of files, coordinates, and data to be plotted can all be done using descriptive names. To streamline the process of defining map parameters, many of the less frequently used options in CPS1 are not directly accessible to the user. The parameters are saved in a file, however, so a more experienced user can make customized changes with a text editor, and thus have access to the full range of options. Normally, plotting jobs are submitted as batch jobs, rather than having the user wait at the terminal. Multiple plots can be created in a single session, and common parameters need be defined only for the first. This saves a considerable amount of time, as it is quite common to produce several maps covering the same area. In this case, the menu which defines map coordinate limits and scale is skipped on the second and succeeding passes through the program.

MAPS provides a variety of display options. Several sets of data can be plotted on the same map, in posted, contour, or stacked profile form. To plot multiple files, different symbols or line thicknesses are used to distinguish the variables. A complete data legend is automatically drawn, so that the information presented on the map can always be clearly identified.

Some other plotting tasks are run with a similar approach. A program very much like MAPS is SECTION, which creates parameters for plotting cross sections showing data associated with drill holes, which are used for direct sampling of potential buried bodies of mineral ore. In this case, different CPS1 functions are used, to prepare the specific types of displays required for a cross section.

Other graphical displays can also be produced from any file in the database structure. As noted above, STATS creates simple printer histograms and scatter plots. Ternary diagrams can be plotted by a separate program which plots directly (instead of using CPS1). Profile plots (i.e., plots with one variable plotted along a coordinate axis) are run using a data selection program which retrieves specified fields from a data file and prepares a standard format for plotting by a fixed CPS1 run stream.

5. Use of the Complete System

1. Files are created by a variety of programs, and verified by special data checking routines, or by inspection of LISTDF output. If corrections are required, the standard text-editing program provided with the computer system is normally used.
2. SMERGE and COORD are often used to combine different sets of related information.
3. SELECT and STATS can be used in a iterative sense, to separate different groups of data for basic statistical analysis.
4. Various data files or fields from one file can be plotted using MAPS, SECTION, or other plotting programs.
5. Subsets of data from SELECT can also be plotted. As in item 3, this often entails multiple cycles of data selection and plotting.

6. Training

The objective of all programs is to be completely self-contained, that is, to be usable without reference to documentation. A guidebook with recommended procedures and an outline of program functions is available to aid novices. It also includes an overview of how to use the various programs in a coordinated fashion, something which can not be easily described in the interactive prompting messages of each program. One or two demonstrations from an experienced user will make most people comfortable with a program. The interactive menus used in each program are very similar (in fact identical in many respects), so the overall system presents a consistent face to the user. This helps to reduce the learning period for any new program.

One major benefit of developing this system is that many people now run computer studies themselves instead of passing the task on to the staff of the computer department. This makes it possible for them to gain a more intimate knowledge of their data and to obtain final results more quickly (since there are fewer instances of delays caused by conflicting priorities). Another bonus is that the computer staff have more time for new developments and improvements to the system, since they are less involved in routine "production" work.

REFERENCES

There are a vast number of books and articles on data analysis and computer applications. A thorough survey of the literature would comprise a book in itself. In this section, I note some sources that contain more complete treatment of these subjects, or that illuminate particular points. This is necessarily a personal selection, and is not intended to be complete. As noted below, some of the books have extensive reference lists, for those who wish to pursue specific topics in more detail.

Data Analysis

Data Collection and Analysis
Robert M. Thorndike
Gardner Press, New York, 1982

Exploratory Data Analysis
J.W. Tukey
Addison-Wesley, Boston, 1977

Applications, Basics, and Computing of Exploratory Data Analysis
Paul F. Wellerman and David C. Hoaglin
Duxbury Press, Boston, 1981

An Introduction to Data Analysis
Bruce D. Bowen and Herbert F. Weisberg
W.H. Freeman, San Francisco, 1980

This a non mathematical account, oriented toward the social sciences.

Statistical Analysis of Geological Data
G.S. Koch and R.F. Link
John Wiley, New York, 1970-71 (Dover reprint 1980)

This book contains a detailed exposition of applications of data analysis to the specialized field of geologic exploration for minerals.

Computers and Computer Applications

Introduction to Data Processing, third edition
Carl Feingold
Wm. C. Brown, Dubuque, 1980

Digital Computer Fundamentals, fifth edition
Thomas C. Bartec
McGraw-Hill, New York, 1981

James Martin is the premier author in the field; he has written many books that have become standard texts. For further insight into communications, database techniques, software design, and other topics, his work is a good place to start.

Computer Applications in the Earth Sciences
Daniel F. Merriam, Editor
Plenum Press, New York, 1981

This book contains proceedings of a 1979 symposium, consisting mainly of review papers on how computers are used in various earth sciences. Many of these papers have lengthy reference lists.

Statistical Methods

Many good basic texts on this topic are available, and most people who wish to use these methods will probably already have introductory books. See also the books listed under Data Analysis.

Statistics — Schaum's Outline Series (published by McGraw-Hill) is a good summary of the mathematical methods, with many worked examples.

Analysis of Straight-Line Data
Forman S. Acton
John Wiley, New York, 1959 (available in a Dover reprint)

This is detailed investigation of methods for studying the relationships of two numeric variables.

Quick Statistics, An Introduction to Non-Parametric Methods
P. Sprent
Penguin Books, London, 1981

"An Efficient Point-in-Polygon Algorithm"
Kenneth B. Salomon
Computers and Geosciences, vol 4, pp. 173–178, 1978

This is a complete listing of a FORTRAN program for doing polygon selection

Applications of Probability Graphs in Mineral Exploration
A.J. Sinclair
Special Publication 4, Association of Exploration Geochemists, Rexdale, Ontario, 1976

This book demonstrates simple graphical techniques for probability graphs. As noted in the title, examples are all drawn from mining, although the methods can be used in other fields.

Computer Graphics and Mapping

Fundamentals of Interactive Computer Graphics
J.D. Foley and A. Van Dam
Addison-Wesley, Boston, 1982

This is a massive work, which concentrates on programming principles and techniques, but also includes discussions on hardware and a variety of graphics applications. Includes descriptions of graphics standards.

Computer-Assisted Cartography: Principles and Prospects
Mark S. Monmonier
Prentice-Hall, Englewood Cliffs, N.J., 1982

This book reviews methods for using computers to draw maps, and includes an introduction to computers and graphics technology, and a fairly extensive list of references.

Elements of Cartography, fourth edition
A. Robinson, R. Sale, and J. Morrison
John Wiley, New York, 1978

This is an excellent introduction to the techniques of map making.

The Harvard Library of Computer Graphics Mapping Collection
Laboratory for Computer Graphics and Spatial Analysis
Harvard University

Many of the proceedings of the annual Harvard Computer Graphics conferences are included in this 17-volume set. Papers include reviews of technology, basic principles, and a wealth of example applications.

Computer Graphics World
Pennwell Publishing, San Francisco

This magazine reviews new developments in computer graphics, in a largely nontechnical style. Most of the firms developing graphics products advertise here.

Method-Produced Error in Isarithmic Mapping
Joel L. Morrison
American Congress on Surveying and Mapping, Falls Church, VA

A monograph which examines the problems of modeling surfaces and drawing contours with a computer.

Advanced Statistical Methods

Mining Geostatistics
A.G. Journel and C.J. Huibregts
Academic Press, New York, 1978

This is the primary reference book for geostatistics, and contains a full theoretical development with numerous examples.

Practical Geostatistics
Isobel Clark
Applied Science Publishers, London, 1979

A brief introduction to geostatistics and its applications.

Spatial Statistics
Brian D. Ripley
John Wiley, New York, 1981

This book reviews many statistical methods applicable to spatial data, and contains an extensive list of recent references.

Statistical Methods for Digital Computers
K. Enslein, A. Ralston, and H. Wilf, Editors
John Wiley, New York, 1977

This volume contains a collection of papers on such multivariate techniques as stepwise regression, factor analysis, and discriminant analysis.

Computational Methods of Multivariate Analysis in Physical Geography
P. M. Mather
John Wiley, New York, 1976

This is an excellent in-depth review of such methods as multiple regression, trend-surface analysis, and cluster analysis. The book includes full listings of working FORTRAN programs, many examples, and extensive references.

Graphical Representation of Multivariate Data
Peter C.C. Wang, Editor
Academic Press, New York, 1978

This is a collection on graphics applications for multivariate analysis. It concentrates on the use of special figures like Chernoff faces.

Graphical Methods for Data Analysis
J.M. Chambers, W.S. Cleveland, B. Kleiner, and P.A. Tukey
Duxbury Press, Boston, 1983

Array-Oriented Processing

Time Series and Systems Analysis with Applications
S.M. Pandit and S.M. Wu
John Wiley, New York, 1983

This is a thorough treatment of the ARMA model for time series. It includes some programs, numerous complete examples, and a basic list of historical references.

The Measurement of Power Spectra
R.B. Blackman and J.W. Tukey
Dover Publications, New York, 1958

This is the classic work on analysis of frequency spectra.

Fourier Analysis of Time Series: An Introduction
Peter Bloomfield
John Wiley, New York, 1976

Nonlinear Maximum Entropy Spectral Analysis Methods for Signal Recognition
C.H. Chen
John Wiley (Research Studies Press), New York, 1982

This is a research monograph on sophisticated methods for spectral estimation.

Time Series Analysis and Applications
Enders A. Robinson
Goose Pond Press, Houston, 1981

This is a collection of papers by one of the major figures in the field. It includes examples from geophysics, econometrics, and other fields.

An Introduction to Information Theory, second edition
John R. Pierce
Dover Publications, New York, 1980

This is a basically nontechnical review of applications of signal detection.

Remote Sensing Principles and Interpretation
Floyd F. Sabins
W.H. Freeman, San Francisco, 1978

Manual of Remote Sensing, second edition
American Society of Photogrammetry, Falls Church, VA, 1983

This is a massive compilation (two volumes, 2400 pages) on all aspects of the subject.

Remote Sensing for Resource Management
Soil Conservation Society of America, Ankenny, Iowa, 1982

This book contains 55 papers, primarily dealing with various uses of remote sensing by industry and public agencies.

"Image Processing by Computer"
T.M. Cannon and B.R. Hunt
Scientific American, vol. 245, no. 4, October 1981

"Supercomputers"
Ronald D. Levine
Scientific American, vol. 246, no. 1, January 1982

Modeling and Interpretation

System Simulation, second edition
Geoffrey Gordon
Prentice Hall, Englewood Cliffs, N.J., 1978

Digital Computer Simulation
Fred J. Maryanski
Hayden Book Co., San Francisco, 1980

These two books are introductions to the general principles of simulation using computer models.

Introduction to the Mathematics of Inversion in Remote Sensing and Indirect Measurements
S.W. Twomey
Elsevier, North-Holland, New York, 1977

Numerical Prediction and Dynamic Meteorology
G.J. Haltiner and R.T. Williams
John Wiley, New York, 1980

Theory of Climate
Barry Saltzman, Editor
Academic Press, New York, 1983

These books are examples of detailed monographs on the complex mathematics involved in many large-scale modeling problems.

The Fractal Geometry of Nature
Benoit B. Mandelbrot
W.H. Freeman, San Francisco, 1983

This is an interesting review of a new mathematical formulation that allows successful empirical models to be built for a wide variety of phenomena, including landforms, shapes of coastlines, galactic structure, and stock market fluctuations.

Mankind at the Turning Point
Mihajlo Mesarovic and Eduard Pestal
E.P. Dutton/Reader's Digest Press, New York, 1974

This is the sequel to *The Limits to Growth,* which considers policy alternatives for projected economic disruptions in the near future.

"The Future of the Universe"
D. Picus, J. Letaw, D. Teplitz, and V. Teplitz
Scientific American, vol. 248, no. 3, March 1983

"A Computer-Generated Cosmic Portfolio"
Penny D. Sackett
Science News, vol. 124, no. 18, October 29, 1983

These two articles review recent modeling studies in cosmology.

GLOSSARY

What follows is a brief list of common terms used in data processing and graphical display with a computer. More complete discussions are given in the text, primarily in Chapters 2 and 6. These definitions are informal, and are intended to describe the popular usages of the terms, rather than a more restricted context which might be preferred by computer scientists.

APPLICATIONS SOFTWARE The set of programs which perform the tasks of interest to the computer users, as opposed to SYSTEM SOFTWARE

ARRAY PROCESSOR A specialized computer attached to a large general purpose machine, for very fast calculations on arrays of numbers

BATCH Data processing jobs run completely under the control of the operating system, to be performed according to the availability of computer resources. Also called background jobs. The opposite of foreground or INTERACTIVE jobs

BINARY SEARCH A procedure for quickly locating an element of an ordered array: First determine if the desired value is in the first or last half, then subdivide the chosen area in half again, and continue until the desired entry is found

BIT A binary digit, which can have a value of 0 or 1. The bit is the basic form for coding any information in a computer

BYTE A series of bits used together as a code for a single character. Most commonly there are eight bits in a byte

CAD Computer Aided Design: specialized computer systems employing graphic displays and extensive software packages for drafting, mechanical design and similar functions

COMPILER A system program which translates statements written in a particular programming language into machine-readable instructions; normally includes extensive error checking, to ensure that the program is executable

COMPUTER GRAPHICS Use of a computer to create such graphic displays as maps, charts, and animation; requires special equipment like plotters and graphics terminals

CONTROL LANGUAGE The set of commands with which a user can issue instructions to the computer's operating system

COORDINATE TRANSFORMATION Any operation which allows spatial data to be expressed in terms of different coordinate systems

CORE The graphics standards adopted by SIGGRAPH (Special Interest Group on Graphics of the Association for Computing Machinery)

CPU Central Processing Unit: the heart of a computer system, which does the actual calculations, and controls the functions of all other devices

DATA ENTRY The process of encoding any data into a form which a computer can understand, and loading the data into a computer file

DATABASE A set of data with at least some common characteristics, which may be highly structured to allow easy access to particular subsets of data

DATABASE SYSTEM The software used to manipulate the data in a database, which typically includes programs for selective retrieval of data, editing, sorting, generating reports, etc. Often called a DATABASE MANAGEMENT SYSTEM (DBMS)

DEVICE INDEPENDENCE The practice of developing software which can produce output on any appropriate device, especially in computer graphics

DIGITAL The representation of any continuous phenomena as a series of discrete numbers is referred to as a digital format

DIGITIZER A device for converting graphic data to digital format for computer processing (e.g., creating a file representing topography from a contour map)

DISK A device for secondary storage of computer data, consisting of a number of rapidly spinning platters, each with many "tracks" of magnetically coded data

DISTRIBUTED PROCESSING The use of a number of separate computers in a coordinated network, each performing tasks for which it is most suited

DOCUMENTATION The written instructions on how to use a computer, various programs, and so on

DOUBLE PRECISION For numeric calculations requiring high accuracy, precision is extended by using two words to represent a number, instead of the normal one

DRIVE The hardware device for reading data from a magnetic tape or disk (normally referred to as "tape drive" or "disk drive")

ELECTROSTATIC PLOTTER A plotting device which creates a display as a large array of closely spaced black or white dots, by placing an electric charge at each black point on the paper. The charge attracts carbon particles from a "toner" solution. A RASTER device

FILE A single set of data stored on tape or disk

FIRMWARE Software permanently encoded in storage devices to provide extended capabilities to a piece of hardware

GKS Graphical Kernel System: the graphics standard most popular in Europe

GRAPHICS STANDARDS Rules on design of software for computer graphics, to ensure device independence and easy transfer of programs between different computer systems

GRAPHICS TERMINAL A special computer terminal which can display graphic images in addition to printed characters

HARDWARE The mechanical and electronic components of a computer system

INPUT The data and parameters supplied to a computer program as "raw material" for its calculations

I/O Input/Output: An acronym to describe devices for transferring data to and from the CPU, and the process of data transfer

INTERACTIVE A mode of use of a computer, where the user can immediately respond to prompts from the operating system or an applications program. The opposite of BATCH. Sometimes called "foreground"

INTERFACE Any link between different components of a computer system

LANGUAGE Rules and syntax required to write computer programs in a form acceptable to a compiler

LIBRARY Collection of commonly used routines which can be "called" into an applications program

LIGHT PEN A device for pointing to a specific location on a graphics terminal display (by directly touching the desired spot)

MAINFRAME A large general-purpose computer, capable of supporting many peripheral devices, and many concurrent users. The distinction between this and a large "minicomputer" is no longer clear

MEMORY Fast access storage of data and program instructions for direct use by the CPU when executing any program

MENU Presentation of a number of program parameters and options in a list, as part of an interactive program

METAFILE A data file containing complete coded instructions for a computer graphics display, which can be adapted as required to produce output on any plotting device

MICRO Short for microcomputer, which normally means a small "personal" computer that can only be used by one person (although some allow a limited number of concurrent users)

MINICOMPUTER A computer system of intermediate size between a micro and a mainframe

MOUSE A device for marking a position on a graphics terminal screen. The mouse is moved anywhere on a desktop; a moving arrow appears on the screen. A particular location can be marked by pushing a single key

OPERATING SYSTEM The collection of software that controls all of the basic functions of the computer system: I/O operations, loading programs into memory, monitoring concurrent jobs, and so on

OUTPUT The results of calculations performed on input data by a computer program

OVERPOSTING A problem in computer graphics, where adjacent points are so close that annotated data overlaps

PERIPHERAL Any device attached to a computer: printers, tape drives, and so on

PLOT VECTOR The basic element of a plot file, in general of the form X, Y, CODE: the plotting device moves from the current position to (X,Y), and performs the action defined by CODE (e.g., draw a line, move without drawing)

PLOTTER An output device capable of drawing lines, special symbols, etc., rather than just printed characters (as on a "lineprinter"). May also have the capability to use different colors

RASTER Representation of a graphic image as a series of points on a finely spaced grid. Such data are called "raster data," and the process of converting from a vector format is called "rasterizing." A plotter or terminal that creates graphical output this way is called a raster device

RECORD A single entry from a computer file, generally containing all data associated with a single sample or event, or a single line from a file of free-form text

RUN The term used to denote the use of a program: for example, we might "run" a program called HISTO to plot a histogram. An alternate term is "execute." Also used as a noun, for instance, "this run is incorrect."

SESSION The period of time during which a user is using a terminal in interactive processing

SOFTWARE The coded instructions (programs) that tell the hardware what to do

SORTING Rearranging the sequence of records in a file (or items in an array) according to the value of one or more data fields

SOURCE CODE Software in the syntax of a programming language (i.e., in the original form in which it was written)

STORAGE TERMINAL A graphics display in which the plot vectors stay on the display surface until erased, and do not have to be continually redrawn

SUPERCOMPUTER A large mainframe making extensive use of "vector processing" to allow tremendous speed in scientific problems involving large data arrays

SYSTEM SOFTWARE The subset of all software devoted to basic tasks of the computer (including the entire operating system, and links to operating system functions from an applications program)

TABLET See Digitizer

TAPE Secondary storage medium used for large volumes of data, backup of disk files, and so on

TERMINAL The primary link between the user and the computer system, incorporating a display screen for output from the computer, and a keyboard for entering instructions

TEXT EDITOR A computer program for revising data files, normally by typing new text or changes on a terminal

USER Anyone who uses a computer system

UTM Universal Transverse Mercator: a widely used coordinate system for converting latitude-longitude into an orthogonal projection suitable for accurate plotting of maps

VECTOR In spatial analysis, an ordered pair of coordinates; in computer graphics, a vector device creates plots as a series of line segments, each of which is considered a single vector

VECTOR PROCESSING Computer systems designed to take advantage of ordered data, that is, regular arrays. Special hardware and software techniques allow much faster calculations on arrays than is possible with a conventional "scalar" computer (which treats each element of the array as independent)

WORD The basic element of memory and storage, typically 32 or 36 bits on a mainframe computer. Normally the unit of memory sufficient to store a single number with adequate precision

INDEX

Many of these items are defined in the GLOSSARY, as well as being discussed in the main text on the cited pages.